Europe Old and New

Europe Old and New

Transnationalism, Belonging, Xenophobia

Ray Taras

ROWMAN & LITTLEFIELD PUBLISHERS, INC.
Lanham • Boulder • New York • Toronto • Plymouth, UK

ROWMAN & LITTLEFIELD PUBLISHERS, INC.

Published in the United States of America
by Rowman & Littlefield Publishers, Inc.
A wholly owned subsidiary of The Rowman & Littlefield Publishing Group, Inc.
4501 Forbes Boulevard, Suite 200, Lanham, Maryland 20706
www.rowmanlittlefield.com

Estover Road, Plymouth PL6 7PY, United Kingdom

Copyright © 2009 by Rowman & Littlefield Publishers, Inc.

British Library Cataloguing in Publication Information Available

Library of Congress Cataloging-in-Publication Data
Taras, Ray, 1946-
  Europe old and new : transnationalism, belonging, xenophobia / Ray Taras.
    p. cm.
  Includes bibliographical references and index.
  ISBN-13: 978-0-7425-5515-0 (cloth : alk. paper)
  ISBN-10: 0-7425-5515-1 (cloth : alk. paper)
  ISBN-13: 978-0-7425-5516-7 (pbk. : alk. paper)
  ISBN-10: 0-7425-5516-X (pbk. : alk. paper)
  eISBN-13: 978-0-7425-5734-5
  eISBN-10: 0-7425-5734-0
  1. European Union countries—Relations. 2. Europe, Western—Relations—
Europe, Eastern. 3. Europe, Eastern—Relations—Europe, Western. 4. National
characteristics, European. I. Title.
  D2025.T37 2009
  320.54'9094—dc22

                                                        2008012559

Printed in the United States of America

Contents

Acknowledgments

Like all faculty working at universities that had to be temporarily closed down after Hurricane Katrina ravaged the Gulf Coast in August 2005, I became indebted to other institutions that generously opened their doors to evacuees like myself. In my case, the University of Colorado's Political Science Department and Stanford University's Center for Russian and East European Studies offered congenial academic homes where I could continue working on this book project. I am especially grateful to Mary Dakin at Stanford and William Safran in Boulder for their support and understanding.

Individuals to whom I wish to express my gratitude for their intellectual and other contributions to the writing of this book include Rainer Bauböck (European University Institute, Florence), George Bernstein (Tulane University), Ulf Hedetoft (University of Copenhagen), Alkmini Koundouroff (San Antonio), Peter Olofsson (Trinity University), Irina Paperno (University of California, Berkeley), Muhammad Siddiq (University of California, Berkeley), John Wrench (Fundamental Rights Agency, Vienna), Hakan Yavuz (University of Utah), and Marshal Zeringue (Campaign for the American Reader, St. Charles Parish, Louisiana). I was fortunate to receive highly constructive critiques of this project from three anonymous reviewers in its early and late stages. Finally I am grateful to Susan McEachern, senior editor at Rowman & Littlefield, for embracing this project and keeping it on track from start to finish.

Introduction

Europe Old and New

Clashes *within* civilizations may have as much impact on the shape of world politics as the well-publicized clash between civilizations. Europe is a case in point. The accession process that brought twelve new members into the European Union (EU) beginning in 2004 served to juxtapose the persisting cultural divide between "old" and "new" Europe. To the fanfare of "the iron curtain is finally down," the popular refrain on the unification of western and eastern Europe was "So Happy Together."

Few Europeans paid any attention to the version of this popular hit song from the 1960s performed by Finnish rock band Leningrad Cowboys backed up by the Red Army Choir in Helsinki's Senate Square in 1993—as symbolic a "border" site as there is in Europe. Just about all Europeans agreed at the time that there was no place in reunified Europe for any part of the former Red Army or, for that matter, for any vestiges of the collapsed Russian empire. Yet in hindsight, the mantra "So Happy Together" seems at once a pastiche of European integration and an omen that such an idyllic state may not be achieved any time soon.

This book is about European leaders' and citizens' contrasting understandings of their political homes—of who belongs to them—whether political home is regarded as the EU or as the nation-state. The initial reservations drawn by European specialists were that contrasting views about belonging did indeed separate the two Europes.

Belonging and citizenship are closely related: "If citizenship signifies the participatory dimension of belonging, identification relates to the more emotive dimension of association. Feeling that one is part of a collectivity, a community, a social category, or yearning to be so, is not the same as actually taking part in a political community with all the rights and responsibilities involved."[1]

The west's idea of belonging, so it was held, was liberal, inclusive, and bound to a civic and multicultural approach. The east was purportedly paranoiac, exclusionary, and committed to promoting an ethnic reading of the state and its inhabitants. EU enlargement was designed in part to supplant the east's ideas about belonging, as it was supposed to snuff out eastern backwardness in many other areas. Before enlargement, little effort was made to debunk myths about the supposedly backward east, in part because they supplied the very raison d'être of enlargement.[2]

Enlargement removed various borders between the two former geopolitically defined parts of Europe. Standardized trade and legal regimes are well-known examples; the expanded Schengen zone (for unrestricted travel within the EU which, beginning in late 2007, permits a passport-free trip from Portugal to Estonia) is a more recent one. But other borders have taken longer to dismantle, for example, the Eurozone (where the European currency has been introduced) and the labor market.

Because they were intangible and ephemeral, some borders could not be taken down. These include socially constructed borders, as observed in the 2005 French referendum on the EU constitution draft when voters expressed their fears about the specter of the "Polish plumber" ready to invade that country's workforce. Yet other borders were imagined: the postmaterialist, tolerant values of old Europe versus the materialist, nationalistic ones of the east. If the French electorate seemed paranoiac, then two prominent British social theorists added, "The 'new Europe' has been troubled by rising xenophobia and cultural backlashes."[3]

DIFFERENTIATING THE OLD FROM THE NEW

Different ideas about who belonged to their political homes were not the sole schism between the two Europes. The notion of a persisting cultural border spilled over into the foreign policy realm and helped popularize the theory of the two Europes.[4] The U.S. defense secretary at the time played a pivotal role in anchoring this conception. In January 2003, much of the world was bracing for the start of a U.S. attack on Iraq. Commemorating the fortieth anniversary of the Élysée Treaty between their countries, French president Jacques Chirac and German chancellor Gerhard Schröder promised to work together to oppose this war. But American defense secretary Donald Rumsfeld sought to minimize the significance of this declaration. He retorted: "You're thinking of Europe as Germany and France. I don't. I think that's old Europe." He inveighed: "vast numbers of other countries in Europe, they're not with France and Germany . . . they're with the U.S."

When German and French leaders expressed their indignation at Rumsfeld's remarks, he put forward his understanding of an "old Europe" by signaling the eastward expansion of NATO as far as the three Baltic republics. "If you look at the entire NATO Europe today, the center of gravity is shifting to the east," to what he labeled "new Europe."[5]

It was the inferences Rumsfeld was making that caused the greatest controversy. Old meant just that: obsolete, out of date, outliving its time. New suggested fresh, forward looking, the future. Paradoxically, in terms of foreign policy orientations "new" Europe was not that at all. It had appropriated the Atlanticist, NATO-anchored alliance system for itself. By contrast, the foreign policies of France and Germany were "new" in refusing to be bound to U.S. policy on Iraq merely by the existence of that alliance system.

In January 2003, "an open letter of support for the U.S." was signed by a mix of old and new European states. This "letter of the eight" was endorsed by leaders of five of the then fifteen EU members, led by Tony Blair of Britain and José María Aznar of Spain and also including Denmark, Italy, and Portugal. The three accession states to sign were the Czech Republic, Hungary, and Poland.

The following month, ten ex-communist states meeting in the Lithuanian capital Vilnius signed their own letter supporting U.S. policy on Iraq. This so-called Vilnius group, made up mainly of countries that were EU applicants, included Albania, Bulgaria, Croatia, Estonia, Latvia, Lithuania, Macedonia, Romania, Slovakia, and Slovenia. Seven of these ten Vilnius signatories had not even been independent states fifteen years earlier.

The dividing line on supporting the Bush administration's policy towards Iraq was not reducible to a stark old Europe versus new Europe, though, to be sure, western publics were far more critical of the United States than their eastern counterparts. Timothy Garton Ash and Ralf Dahrendorf candidly explained why some eastern political leaders bucked their own public's skeptical views about the need for war and backed Bush. The letter of the eight was "signed by statesmen who are known for their obsequiousness, such as Václav Havel."[6] The Vilnius letter was agreed to by leaders who may have been even more obsequious given their applicant status.

The old-versus-new dichotomy has been used in non-Rumsfeldian ways. Old Europe is identified with the Europe of nation-states that existed prior to the establishment of the EU. New Europe is associated with the emancipatory development of a postnational federal Europe. In literal terms, old Europe can simply mean those countries that have been members of the European community for a long time; new Europe can mean those who joined the EU beginning in 2004. Nevertheless, the meaning that the since-disgraced Rumsfeld impugned to old and new has taken hold.

A cultural divide may indeed lie underneath the veneer of EU unity and the idea of two Europes should not be dismissed *prima facie*. Hungarian

Nobel literature laureate Imre Kertész, for one, acknowledged this divide: "A lot is said nowadays about 'old Europe,' about traditions, about European culture, and there can be no doubt that the crisis, indeed division, to which we are witness across Europe is, in large part, cultural in nature."[7]

THE VALUES GAP OR VALUES CONVERGENCE?

There is greater complexity to the European divide than its political manifestations. The search for the antecedent causes of the divide requires an examination of the values and attitudes of citizens in the former Soviet bloc and an assessment of whether they have come to resemble those in western European states. When values increasingly become shared across Europe, it is possible to speak of an incipient form of transnationalism.

Ideally, emerging shared values would be those alluded to and championed by EU elites. Social cohesion is perhaps the most important of these, though it is formulated in often arcane ways. An Open Society Institute study listed EU "commandments" that represent its principal prescriptive values. These include three that concern social cohesion. One is "Thou Shalt Provide for Social Cohesion between People, Regions and States." Another commandment is "Thou Shalt Reject Nationalism and Favor the Multiple Identity of Citizens." Finally, the social cohesion value must be projected internationally: "Thou Shalt be Open, Inclusive and Integrative Toward Neighbors that Adhere to the Above."[8]

There is another possibility related to shared European values—that it is the illiberal ones producing xenophobia and racism that are spreading across and making moot the European divide. Intellectuals in western Europe have generally played an important role in exposing racism and xenophobia in their part of the continent. One specialist on these pathologies lamented, however, that "academics have been almost absent in the debate over, as well as the struggle against, racist extremism in Central and Eastern Europe."[9] Notwithstanding respective efforts to address the imperative of social cohesion, an unsavory form of transnationalism anchored in anti-foreigner, anti-immigrant, anti-minority sentiments is making headway as Europe's shared value system.

The role of the EU has been to promote convergence between west and east around a core set of liberal values, in the process creating a "Europe undivided."[10] EU elites seek to contain the spread of unsavory transnationalism by sanctioning individual states that vote xenophobic parties into government, as in Austria in 2000 and Switzerland in 2007. EU admission criteria rule out membership for countries which practice ethnic cleansing; Serbia is the best-known example from the former socialist bloc. But there are fuzzy areas where there is an acceptance that EU and national values have to cohabitate. Thus, some national elites have given high priority to protecting their societies' ingrained religiosity from EU-sponsored secularism; Poland has been a case in point. EU practice in such circumstances has been to acquiesce rather than sanction. As we know from current affairs, however, where religious fundamentalism has breathing space there may follow overlapping cleavages (in the areas of ethnicity, language, and territory) that create illiberalism, intolerance, and strife.

The east-west divide may be narrowing in ways that the EU is oblivious to. Thus in new Europe an initial admiration for a mythical West—whether embodied by Britain, France, or the United States—that did not really exist has produced an "expectations crash." From greater freedom of travel and information, east Europeans discovered that western states had serious flaws and were not economic or even ethnic utopias. A more skeptical Occidentalism has recently emerged in the region that highlights the West's shortcomings. Paradoxically, the more hardheaded eastern critique of the other side of the continent may help bridge the cultural gap between east and west.

What are the tangible differences between the two Europes today? While we can explore their contrasting political values, processes, and behavior—through the study of political culture, institutions, and electoral behavior—this book is concerned with an antecedent stage: the cultural pathways followed by a nation. This approach is guided by the observation made by Nobel literature laureate Wole Soyinka that "Before politics, there was clearly culture. . . . This hierarchy of evolution also explains why man resorts to his cultural affiliations when politics appear to have failed him, never the other way around."[11]

In examining Europe's problematic cultural unity, we need to go beyond institutional frameworks and put cultural dynamics first. We need to examine contestations triggered by multiple perspectives on European transformation. We have to express "a dissatisfaction with the ways in which questions of European transformation have been framed within political science discourses on the EU."[12] Accordingly, we need to reject the reductionist formula that "The challenge for Europe is not culture but politics."[13]

AN ANALYTIC FRAMEWORK FOR STUDYING EAST-WEST DIFFERENCES: FUSING INSTITUTIONAL, DISCURSIVE, AND CULTURAL PERSPECTIVES

For too long cross-national social science research has been fixated on meeting the canons of the comparative method. For starters, selection of case studies is supposed to be guided by their essential comparability or their representativeness of a larger number of cases. Data sets used in this book comprise attitudinal survey results taken from both parts of Europe. In a perfect world, these data would be uniformly available—and they would always be comparable—for all EU member states. Fortunately or unfortunately as the case may be, the EU has not yet attained such perfect standardization.

Where quantitative data may be imperfect, the social science canon insists that empirical investigation should involve qualitative case study research, above all when the number of cases is small. This book's examination of institutional arrangements, elite discourses, and narratives of belonging would satisfy this qualitative requirement if all cases were studied in exactly the same way. But the EU consists of twenty-seven cases. Furthermore, such rigor in research design may actually handcuff the investigator, requiring giving equal attention to variables whose real importance differs from country to country. For example, it makes little sense to examine the legacy of authoritarianism in western Europe, whereas this factor is of great significance in the east. What is the researcher skeptical of the social science canon to do?

An interdisciplinary approach is often advanced as a methodological panacea for parsing complex problems. There is great intellectual appeal in seeking to enhance the explanatory power of a research inquiry by combining a mix of discrete paradigms taken from diverse disciplines. The rigor advocated by the political science canon can be blended with the flexibility and open-endedness characterizing cultural studies, the structural framework favored by institutionalists can be integrated with the decentered sociological imagination, and the trend lines of empirically driven econometrics can be complemented with trace analysis of distant events used by historians. As we may suspect, however, such interdisciplinary methods may prove overly ambitious for most scholars. At the end of the day, most take refuge in their disciplinary homes. It is therefore uncommon to encounter an interdisciplinary research design.

This study also comes up short in terms of its ability to apply a methodologically interdisciplinary framework, but it makes every effort to place itself in an interdisciplinary spirit. The literatures examined in this book encompass the social sciences as well as fictional narratives. The texts analyzed range from the official discourse of political leaders to the polemics of essayists. Empirical data subsume public opinion polls and also literary reflections. The perspectives adopted focus on political institutions and processes as well as historical contexts and ideological orientations. I would characterize this composite analytic framework as providing a multidisciplinary observation point that offers the best shot of trawling up the elusive idea of Europe as it is understood by the divergent communities spread out on the continent and across the British Isles.

The idea of one Europe has sparked the imagination of thinkers for several centuries. Implementing the idea of a Europe having its own supranational institutions has been the labor of hardnosed bureaucrats of recent vintage. The recent enlargement of the EU has drawn the attention of scholars who study the role of institutions in shaping politics. Some institutionalists, as they are known, have adopted a statecentric approach, others focus on how political integration can be accelerated by institutions, and still others have been informed by governance or constitutional theories.

Institutionalists have made a major contribution to our understanding of how the EU works and where the roadblocks are. Like the advantage an aspiring artist who has studied art history has in being able to contextualize creativity and knowing how to break new ground, it would be remiss for us to overlook the fifty-year-long process of European integration, which has been driven by deepening institutional arrangements and periodic reconfigurations. Accordingly, chapter 1 describes how during the Cold War era many Europes were institutionally—and politically—configured into two blocs, then welded into one in the new century.

Chapter 2 addresses the topic of disagreements and conflicts over institutional arrangements within the enlarged Europe. We will find that Cold War divisions were not easily swept away. After enlargement, east European assertiveness within EU structures took some western leaders by surprise. The efforts to draft an EU constitution acceptable to all proved to be a lightning rod that instigated many quarrels. The Reform Treaty agreed to in 2007 seemed to put an end to the quarrel over institutions, but it did not reconcile the competing value systems that individual states espouse. Exhibit A was Irish voters' rejection of the Treaty in a June 2008 referendum.

European integration involves much more than institution building and constitution making. There is a subjective dimension that involves the strength of the general will, made up of Europe's citizens, to construct an integrated Europe. A constructivist approach is better equipped to make sense of this subjective process than institutionalism. Europeanization is the term we can use to refer to the open-ended process of constructing a supranational European society. The late political theorist Cornelius Castoriadis argued, "Each society is a construction, a constitution, a creation of the world, of its own world. Its own identity is nothing but this 'system of interpretation,' this world that it creates."[14]

Citizens' efforts to arrive at a social imaginary that would explain their identities and trigger relevant change can be seen to be at the heart of the process of European integration. Studying how national societies change in the context of EU-led integration processes is closely connected to popular social constructions of Europe. Europeanization entails negotiating differences and divergences within Europe in order to implement a shared social imaginary.

The purpose of chapter 3 is to review contrasting constructions of Europe advanced by its political and intellectual elites. Official discourse on European integration reflects an imaginary model of Europe. Successive presidents of the European Commission have engaged in discursive practices that also imagine a future Europe. For example, while serving as EU president, Romano Prodi envisaged a united Europe linked historically to the times of Charlemagne. The pronouncements of individual state leaders on the idea of Europe are acts of social construction. Their expectations and imaginaries of Europe, expressed on the occasion of EU enlargement in 2004, then again on the fiftieth anniversary of the Treaty of Rome in 2007, are indicators of whether elites from old and new Europe speak with one voice.

In reality, there seem to be many Europes. As a countervailing force to this, EU elites have adopted metacultural, transnational discourses and practices intended to bring them together. European elites are in the business of constructing a Europe that is "happy together"—one in which racism, xenophobia, division, and hatred would disappear. Chapter 4 introduces a number of concepts that can be used to examine the extent to which the politics of phobias shape Europe. The paranoias of new Europe, in great part informed by supposed ancient hatreds, are identified, then contrasted with those of old Europe, which largely obsess about recent waves of immigration. This chapter compares the emergence of transnational values west and east. The everyday practices of inclusion and exclusion are described.

The modal Europe—the one that actually exists—is where its citizens live and act. The modal Europe depicted in chapter 5 differs markedly from elites' model Europe. Here, politicians' platitudes are juxtaposed with public attitudes. We are led to the inescapable conclusion that Europeanness seems to be a reification of its elites more than it is a reflection of its public's cultural pathways. Presenting survey data on citizen attitudes towards other EU nationalities, minorities, immigrants, and nations not part of the EU, we discover a Europe of often-conflicting norms. Public opinion results provide a sometimes brutally frank set of answers to the questions of who "belongs" in a particular EU state and who "belongs" in Europe generally. Opinion polls measure whether European citizens generally adopt an inclusionary approach in their construction of their societies—in other words, do they buy into transnational elites' discourse about deepening integration of all kinds? Or are they protective of their national or religious identity, even going as far as to exclude those who do not belong? Three case studies—of Germany, Poland, and Sweden—take us beyond a normative snapshot and provide comparative qualitative answers to these questions.

Chapter 6 is concerned with specific public phobias that define today's Europe. If citizens in EU countries create ethnic hierarchies in which people they like and dislike are put in rank order, then where do two of their great antipathies today fit in—Islamophobia and anti-Americanism? Again employing survey data, the chapter compares attitudes towards Muslims in various EU states. A case study of Britain adds qualitative data. Similarly, the chapter assesses whether anti-Americanism in both old and new Europe serves as a marker of Europeanness.

Using institutional, constructivist, and normative frameworks provide us with a multidimensional picture of Europe viewed from a number of vantage points. Chapters 7 and 8 add an additional framework and vantage point—narratives about Europe written by contemporary European novelists. Engaged in cultural production, these authors imagine Europe in diverse ways. Some advance transnational understandings of Europe as home. Others embrace fragmented, polyvocal understandings in which belonging is strictly bounded culturally.

Chapter 7 analyses narratives of a political home that aspire to transcend national borders. In particular, it reviews the writings of three novelists originating in eastern Europe: 1) Mircea Cărtărescu, a Romanian who insists on a pan-European identity; 2) Andreï Makine, born in Russia and living and writing in France, whose characters are often entangled in a transnational Russo-French culture that breeds nuanced hybridity; and 3) Dubravka Ugrešić, a Croatian living in exile in Holland and identifying with a country that no longer exists (Yugoslavia), whose characters struggle with a cultural cosmopolitanism they did not choose.

Chapter 8 examines writers who emphasize—though they do not necessarily endorse—exclusionary notions of home and belonging. These include: 1) Ismail Kadare, an Albanian writer living in Paris, who details the complex religious and ethnic identities and conflicts found in Europe's southeastern borderlands; 2) Emine Sevgi Özdamar, born in Turkey and living in Germany, who narrates problems of belonging for migrants and the national stereotypes that influence it; 3) Dorota Masłowska, a young writer very much the product of postcommunist Poland, who documents the angst and identity crisis of young people living in a rapidly transformed capitalist society; and 4) Michel Houellebecq, very much the product of agnostic France, who conveys contemporary European racism through many of his protagonists. All four agonize about the antipathies and prejudices that structure belonging in societies east and west.

The analytic framework for these cultural narratives includes an examination of the literary devices used to map national and transnational belonging. Among these are alterity (positing a notional "other" to demarcate and frame one's own culture), stereotyping and heterotyping, scapegoating and xenophobia, and even "civilizational chauvinism"—the universalist pretenses of an otherwise culture-specific narrative.

The book concludes with an assessment of the appeal of the culturally bounded European home. While EU integration, European identity, and transnationalism have made considerable headway, cultural boundaries in Europe have not been removed, sometimes not even blurred. Chapter 9 also reevaluates the wisdom of the proposition that diversity within a nation-state is to be celebrated but polyvocality—the resonance of many national voices—within the EU is to be overcome. Should it not be the other way round, we ask? Given deep-seated and intensely felt public attitudes on identity and belonging, it seems imperative that the construction of an attractive—if less politically correct—political home needs more accurately to reflect the values of citizens—warts and all—than elite propositions, which anyway may go down as the false consciousness of our age.

A EUROPEAN EXPERIENCE: ONE TRAJECTORY

The way this book has been researched cannot be separated from the author's professional and personal experiences living in Europe. I lived, studied, and worked for many years in a number of countries of old Europe. Setting aside study and work, I remember in the summer of 1968 frequenting a small West Indian nightclub in the Moss Side area of Manchester, where no native Mancunians dared set foot. A musical genre called reggae was just emerging, and these clubs were playing it and letting Rastafarianism out into the light.

But 1968 was also the year the Commonwealth Immigration Act was passed, making immigration to Britain from Jamaica and elsewhere more difficult. An erudite Conservative Party shadow minister, Enoch Powell, had made his "rivers of blood" speech that year, warning that Britain's lax immigration policy would lead to racial conflicts and the spilling of blood, as it had into the river Tiber that Virgil had described in *The Aeneid*. To this day, some older Britons—and even younger politicians on the right—remark, "Enoch was right."

When I return to parts of old Europe now, it is more modern, vibrant, and "cooler" than ever. Britons of West Indian background speak with local accents, not in patois. Most prefer soccer to cricket. On the continent, I am struck by the ease with which a Belgian or Dane may move to Budapest to work as a financial consultant or go to Timişoara—the Romanian town where in 1989 the country's anticommunist revolution began, today a shopping mecca—to set up a distribution business. Bureaucratic obstacles have disappeared, borders are notional, cheap air flights make intra-European travel commonplace, and mindsets have few limits.

I also lived, studied, and worked in what was then communist east Europe. In late 1991, I was on a boat on the Danube sailing past the Croatian city of Vukovar. It had just fallen to Serb forces who had massacred much of the population and shelled almost all of the buildings. A small motorboat pulled up alongside us for a few minutes. In it, teenage Serb boys proudly polished their guns, which glittered in the sun. These months proved in the end to be the death knells of the socialist Yugoslav state. A few years later, I was invited to a conference in Zagreb sponsored by the Croatian ministry of culture. The city is now a jewel of European culture, far removed in every way from what I had witnessed in Vukovar.

Today, new Europe is characterized by very different political and economic relations; by new buildings, transport, and consumer products; by young people with little historical baggage encumbering them. I see how seamlessly they slot in among the shoppers at Camden Town market when they move to "the west" or drive the bus up into the Vienna woods. To be sure, most of these east Europeans are not in London or Vienna as financial consultants or sales representatives, but instead are drawn by better job opportunities in these older free-market economies.

Rarely are the seedy side effects of this transnational mobility visible. However, the fact is that human nature causes people to harbor antipathies, paranoias, dislikes, and hatreds of others. On occasion these are based on our sense of ourselves as well as our evaluation of someone else's race, citizenship, ethnicity, place of birth, and religion. The question is why such irrational—or are they in fact occasionally rational?—constructions should appear at a time when Europeans from two former geopolitical parts are enjoying unprecedented levels of prosperity.

For me, home has for the last two decades been New Orleans—a city in many ways more Creole and European than American. It is not a prosperous or dynamic city like the capitals of the east European accession states have become. But its cultural gumbo is every bit as rich as what any European city can serve up. A while ago I lived in a boardinghouse not far from Commander's Palace, the celebrated restaurant in the city's Garden District. I was the rare lodger who was neither black nor employed at the restaurant and so the inquisitive elderly black landlady who still sang at the local gospel church asked where I came from. "Canada," I said, referring to my birthplace. She immediately tried to console me: "Tha's all right, honey chil', we all God's chil'ren."

Amen. Whether Canadian in New Orleans (hardly a disadvantageous status), Turkish in Germany, or Roma in the Czech Republic, we are all relatives. But unlike my former landlady, not everyone accepts this notion. Across all Europe, there is spreading anxiety about the many who arrive from elsewhere, who do not really belong. Even as the European Union pushes for integration, ordinary people seem poised for culture wars. This study seeks to capture and gauge these countervailing pressures across the continent and the British Isles.

This book presents four contrasting perspectives on Europe: 1) the Europe of an interlocking web of institutions and processes; 2) the Europe that is a construction of its supranational and national elites; 3) a conflicted Europe made up of competing values that its diverse citizenry cobbles together; and 4) a Europe of belonging and exclusion, of a transcendental culture and of knee-jerk hatreds, that its literary intelligentsia narrate. Whether the continued existence of a divide within Europe—running roughly along the line of the Cold War Iron Curtain—is confirmed by each of these perspectives is the subject of this book.

NOTES

1. Nira Yuval-Davis, "Belongings: In between the Indigene and the Diasporic," in *Nationalism and its Futures*, ed. Umut Ozkirimli (London: Palgrave, 2004).

2. A study that influenced my thinking on this subject is John M. Hobson's revisionist *The Eastern Origins of Western Civilization* (Cambridge: Cambridge University Press, 2004). His East refers not to a part of Europe but, essentially, all non-European civilizations. In this book, West (in uppercase) is used as shorthand for the Western world. When referring to the two parts of Europe, west and east (in lowercase) are employed.

3. Gerard Delanty and Chris Rumford, *Rethinking Europe: Social Theory and the Implications of Europeanization* (London: Routledge, 2005), 29.

4. I use the convention "western" Europe to refer to the fifteen EU member states before May 2004. In turn, "eastern" Europe consists of ten of the twelve states that joined beginning in 2004 (Cyprus and Malta are excluded).

5. *BBC News*, "Outrage at 'olde Europe' Remarks," January 23, 2003.

6. Timothy Garton Ash and Ralf Dahrendorf, "The Renewal of Europe: Response to Habermas," in *Old Europe, New Europe, Core Europe: Transatlantic Relations After the Iraq War*, eds. Daniel Levy, Max Pensky, and John Torpey (London: Verso, 2005), 143.

7. Imre Kertész, "Europe's Oppressive Legacy" (keynote speech at the Perspective Europe conference, Academy of Arts in Berlin, June 1, 2007). www.signandsight.com/features/1382.html

8. Michael Emerson, "What Values for Europe?" in *Islam and Tolerance in Wider Europe*, ed. Pamela Kilpadi (New York: Open Society Institute, 2007), 10–11.

9. Cas Mudde, "Central and Eastern Europe," in *Racist Extremism in Central and Eastern Europe*, ed. Cas Mudde (London: Routledge, 2005), 279.

10. Milada Vachudova, *Europe Undivided: Democracy, Leverage, and Integration after Communism* (New York: Oxford University Press, 2005).

11. Wole Soyinka, *The Open Sore of a Continent* (New York: Oxford University Press, 1997), 129.

12. Delanty and Rumford, *Rethinking Europe*, 7.

13. Delanty and Rumford, *Rethinking Europe*, 66.

14. Cornelius Castoriadis, *World in Fragments: Writings on Politics, Society, Psychoanalysis, and the Imagination* (Stanford, CA: Stanford University Press, 1993), 9.

1

Europe's Institutions and Millennial Expansion

INEVITABLE CONVERGENCE?

Even before Europe became a union of twenty-seven sovereign states, well before it adopted a common currency and passport, even before the states had started selling goods tariff-free to each other, the continent was a standard-setter for the rest of the world. Zygmunt Bauman, a sociologist originally from Poland who spent three decades teaching in England during the Cold War period, drew attention to "the unchallenged position of Europe as the reference point for the evaluation, praise or condemnation of any other form of human life, past and present, and as the supreme court of law where such an assessment was authoritatively pronounced with no right of appeal."[1] In his many books on Africa and other developing regions of the world, the late Polish journalist Ryszard Kapuściński repeatedly highlighted how it was sufficient just to be a European in order to feel like a ruler everywhere else.[2] These observations had been incorporated into a fictional narrative by another Pole writing a century earlier. In 1902, Joseph Conrad published *Heart of Darkness*, a study that contrasted barbarism in the Congo with the light of European civilization.

If a normative regime for the world exists today that establishes a set of prescriptive values, it is European-made. This is the result of Europe having built up its political capacity and credibility and reflected this in its track record—an unprecedented continentwide project of economic and political integration. In 1795, German philosopher Immanuel Kant could propose the "universal unification of the human species," but around him Europe's empires were uniting peoples by military force and political partition. Some two centuries later, in 2002, French philosopher Étienne Balibar advanced the more modest idea of forging a "transnational public order" in Europe. The continent had taken to heart the "lesson of tragedy" that was the two world wars and was moving ahead with spreading this transnational public order across the breadth of the continent.[3]

Considering that history's two bloodiest world wars were fought largely on European soil in the twentieth century, it is extraordinary that much of the world turns to Europe today for moral guidelines. Given that in the view of some radical historians it was Europe that for over a millennium and a half emulated eastern civilizations—not the other way around—the turnaround seems miraculous.[4] Considering that in the 1960s, after destalinization had been initiated in the Soviet bloc, Samuel Huntington and Zbigniew Brzezinski remained skeptical that real convergence between eastern and western Europe was in the making, a Europe of twenty-seven member states stretching from Ireland across three seas to Estonia, and from Portugal over the landmass to Bulgaria—all accepting being bound by the EU's accumulated laws, or *acquis communitaire*—seems like a mirage, too good to be true.[5]

Recent European Union expansion has more than doubled the number of member states from twelve in 1995 to twenty-seven in 2007. In the process, the EU was transformed from a purely western European organization—Greece was, in geographic if not philosophical terms, the exception—to one spanning the entire continent. Most Nordic and certain Balkan countries were added in this frantic era of enlargement.

Given this rapid expansion, it is easier today to remember which European countries are *not* members of the EU than which are. Affluent Switzerland and Norway have not joined. On Europe's eastern periphery are Belarus, Moldova, Ukraine, and the Russian Federation—all quasidemocracies, at best, and not involved in accession talks. In the Balkans, Albania and Macedonia jumped through the initial hoops set up on the road to full membership. By contrast, Serbia had accession talks delayed because of disagreements over Kosovo's future as well as its lack of cooperation in handing over war criminals to The International Criminal Tribunal for the Former Yugoslavia based in The Hague. Turkey, with Croatia, officially began membership negotiations in 2006. For many different reasons, the prospects for Turkey remain dim. Then there is Iceland, in the mid-Atlantic, on its own and not in the EU.

These recent waves of EU enlargement were presided over by an uncharismatic low-key Italian, fittingly known as *il professore*. President of the European Commission until 2005, Romano Prodi had been called Europe's "first prime minister" (as it happened he was fortunate merely to become Italy's prime minister). By 2007, the EU had nearly 500 million citizens, functioned in twenty-three official languages, used three different alphabets (Latin, Greek, and Cyrillic) and sprawled from the Atlantic to the borders of Russia. Prodi consciously associated his vision of European unification with that carried out—by force of arms—during the reign of Charles the Great (768–814). Known as Charlemagne, Charles the Great expanded the Carolingian empire from what is today France to Bavaria and Saxony in the north, and to Italy and parts of Spain in the south.

Even as today there are those who insist on Europe's "unique" and "historically determined" road to political integration, many centuries ago what seemed unique about Europe was just the opposite—its uncanny ability to create divisions of all kinds. Europe was the region of the world where the establishment of rigid national boundaries first took place. Emerging national elites competed with each other in claiming they were the most qualified agents and advocates of Europe as a whole, even as they fought each other for influence.

The invention of the balance of power system after the religious wars, the distinctions drawn between racial and cultural groups, the exclusion of Russian- and Turk-conquered areas of Europe from the rest of the continent, and even the reification of climatic zones contributed to the emergence of a checkerboard of states by the nineteenth century.[6] The signing of the Treaty of Westphalia in 1648, acclaimed by international relations specialists as the origin of modern state sovereignty, could equally be regarded as blazoning the prototype of the territorial state consumed with maintaining its borders and flaunting its uniqueness. England, France, and Holland were such statist prototypes. In 1815, the Congress of Vienna represented an effort to resurrect a pre-Napoleonic Europe of states. But no accommodation was made for eastern European nations, which were left under the domination of tsarist, Austrian, and Ottoman empires. An altogether different prototype—the making of an iron curtain dividing Europe—was being designed.

Over the centuries, visions of a united Europe had appeared in the thought of numerous philosophers and political leaders. In 1306, Pierre Dubois, a counselor for the Duke of Burgundy, appealed for a European federation. In 1693, the English Quaker William Penn conceived of a united states of Europe with its own parliament, or *dyet*. A century later, in 1795, the great German thinker Kant drafted a philosophical sketch for a perpetual peace among states. Russia's tsar Alexander I, vanquisher in 1812 of the army of Napoleon and harboring his own ambition to unite Europe, proposed the Holy Alliance of Christian states in Europe. The educating state sketched in the post-Enlightenment theories of Jean-Jacques Rousseau and Hegel held out the prospect of a future moral unity and common identity.

Early socialist thought addressed the importance of reforming Europe. In 1814, Claude Henri de Rouvroy Saint-Simon, a Frenchman of noble birth, published a work entitled *The Reorganization of European Society* in which he called for the creation of a new set of universal institutions.[7] Europe was in "critical disequilibrium," he asserted, and outdated institutions, as found in Europe preceding the Congress of Vienna, retarded the evolution and progress of society. In his books Saint-Simon argued that new institutions would promote industry, combat poverty, eliminate privilege, and forge greater unity within Europe. Saint-Simon also became an advocate for a secularized form of Christianity that could provide Europe with a modicum of spiritual unity.

Apart from philosophers, many artists, writers, and composers expressed their creative visions of a Europe at peace and in harmony. In 1823, Ludwig van Beethoven completed his Ninth Symphony, the fourth movement of which was set to the words of German poet Friedrich von Schiller's "Ode to Joy." Written in 1785, the ode acclaimed a day when "all men will become brothers." In 1985, Beethoven's hymn was formally adopted as the anthem of the EU, though it lost this status when the 2007 Lisbon Treaty opted to remove supranational EU symbols.

Arguably, the most prescient vision of a united Europe of the future was that captured by France's great nineteenth-century poet Victor Hugo. Although radical in his humanist politics, Hugo acknowledged the importance of capitalism and democracy: "A day will come when the only fields of battle will be markets opening up to trade and minds opening up to ideas. A day will come when the bullets and the bombs will be replaced by votes, by the universal suffrage of the peoples, by the venerable arbitration of a great sovereign senate which will be to Europe what this parliament is to England, what this diet is to Germany, what this legislative assembly is to France."[8]

Box 1.1 Victor Hugo's Prophecy

"A day will come when your arms will fall even from your hands! A day will come when war will seem as absurd and impossible between Paris and London, between Petersburg and Berlin, between Vienna and Turin, as it would be impossible and would seem absurd today between Rouen and Amiens, between Boston and Philadelphia. A day will come when you France, you Russia, you Italy, you England, you Germany, you all, nations of the continent, without losing your distinct qualities and your glorious individuality, will be merged closely within a superior unit and you will form the European brotherhood."

Source: Victor Hugo, "Opening Address to the Paris Peace Congress 1849" (August 21, 1849), http://www.ellopos.net/politics/eu_hugo.html.

Where such great political thinkers and artists failed to make inroads into constructing a Europe in harmony, a very unlikely force did. The bureaucrats of Europe after World War II recorded the first major institutional successes for uniting Europe. We discuss these fathers of Europe (as they are now frequently described) below.

Alongside grand liberal utopias came a number of unification projects for an illiberal Europe. Hitler's Third Reich is one example. Vichy France, for example, can be construed as a regime embracing a German-led unification process.[9] Stalin's Cominform, founded in 1947, is another illustrative case. Its transparent agenda for a Soviet-led political bloc across Europe spawned resistance in the form of national communism in the east[10] and indirectly, later, of Eurocommunism, a democratizing movement within west European communist circles.[11] Although it was focused on proletarian unity, the late nineteenth-century Socialist International inspired by Karl Marx has sometimes been classified as the first illiberal communist-inspired unification project.

A more recent, if short-lived, example of an effort to promote European unity on the basis of an illiberal project was the establishment in 2007 of a coalition of right-wing parties as an official parliamentary bloc at the center of the network of European institutions—the European Parliament (see chapter 2). It survived for just a few months. Nevertheless, the bloc's existence raised the question whether a new type of European unity based on shared fears of ethnic, religious, and immigrant minorities is in the making.

Is the noble project of a common liberal European home being hijacked today by xenophobes and, increasingly, Islamophobes? The symbolism stemming from a far-right parliamentary group from Romania—elected at the time that country joined the EU—putting the xenophobic bloc in the European Parliament over the threshold needed to received formal recognition raises a related question. Has enlargement into central and eastern Europe increased the chances of the EU becoming illiberal, exclusionary, and intolerant? How much substance is there in the claim that a more nationalistic group of central and eastern European states—still not recovered from having their identities repressed by Soviet-imposed communism for half a century—is eroding Schiller, Beethoven, and Hugo's idealistic conceptions of European harmony? Going one step further, is Kant's notion of perpetual peace jeopardized by the newfound fractiousness of the enlarged EU?

To address these questions we need to review the postwar histories—they are distinct enough from each other to be termed histories—of western and eastern Europe. For the west, we need to understand why European integration became a political imperative and how it was promoted. In the east, we need to describe the experience and legacy of communism, which included a perverse Soviet model of political and economic integration that made east European nations feel un-European.

THE INTEGRATIONIST MOMENTUM OF THE WEST

"Europe has seen two of the world's grandest attempts at large-scale social steering," observed Göran Therborn, "building socialism in the East and uniting the nation-states of the West."[12] The next sections inquire into these processes and make the case that the separate steering systems helped keep the two Europes apart for nearly half a century.

Box 1.2. Commonplace Terms Used to Describe Europe
"The discourse of Europeanization is dominated by superficial metaphors suggesting a teleological project legitimated by grand EU narratives, such as 'widening' and 'deepening' or 'ever closer union'; vague, if not inaccurate, sociological terms, such as 'integration' and 'inclusion,' and morphological metaphors such as 'multi-leveled' governance."

Source: Gerard Delanty and Chris Rumford, *Rethinking Europe: Social Theory and the Implications of Europeanization* (London: Routledge, 2005), 3.

No systematic theory about Europeanization has been developed. No doubt Europeanization was kick-started by a set of practical imperatives that initially spurred cooperation among western European states. Cooperation among economically advanced countries was regarded as a process to end all wars—a self-evident proposition but by no means a historically inevitable development.

Few historians would contest that the Yalta and Potsdam treaties of 1945, concluded by wartime allies Britain, the United States, and the USSR, had countenanced a Soviet sphere of influence in eastern Europe. An overlooked and unintentional effect of the treaties was to distinguish a geographically compact, politically Atlanticist western Europe. Political structures were constructed in the west to reflect this emerging geopolitical reality while still incorporating the overriding concerns of all states: security, peace, prestige, prosperity, and protection of national values. Ensuring lasting postwar peace on the continent was the overriding priority, and to achieve this goal Franco-German reconciliation was indispensable.

There was no substitute for increased direct bilateral cooperation between the two countries. Churchill's Britain had played an indispensable part in the liberation of France and the defeat of Germany. The United States had done both these things *and* put together the Marshall Plan in 1947 to help western Europe recover economically from the devastation of

World War II. But any semblance of an Anglo-American condominium was a cause for concern on the continent. The only authentic continentalism had to be a product of countries in western Europe.

From the 1950s, international relations specialists became fascinated with the subject of regional integration. It has been defined as "the process whereby political actors in several distinct national settings are persuaded to shift their loyalties, expectations, and political activities toward a new and larger center, whose institutions possess or demand jurisdiction over the pre-existing national states."[13] International relations theorists have identified two general approaches to regional integration.

The first is federalism, which entails the creation of transnational political organizations leading to a political union of independent territories. A "United States of Europe" in which a single supranational authority would appropriate sovereignty from individual states would constitute such a federal system. Proponents of European federalism have included Jean Monnet, who in 1951 became the first president of the European Coal and Steel Community (ECSC), a pioneering supranational European organization. Another European federalist was Jacques Delors, European Commission president from 1985 to 1995.

More recently, the process in the EU leading to the adoption of a supranational constitution has engaged federalist supporters with advocates of a second, more gradual, approach to integration. Sacrificing state sovereignty is the issue that divides federalists, who advocate "full steam ahead" to supranationalism, from gradualists, who are squeamish about the sudden disappearance of sovereignty. Danish social theorist Ulf Hedetoft has captured EU dynamics around the issue: "the factual neutralization of sovereignty is effected by means of direct bargaining and codified in treaties and institutional mechanisms for interest maximalization. There is a *quid pro quo* at work: interests for sovereignty."[14] Put another way, "Sovereign behavior and EU integration are incommensurable—it is one or the other, not both at the same time."[15]

The gradualist approach to integration, pursued by the founders of the early European communities of the 1950s, involves functionalism. The idea here is that integration of national states can best be brought about by first creating a central organization to oversee technical and economic tasks. Piecemeal nonpolitical cooperative ventures can then create a demonstration effect where cooperation spills over from one area to another. State sovereignty is eroded over time rather than done away with by decree.

International relations specialists usually single out three types of regional organizations: economic, military, and political. Generally, political integration is most difficult to achieve because of states' reluctance to part with sovereignty. The postwar history of European integration substantiates this proposition. The first postwar transnational organization in Europe was the Council of Europe, founded in 1949, which was designed to enforce human rights norms among its member states. It was not a political organization, therefore, but was intended to serve as the embryo of European political unification.

Also in 1949, a U.S.-led military alliance—the North Atlantic Treaty Organization (NATO)—was established by fourteen European countries, together with the United States and Canada, to counter the rising threat of Soviet expansionism. It was not long, however, before efforts were made to reinforce Europe's independence from the United States. In 1950, the French prime minister proposed setting up a European Defense Community that would be anchored by an all-European army—an idea subsequently rejected by the French parliament itself. A draft for a European Political Community was also prepared but went nowhere. These initial projects were ambitious but unrealistic, imposing transnational responsibilities on western Europe that it was not yet mature enough to carry out.

Inspired by Monnet's thinking about European federalism, it was France's foreign minister Robert Schuman who is credited with launching the plan for European economic integration—an area less contentious than setting up a European army. The ECSC was established in 1951 to manage the energy needs of six west European industrial states: France, West Germany, Italy, and the Benelux countries (Belgium, The Netherlands, and Luxembourg). These same countries quickly agreed to set up the European Atomic Energy Community (Euratom), which was to manage, regulate, and develop this energy resource. The attachment to national sovereignty had not been snuffed out, however. On becoming president of the French Fifth Republic in 1958, Charles de Gaulle announced that his country would go it alone in the development of atomic energy. France subsequently took no active part in Euratom.

The jewel in the crown of European integration was the signing of the Treaty of Rome in 1957, which created the European Economic Community (EEC). Over the next three decades, the EEC's name was changed several times before it finally became known as the European Union in 1993. For the sake of simplicity, we use the term European Community (EC) to refer to this organization between 1957 and 1993.

In the formative period of European integration, we can distinguish five principal ways that nation-state identity was constructed. The first was the idea of *a Europe of nation-states* that recognized the primacy of the state as the basis of intergovernmental structures and relations. The second was Europe as *a community of values*, championed by President de Gaulle in his notion of *l'Europe des patries*. The third was Europe as *a third force*—a democratic socialist alternative to capitalism and communism. The fourth was European modernity within the Western community—*an Atlanticist framework* promoted by European Christian Democrats and also the United States (especially through NATO). It centered on liberal democracy as a common denominator. Finally, *Christian Europe* (*Abendland*) was an identity construction largely inspired by Catholic social values and obligations.[16]

Over the next half century European integration steadily dispensed with nation-state constructions other than the first—a Europe of nation-states—and fourth—an advanced Western community. In the decades after the Treaty of Rome was signed, the piecemeal enlargement of the European Community of the founding six was made possible by the dual appeal of building a community of nation-states while promoting economic modernization for all. To be sure, some political leaders may have viewed economic integration as an end in itself. Others regarded it as a prelude to the political unification in Europe. But the immediate payoff understood by all was that economic integration would inevitably lead to Europe's modernization. It also positioned Europe as a major player in the global economy.

The backbone of the European Community was the Franco-German alliance. In 1963, President de Gaulle and Chancellor Konrad Adenauer formalized the relationship by concluding the Élysée Treaty. Among its provision was article one, chapter II on foreign affairs. It stated:

> The two Governments will consult before any decision on all important questions of foreign policy and, in the first place, on questions of common interest, with a view to reaching as far as possible an analogous position. This consultation will bear among others on the following subjects:
>
> - Problems relating to the European Communities and to European political cooperation;
> - East-West relations both on the political and the economic planes;
> - Matters dealt with within the North Atlantic Treaty Organization and the various international organizations in which the two Governments are interested.

This institutionalized form of Franco-German foreign policy coordination did not produce a spillover effect on the community of six. In economic areas, however, the European Community recorded steady advances, including by 1968 a free-trade area in which mutual tariffs were eliminated. The six applied Common Customs Tariffs (CCT) on imports from other countries, in this way achieving a customs union. They forged an economic union when they authorized the free movement of capital and labor across national boundaries. In 1978, the European Currency Unit (ECU) was introduced. It consisted of a basket of European Community currencies that served as the basis for fixing exchange rates among member states while setting a floating rate for the outside world. More and more monetary decisions and, related to them, social policies were decided together by member states. The legitimacy of such policy harmonization was enhanced in

1979 with the first elections held to a European Parliament. An intellectual force behind the creation of such a quasifederal institution had been Italian Altiero Spinelli who, since the 1950s, had supported the idea of a United States of Europe with its own supranational constitution.

When Delors became commission president in 1985, the push for a single market, single currency, and stronger political institutions increased. Two major treaties were concluded during his presidency. The first was the Single European Act of 1987, which specified a time line—1992 was the target date—for the completion of a single market free of tariffs and of other barriers to the exchange of goods and services. The Single Act expanded EC jurisdiction to such new areas as the environment, technological development, employment policy, and, most ambitiously, foreign policy cooperation. The concept of "cohesion policy" was put forward, with the practical element consisting of a doubling of structural funds available to the less economically developed regions of member states. The Single Act laid the groundwork for a deepening of European integration that now entailed both political and social spheres. The road to a European union had been paved.

The Maastricht Treaty of 1993 was the greatest achievement recorded under Delors, but it owed much to the support given by West German chancellor Helmut Kohl and French president François Mitterrand. The Soviet bloc and Soviet Union had just disintegrated and German unification was in the cards. But France needed to be reassured that a greater Germany would remain anchored in Europe. For Mitterrand, the way to achieve this was to establish a single European currency that Germany had hitherto been unenthusiastic about because of the strength of the deutsche mark. A common currency, together with a European Central Bank, would cement an enlarged Germany's commitment to Europe. But the euro, as the new currency was to be called, became a flash point in identity-fostering processes for many other nations. Some states were not possessive about their national currency—for example, the Belgians were not nostalgic about the Belgian franc—and seemed willing to make the jump to an emerging European identity symbolized by the euro. Others dug in and rallied to the defense of their national currencies, such as Britain with the pound sterling and Denmark and Sweden with their respective kronor. One way or another, the introduction of the euro represented an identity-arousing experience.

The Maastricht Treaty formally adopted these two monetary institutions. In an effort to address the "democracy deficit" in the community, the treaty also augmented the powers of the European Parliament. In addition, it created two new "pillars" to go with the European Community, which was the first and central pillar. One was Common Foreign and Security Policy (CFSP), to be considered the second pillar. The other was police and judicial cooperation in criminal matters—the third pillar. These new dimensions had more of an intergovernmental than a supranational character but, again, the assumption was that momentum would carry a cooperative venture into an integrationist one. The Maastricht Treaty named this conglomerate of institutions, pillars, and policies the European Union.

ELITES ON INTEGRATION AFTER MAASTRICHT

Our examination of how western Europe pursued integration has focused on the preferences of the political elite, because that was the group that really carried it out. Popular representation within the European Community was of marginal importance until the Maastricht Treaty. So it is ironic that this ambitious treaty, which took a nuts-and-bolts approach to further integration while positioning the European Parliament closer to the center of decision making, triggered a popular backlash against the Eurocrats in Brussels. More and more citizens in EU member states felt that there had been little democracy during the EC's evolution. They came to believe that Eurocrats had been pushing ahead with an agenda that furthered their own interests. The backlash resulted in an only razor-thin margin of approval of the Maastricht Treaty in a referendum held in France in 1992. The first time around the Danes rejected it out of hand before ratifying it in a second referendum that made no reference to the introduction of the euro. Britain opted out of both the Eurozone and the social chapter related to employment. A legal challenge against Maastricht provisions was mounted in Germany, though it eventually failed. Across member states the EU's governance process had come under attack. The EU was seen as remote from and inaccessible to ordinary citizens.

The wave of Euroscepticism that followed Maastricht led to the convening of an EU Council meeting of all political leaders, which took place in another Dutch city. The Amsterdam Treaty was signed in 1997, but only came into force two years later. Its most prominent provision was giving the European Parliament the right to approve both the commission president and the commissioners themselves. Its assent was also now needed for the majority of decisions that the Commission took. Parliament's control over the executive branch—a moot subject in the early decades of the community—had been formalized.

Another key innovation of the Amsterdam Treaty was "enhanced cooperation" among member states, which would replace the unanimity principle. As the adoption of the euro had highlighted, a minority of member states might not wish to participate in an EU policy initiative, and so the Amsterdam conference agreed that under such circumstances a group of member states could pursue a project by themselves. An early example of such "opting out" was Britain, Ireland, and Denmark deciding not to participate in the project to abolish border controls for EU citizens. This enhanced coop-eration arrangement took on added importance as a way to manage in-tractable disagreements when the EU was enlarged to twenty-seven mem-bers a decade later.

Another milestone in the EU's evolution took place at the Nice summit in late 2000. Attention shifted from deepening integration to widening membership. Twelve candidate countries were put in line for admission and a timetable for enlargement was set. To deal with enlargement, new rules had to be drafted so as to adapt EU institutions. The most significant of these included re-weighting member states' votes, changing the qualified majority voting principle in the EU Council, modifying the composition of the European Commission, and reapportioning and increasing the number of European Parliament seats. These changes are outlined in the next sec-tion on EU institutions.

The Nice summit involved high politics and not merely institutional fine tuning. "At issue was the allocation of national power within Community institutions rather than strengthening them, a subject in which only the Commission was interested."[17] The summit also approved the Charter of Fundamental Rights, though its legal status was to remain unclear for the next few years. The Nice Treaty took effect in 2002.

Nothing in the EU's history compares to the enlargement of 2004 when, at a stroke, ten states—eight of them ex–Soviet bloc nations—joined the or-ganization. This eastern enlargement was qualitatively different from earlier cases. In 1972, the six had become the nine with the admission of Den-mark, Ireland, and the United Kingdom—all consolidated democracies with advanced market economies. At this time Norwegians, protective of their national identity and flush with new revenue from North Sea oil fields, rejected membership in a referendum.

Expansion did not always mean adding members to the Community. Eu-ropean states that maintained close economic links to their former colonies sought a special status for these faraway, now independent states. Accord-ingly, in 1975 the Yaoundé and Lomé conventions assured increased eco-nomic aid and preferential access to EC markets for African, Caribbean, and Pacific (ACP) states. By 2000, nearly all African and Caribbean states had signed the Lomé Convention.

Two decades after the drafting of the Yaoundé and Lomé conventions, a conference in Barcelona launched a Euro-Mediterranean process. Its aim was to create a free-trade area between the EU and countries in North Africa and the eastern Mediterranean. As important as this "reaching out" to non-European lands was, it did not profoundly reshape European identity.

EC expansion proceeded apace when Greece was added as a tenth mem-ber in 1981. Spain and Portugal's admission in 1987 made it a community of twelve. In 1995, Austria, Finland, and Sweden became the first new members of the EU after the Cold War's end. As more prospective members entered into accession negotiations, EU official discourse began to shift to issues related to "deeper integration" of countries with strong economies. There was now talk of two tracks for future political integration, because the candidate states in the east did not appear to have the same commitment to the integration project as the older members. In turn, Euroscepticism—a common phenomenon in the postmaterialist societies of the west—began to surface in some of the accession states.[18] In particular, in central Europe—Poland, the Czech Republic, Slovakia, and Hungary—concerns about national and religious identity, land acquisition by "foreigners," and state borders began to emerge. How cohesive and effective the enlarged EU would be became a fundamental question that shook the complacency of and confidence in the Union.

EU INSTITUTIONS AFTER THE 2007 LISBON TREATY

We have observed that the EU is a web of processes, policies, and institutions—formal and informal—as well as of publics, values, and identities. The Europe of institutions is in itself a complex, evolving set of structures that reflects a mix of integrationist idealism and pragmatic compromises. Belonging to this institutional EU involves a formal process determined by the degree of harmonization of a country's legislation and policy with the EU's *acquis communitaire*—its common, cumulative body of law. By contrast, belonging to Europe has different meanings when invoked in elite discourse, reflected in public attitudes, or narrated by cultural elites. The EU of institutions is neater, has greater legitimacy and appeal, and is less contested (though at times it is subject to fierce debate) than other types of European belonging.

Meeting in Lisbon in late 2007, twenty-six of the twenty-seven leaders of EU member states (prime minister Gordon Brown of Britain symbolically arrived after the official ceremony) signed what had been termed the Reform Treaty—a virtual European constitution that had taken years to complete (see chapter 2 for an account of the constitutional process). In order to achieve unanimous agreement on the treaty, the document had to deny it was a constitution and claimed it set out not to repeal previous treaties but to reform them. Among the most important institutional objectives of what is now known as the Lisbon Treaty was the "modification" of the positions, powers, and processes of existing core EU structures. Governance in the EU of the future was to be adapted in order to bridge the national interests of the twenty-seven member states—and counting—and the EU's supranational agenda. Let us examine how the EU will work when the Lisbon agreement—supposed to go into force in January 2009 but likely delayed because of its defeat in the 2008 Irish referendum—is implemented.

Perhaps the most commonly asked question about the EU is who is its head. There are three EU institutions that have been headed by a president: 1) the European Commission, 2) the European Parliament, and 3) the EU Council. A change effected by the Lisbon Treaty is the creation of a full-time president of the EU Council to go along with full-time presidents of the other two institutions. The intent of the treaty is, then, to elevate the status of the EU Council president so that at some point in the future, when enough support has been marshaled from member states, this president will represent the EU's highest political executive.

Until now, the closest that Europe had to a powerful president was the head of the *European Commission*, an institution that has been at the heart of the process of integration. The Commission supervises the implementation of treaties and manages EU funds, thereby exercising important executive powers. But it also initiates policy and submits policy recommendations to the EU Council and the European Parliament, in these ways exercising legislative initiatives.[19]

Commissioners are appointed by the governments of the member states, but they take an oath to act independently of them. They are therefore expected to think in pan-European terms. This stands in contrast to the EU Council, whose members represent national governments. Before the 2004 enlargement, each of the large member states appointed two commissioners, the smaller states one each. After enlargement, all states appointed one commissioner. The Lisbon Treaty accepted that this arrangement can exist until 2014. Addressing the problem of such a large, unwieldy, and ineffective Commission, the treaty reduces the number of commissioners to two-thirds of member states, that is, eighteen for a twenty-seven-member EU. Members will be chosen by rotation for five-year periods. This streamlined Commission is designed to enhance its efficacy and is purportedly more in keeping with the original vision of the Commission as a European federal executive. Commission president Prodi even called it a European government.

The role of the European Commission president has been open to interpretation. Officially, "The Commission shall work under the political guidance of its President" and he determines its internal structure and assigns responsibilities. The expectation is that he should behave more like a chief executive officer, or manager, than a partisan political executive. But ambitious Commission presidents like Delors and Prodi made much more of their office. In 2004, José Manuel Barroso of Portugal assumed the presidency, and he has been credited with engineering the successful conclusion of the Lisbon Treaty.

The candidate for president is proposed by members of the EU Council and approved by the European Parliament, "taking the European Parliament elections into account"—a clause added by the Lisbon Treaty. The intent is to make the office more politicized and representative of the European electorate, in this way enhancing its democratic legitimacy. Partisan views will now count in selecting a commission president. Here is an example: "In real terms it will be more difficult to hand over Competition or the Internal Market to an over liberal Commissioner if the majority in Parliament after the European elections tends to the left; conversely it will be as difficult to hand over Employment and Social Affairs to a Commissioner who leans too far to the left if the parliamentary majority lies to the right."[20] Adding to the more politicized character of the European Commission, its president is accountable to Parliament, which may dismiss her/him—or the entire Commission—by a vote of no confidence. There is even talk that political groups in the European Parliament—for example, the largest one made up of Christian Democrats—may propose their own candidates for European Commission president.

The *European Council* refers to the regular meetings bringing together the heads of state or government of the European Union and the Commission president. The Council, which most often meets in Brussels, outlines the EU's general political guidelines and therefore is responsible for high-level policy making. The EU Council, as it is referred to here, should not be confused with its close namesake, the *Council of Europe*—a separate international organization that focuses on human rights issues in Europe and even parts of Eurasia.

The *European Council of Ministers* (also known as the Council of the EU) is made up of the ministers of the member states. It meets several times a month though in nine different configurations, depending on the issue area involved. As examples, the General Affairs and External Relations configuration is made up of foreign affairs ministers; the Justice and Home Affairs configuration consists of member states' justice and home affairs ministers. Each member state designates one representative to the ministerial level who is authorized to act in the name of his government. Regardless of which ministerial configuration led to the adoption of a policy, it is officially described as a decision of the Council.

The Council of Ministers performs a number of functions. At a general level, it identifies the major orientations adopted by Europe. Together with the European Parliament, it determines the EU budget. Using the codecision procedure, it enacts EU legislation on the recommendations of the European Commission and European Parliament. For pillars two and three, it strives to formulate a common foreign and defense policy, as well as police and justice activities—above all, on counterterrorism—for member states.

The Council has been best known for its high-profile rotating presidency. Sometimes the *Presidency of the Council of the European Union* was inaccurately referred to as the European Presidency, suggesting it possessed an array of executive powers that it did not. For the first five decades of the

Community's existence, the Council presidency was given to the political leader of an individual country according to a predetermined system of rotation among member states and was held for six-month periods. The first presidency, in 1958, was held by Belgium. In practice, the country holding the position was charged with the responsibility of preparing an agenda and organizing and chairing all meetings of the Council over the six-month period. Naturally, each country also wanted to leave its mark during "its" presidency. Efforts were made by the country's head of government and foreign minister to broker deals furthering EU integration. The highlight of the six-month term was a summit (the EU Council *sensu stricto*) hosted by a city of the country holding the Council presidency.

The Lisbon Treaty wanted to strengthen the office of the president of the EU Council by giving him/her a fixed two-and-a-half-year term, renewable once. Elected by a qualified majority of the EU Council (the political leaders of all member states) and lacking a national mandate or source of legitimacy, the president will now give the EU a voice and face and will represent the EU in international affairs.

As suggested earlier, this office may serve as a prototype of a future EU presidency that is fully entrusted with executive powers. In its effort to have the EU increasingly speak with one voice, the Lisbon Treaty also solidified the office of the High Representative for Foreign Affairs and Security Policy by merging the two hitherto separate positions concerned with EU foreign policy. Also to be appointed by the EU Council and approved by the European Parliament, the High Representative will provide greater coherence to EU external policy. The officeholder will become an EU vice president, though not of the EU Council but of the European Commission. Clear demarcation of institutions and separation of powers have never been the EU's strong point.

The decision-making procedures of the EU's Council of Ministers have always been complex. Three types of voting take place depending on the subject being dealt with. First, for procedural decisions, a simple majority of Council members is needed. Second, qualified majority—a weighted voting system based on the populations of member states—is used for decisions involving specified policy areas including trade, economic affairs, and the internal market. The Lisbon Treaty increased from sixty-three to ninety-six the number of areas where a qualified majority, rather than unanimity, was required—for example, border controls, immigration, and asylum policy. Large EU countries have the right to opt out of a policy decision: Germany reserves the right to exclusively determine its immigration policy, France to design protection of its national culture, Britain to write its own fiscal and social legislation, and Spain to allocate the distribution of regional aid. Third, the Council of Ministers must reach unanimity to make decisions related to taxation and social security as well as pillars two and three: foreign policy, defense, and judicial and police cooperation.

The complexity of the Council's voting system is compounded by weighted voting. Enlargement necessitated re-weighting, and after protracted and rancorous negotiations at the Nice summit the twenty-seven states agreed on the following distribution:

29 votes: Germany, the United Kingdom, France, Italy
27 votes: Spain, Poland
14 votes: Romania
13 votes: The Netherlands
12 votes: Greece, the Czech Republic, Belgium, Hungary, Portugal
10 votes: Sweden, Austria, Bulgaria
7 votes: Slovakia, Denmark, Finland, Ireland, Lithuania
4 votes: Slovenia, Estonia, Cyprus, Latvia, Luxembourg
3 votes: Malta

To achieve a "qualified majority vote," 255 out of 345 total votes are needed. In addition, the Council has operated according to a "double majority system." Following the Lisbon Treaty, laws are adopted by the Council if they are supported by 55 percent of member states (fifteen in an EU of twenty-seven members). These member states must represent 65 percent of the total EU population for a resolution to pass.

This voting system, approved by the Nice Treaty, inevitably raised questions of fairness. Arguably, the most contentious issue that hamstrung treaty negotiations was why Poland was given just two votes less than unified Germany, which had a population double that of its neighbor to the east. Locked into a system that overrepresented its weight, whenever efforts were made to reform the voting system Poland threatened to veto them or to scuttle some other major EU initiative, such as an EU constitution.

The most difficult part of the negotiations over the provisions of the Lisbon Treaty involved overhauling the Council of Ministers' voting system. A hard-fought compromise was reached: as a concession to Poland, a new system would be introduced not before 2014 and, even then, would be gradually phased in over three years. During the transitional period, Poland or any other member could choose whichever voting weight they preferred. "The Nice agreement until 2017" was how the Polish leadership portrayed this compromise.

Poland was also reassured by a change made to the so-called Ioannina compromise, which sets the conditions for blocking a Council decision. Any combination of EU states representing 19 percent of the EU's total population—for example, Poland and France together—will be able to prevent the adoption of any measure by qualified majority voting (the Nice Treaty had stipulated a 26 percent threshold). Alternatively, a "blocking minority" has to be composed of any four states (under Nice it was three states). As if there were not enough safeguards for states dissenting with a qualified majority decision, the Lisbon Treaty introduced a provision for the transitional period to 2014 under which if members opposing a text are significant in number but still insufficient to block the decision, all states commit to seeking a compromise while reserving the option to vote at any time. Even with these changes, the Council of the EU will still be dominated by the most populous countries. Working together and co-opting a few allies, Germany and France will usually be able to push through their agenda.

The EU is notorious for its leviathan bureaucracy. Most of the work of preparing Council briefings and decisions is carried out by the *Permanent Representatives Committee* (COREPER); that is, the permanent representatives of the member states working in Brussels.

The legislative body of the EU is the *European Parliament*, which sits in Strasburg, France. We noted how it was been the chief beneficiary of the effort to rectify the democracy deficit that arose after the Maastricht Treaty. The Lisbon Treaty expanded the Parliament's co–decision making (with the Council of Ministers) to nearly fifty new areas, thereby putting the two on an equal footing in terms of legislative power. In a similar way, the Parliament has now been given equal rights on budgetary decisions with the Council of Ministers. As we have observed, the body's political control over the European Commission was also augmented.

Members of the European Parliament (MEPs) are elected by direct universal suffrage every five years under a proportional representation system, which has some national variations. MEPs are considered delegates, exercising their mandates independently, and so cannot be bound by instructions from their country's government or from a political group. At sessions, they do not sit in national delegations but are grouped in transnational political groups according to their political affiliation. When a group receives official recognition—that is, it crosses the threshold of nineteen MEPs from at least five countries—it becomes entitled to enhanced funding and agenda-setting powers. As a rule, votes in parliament are along political rather than national lines. In most cases, a simple majority is enough to pass a measure.

Although their official names are different, the main groups in the European Parliament are Christian Democrats (284 members at the end of 2007), Socialists (215), Liberals (103), Nationalists (44), Greens (42), a united left (41), and even a Eurosceptic Independence/Democracy group (24). The right-wing bloc of 20 MEPs formed in 2007 fell apart later that year when Romanian MEPs bickered with their Italian counterparts over perceived anti-Romanian attitudes in Italy.

For the period 2004–2009, the European Parliament is composed of 785 MEPs. The total is to be reduced to 751 for the 2009 elections. The number of MEPs representing each member state reflects the size of its population, though political trade-offs also play a part. For example, by the Nice Treaty

Germany was given more seats in Parliament in return for a reduced presence in the European Commission. The distribution of seats by country for the sixth term of the European Parliament (2004–2009) follows. The numbers in brackets give seats numbers for the 2009–2014 term.

99 (96):	Germany
78 (74):	France
78 (73):	Italy, United Kingdom
54 (54):	Spain
54 (51):	Poland
35 (33):	Romania
27 (26):	The Netherlands
24 (22):	Belgium, Greece, Hungary, Portugal, Czech Republic
19 (20):	Sweden
18 (19):	Austria
18 (18):	Bulgaria
14 (13):	Denmark, Finland, Slovakia
13 (12):	Ireland, Lithuania
9 (9):	Latvia
7 (8):	Slovenia
6 (6):	Cyprus, Estonia, Luxembourg
5 (6):	Malta

The European Parliament elects a president for half a parliament's term; that is, two and a half years, renewable for an additional term. If no absolute majority is received by a candidate in the first three rounds of voting, a simple majority in the fourth round is sufficient. The functions of this president are modest: he or she directs its activities and represents the institution to the outside world.

The *European Court of Justice* (ECJ) is currently made up of twenty-seven justices; that is, one from each member state. They are appointed by the common agreement of all members. Based in Luxembourg, justices serve for six-year terms and are responsible for establishing the rule of law in Europe. In 1963, the Court established the principles of the *primacy* of Community law on all member states—that is, its consistent and uniform application—and of *direct effect*—citizens claim their rights in the states' court systems. While it has no means of enforcement proper to a state, the ECJ has final authority on all legal matters and its decisions are binding on states and individuals.

The Court's jurisdiction is clearly defined. Its best-known responsibility involves judging the legality of Community acts, of actions by one member state against another, and of actions against the European Commission. Yet the most common legal cases involve European citizens or other legal persons (such as corporations) bringing litigation involving Community law against each other or against national governments. Such legal action begins in member states' courts but goes to the ECJ if a point of law needs clarification

With the ratification of the Lisbon Treaty, the Charter of Fundamental Rights referred to by the Nice agreement acquires a legal quality. In theory, any European law contrary to the values and objectives identified by the charter can now be declared null and void by the European Court of Justice. For example, the Court may force a rewriting of national laws regarding social and economic policy such as strikes, collective bargaining, and working hours. The Lisbon agreement added new social objectives to the charter, including full employment, eradication of poverty, and rights preventing social exclusion and discrimination. Two countries refused to sign the Charter of Fundamental Rights. Britain cited concerns over its ability to control social and economic policy and Poland was suspicious that its Catholic-inspired moral and family policies would be open to challenge.

The EU's many different institutions and processes are designed to strengthen the sense of belonging of individual states to Europe's community of nations. They promote regional integration while also projecting an image of political unity. If we considered the EU's institutional facade alone, we would find it difficult to identify a continental divide, a clash within European civilization, or different national ideas of political belonging. For the most part, EU political elites maintain the appearance of unity. The reality is different, however, when we turn to the views of nationalistic national elites, of ordinary citizens in each country, and of some cultural narrators.

If over the years western Europe has become battle-hardened by banging out agreements on European integration, this is a relatively new experience for the east. In many ways, the recent political history of eastern Europe stands out as an outlier to the integration process in the west. We turn to east European exceptionalism next.

THE COMMUNIST LEGACY IN THE EAST

Eastern Europe has no history to be proud of corresponding to the making of European unity in the west. The history of resistance to communist rule is its major source of pride. It is not surprising that western European prejudice against the east has appeared in many different guises. There have been unkind ways to explain why new Europe—a term laden with irony—has been slow to integrate into the EU. Former Italian prime minister Giuliano Amato had pressed hard for speedy accession of ex-communist nations into the EU but nevertheless understood why the west initially prevaricated about enlargement. The EU was really telling the east, "Yes, you are European, but only of mixed blood."[21]

Mixed blood can be interpreted in different ways. One view is that it was the east European experience of communism and Russian domination that turned these countries into merely hybrid Europeans. Starkly put, while the west was embracing the idealism of unification after World War II, the east was confronting the harsh reality of Soviet hegemony. As the west constructed ways to integrate national economies, laws, and politics, the east had all autonomy snuffed out as Sovietization created a Potemkin village of contrived unity.

Some political observers, in both the east and the west, held that these two rigid rival blocs did not amount to very much. French philosopher Étienne Balibar referred to the geopolitical division as a "phantom," an "illusory Europe, the *Europe of contradictory illusions* maintained since 1920, and most particularly since 1945, by the very way that each of the two 'blocs' laid exclusive claim to the idea of Europe in its confrontation with the other."[22]

External stimuli have profoundly affected the course of European integration. France, under de Gaulle but also under Chirac, was deeply suspicious of Anglo-American influence on the continent. But for different reasons, so were east European countries after World War II. Political stimuli coming from the West served in a number of cases to reinforce the east's separateness and isolation.

Eastern European nations had taken different cultural pathways before that war. Some were oriented towards western Europe, others towards the east and Russia. But the Yalta agreement of 1945, concluded by the Big Three (Winston Churchill, Franklin D. Roosevelt, and Joseph Stalin), which promised eastern Europe free elections even while it remained under the occupation of the Red Army, facilitated the imposition of Soviet rule in the region. The postwar sources of eastern European separateness from the West can, therefore, be traced back to Yalta. By the 1970s, it was the Kremlin that regularly invoked Yalta to condemn Western meddling in its satellite states. Yalta had become a code word for the Cold War adversaries' mutually recognized spheres of influence in Europe.

Some of the West's policies after World War II—including the integration agenda—reinforced the Iron Curtain separating eastern Europe from west. Winston Churchill's 1946 speech in Fulton, Missouri, was a case in point. Few disagreed with his conclusion that "From Stettin in the Baltic to Trieste in the Adriatic, an iron curtain has descended on the continent." But his invocation of providence as explaining American nuclear hegemony—"God has willed the United States, not some Communist or neo-Fascist state, to have possession of atomic bombs"—resonated of a crude form of messianism. And his call for a fraternal association of English-speaking peoples stood no chance of receiving support anywhere on the continent, west or east.

The Soviet hold on its eastern satellites tightened as the West continued to misplay its cards. A few months after Churchill's Iron Curtain speech, U.S. secretary of state James Byrnes stated that Germany's eastern frontier with Poland, running along the Oder-Neisse rivers, was not final. Many otherwise anti-Soviet Poles began to fear German revanchism. Soviet foreign minister Molotov deftly triggered an eastern European backlash to the 1947 Marshall Plan for economic recovery, claiming it would divide Europe, undermine national sovereignty, and revive Germany. Two years later Stalin announced the creation of the Council for Mutual Economic Assistance (CMEA), a self-help organization for the Soviet bloc that had been excluded from Marshall aid.

The political geography of Europe was shaped by these opening moves in the Cold War game. In 1949, the establishment of a separate Federal Republic of Germany and of a Western military pact, NATO, provoked the Kremlin six months later to create the German Democratic Republic—its own puppet state—and six years later to establish its own military alliance system, the Warsaw Pact.

The east's separation from the west was above all the consequence of Soviet rule. But an ancillary factor was the process of western integration and the discourse justifying it, which had the effect—presumably unintended—of leaving the east out in the cold. International systems theory asserts that under bipolarity, when two great powers dominate world politics, small and medium powers are left little room for maneuver; they must join the alliance system of one or the other of the two hegemons. Yugoslavia was exceptional in this regard, but it had cleverly crafted a foreign policy that might bring on a world war if either military bloc violated its nonaligned status.

Setting aside other factors, therefore, the very nature of the international system during the Cold War forced eastern Europe into political and economic dependence on the USSR, its superpower neighbor. If international factors determined the region's fate, domestic consequences followed.

Arguably, the legacy of communism manifests itself most acutely in the retarded economic development of the east. With the 1989 democratic breakthrough, the east was desperate to join European structures, adopt a market economy, build its material base, and begin to approach the living standards of core EU members. The social attitudes and foreign policy orientations of these countries from the early 1990s on reflect these aspirations. But they have sometimes stood at odds with the postmaterialist values and conciliatory foreign policies characteristic of much of west Europe.

The international political economy of the Cold War period is important in explaining divergent paths of development. An increasingly interdependent world meant that a regime's capacity to maintain growth was affected by external processes and actors. Global economic cycles of recession or boom, an expansion in world trade, and increasing aid from international organizations, foreign governments, and commercial banks could push one bloc of countries forward and leave another one behind. Beginning in the 1970s, Poland and Hungary sought to break out of the insulation of the CMEA and they managed to secure billions of dollars in credits from governments and private banks in capitalist countries. Their plan was to use these credits to purchase Western licenses, technology, and consumer goods, which, in turn, would generate export-led growth. The risk involved was not simply antagonizing the USSR, which at the time was mired in "the era of stagnation." Rather this "goulash communism" that offered more consumer goods to citizens made Hungary and Poland vulnerable to the economic cycles of the West. Deteriorating terms of trade for eastern European agricultural and energy (coal) products were exacerbated by a rising interest burden fueled by double-digit inflation in the United States and western Europe.

By the 1980s, the east's external indebtedness—Romania was an exception because its nationalist leader Nicolae Ceauşescu had refused on principle to borrow from the West—led to austerity measures rather than growth. Even the Soviet Union was no longer a secure trading partner as its geopolitical position became increasingly shaky and its economic decline required that it slash its subsidized energy exports to eastern Europe and instead concentrate on selling energy at world market prices to capitalist states. The international economic trends of the 1980s conspired to throttle communism by the end of the decade.

In 1989, the economies and societies of the West were predominantly service sector–based, postindustrial, and consumer-oriented. On the eve of its disintegration, the Soviet bloc was still wrestling with how to modernize its industrial and manufacturing juggernauts—not how to transcend them. Production for the consumer market remained a low priority. In the West, agriculture had been fully mechanized and the rural population was in rapid decline. In the east, a remarkably high proportion of the population—40 percent in some countries—still worked on the land in the late 1980s. Western European governments were beginning to address the problem of environmental degradation, while those in the east were concerned primarily with maintaining the fiction of a full employment economy in which environmental regulations had no place. The communist economies had reached a breaking point. By the late 1980s, they faced the conundrum "damned if you do, damned if you don't."

In the 1970s, people's incomes in eastern Europe had increased, but then what we may call "Huntington's law" kicked in. Named after political scientist Samuel Huntington, who had earlier written on convergence between the Cold War blocs, then on the new wave of democratization beginning in the late 1970s, and was later to write on the clash of civilizations, this "law" established a correlation between economic development and democratization. Huntington found that three-quarters of countries that were nondemocratic and had per-capita GNPs of between $1,000 and $3,000 in 1976 had democratized significantly by 1989. This was the "transition zone" to democracy. But his analysis identified another factor triggering change: "the combination of substantial levels of economic development and short-term economic crisis or failure was the economic formula most favorable to the transition from authoritarian to democratic government."[23]

Many other variables can be cited, of course, for communism's collapse: the organization of civil society in the east, the revolutionary impact of Lech Wałęsa's independent trade union Solidarity in Poland, more liberal foreign travel for eastern European citizens, their decreasing fear, Soviet military defeat in Afghanistan, the rise and fall of Mikhail Gorbachev in the Kremlin, perhaps even the threat of Ronald Reagan's Star Wars antimissile project. But special mention must be given to the 1975 Helsinki Agreement concluded by thirty-five European and North American states. It pledged signatories to respect human rights and fundamental freedoms and, against the odds, ended up boxing communist governments in. As citizen groups formed Helsinki committees in eastern European states, communist authorities found their societies opening. Through underground educational and communications networks organized by dissidents, citizens were able to increase their political knowledge and develop more participatory values. The Vatican, too, played a pivotal role in triggering democratization movements in the east by delegitimizing their authoritarian regimes. This was never more the case than when a Polish cardinal became Pope John Paul II in 1978.

Communism had required a political culture at once compliant and engaged. Citizens were expected to take an active part in the construction of the socialist order while, at the same time, never meaningfully participating in the political process. The atheist world outlook espoused by communism was alien to most citizens in the east whether they were Catholic, Orthodox, Protestant, or Jewish. The supposed superiority of class solidarity over patriotic values also left them cold. Finally, Karl Marx's ideal of work as having an intrinsic value that would promote human emancipation and self-fulfillment was deformed by the communist system into work that was fundamentally alienating and unremunerative.

Eastern European societies developed pathological features, therefore, that made them very different from those in the West. In many respects, the two parts of Europe became "two solitudes."

This changed with the end of the Cold War. In a provocative synopsis, French sociologist Jacques Rupnik observed that the "collapse of communism has had a dual impact on Europe. It affirms a European identity vis-à-vis non-Europe (Islam) or 'semi-Europe' (America and Russia). But it also brings back into the open some intra-European divides . . . . There are different ways of belonging to 'Europe.' One is always someone else's 'barbarian.'" The juxtaposition between the "established" Europe of the west and the "emerging" Europe of the east was one of the first telling reconceptualizations after the Cold War's end.[24]

Swedish sociologist Göran Therborn also sensed the persisting schism between east and west at Cold War's end: "Like all collective identities, European identity formation has faced two kinds of Others: one outside, beyond the range of the (potential) collective, the second inside, dividing the self to be made. A persistent problem of Europeanism . . . has been that the unifying Other outside has been distant, weak or nebulous, and therefore largely irrelevant to most people of the continent, whereas the divisive Other within has been close and strong, in many cases stronger and closer than in other parts of the world."[25]

Much of the 1990s in Europe was taken up with the question of how to resolve "the divisive Other within." The EU once again reached for its stock-in-trade tool—institutionally driven integration—to bridge the divide. Copenhagen became the site of the key meetings seeking to purge the divisive Other within Europe.

NOTES

1. Zygmunt Bauman, *Europe: An Unfinished Adventure* (London: Polity, 2004), 29.

2. Ryszard Kapuściński, *Lapidarium V* (Warsaw: Czytelnik, 2003). These notes by Kapuściński, identified as "the Herodotus of our times," systematically take up questions of globalization, identity, culture, and morality.

3. Étienne Balibar, *We, the People of Europe? Reflections on Transnational Citizenship* (Princeton, NJ: Princeton University Press, 2004), 222.

4. An excellent starting point for examining this view is John Hobson's *The Eastern Origins of Western Civilization* (Cambridge: Cambridge University Press, 2004).

5. Samuel P. Huntington and Zbigniew Brzezinski, *Political Power: USA/USSR* (New York: Viking Press, 1964).

6. John Agnew, "The 'Civilisational' Roots of European National Boundaries," in *Boundaries and Place: European Borderlands in Geographical Context*, eds. David H. Kaplan and Jouni Häkli (Lanham, MD: Rowman & Littlefield, 2002), 25.

7. Henri Saint-Simon and Augustin Thierry, "The Reorganization of European Society," in Saint-Simon, *Selected Writings on Industry, Science, and Social Organization*, ed. Keith Taylor (New York: Holmes and Meier, 1975), 130–36.

8. Victor Hugo, "Opening Address to the Paris Peace Congress 1849" (August 21, 1849), www.ellopos.net/politics/eu_hugo.html.

9. See Robert O. Paxton, *Vichy France, Old Guard and New Order, 1940–1944* (New York: Columbia University Press, 2001).

10. See the example of Yugoslavia in Adam Ulam, *Titoism and the Cominform* (New Haven, CT: Greenwood Press, 1971).

11. Carl Boggs and David Plotke, eds., *Politics of Eurocommunism: Socialism in Transition* (Boston: South End Press, 1980).

12. Göran Therborn, *European Modernity and Beyond: The Trajectory of European Societies 1945–2000* (London: Sage, 1995), 334.

13. Ernst B. Haas, *The Uniting of Europe: Political, Social and Economic Forces 1950–57* (Stanford, CA: Stanford University Press, 1958), 16.

14. Ulf Hedetoft, "Sovereignty Revisited: European Reconfigurations, Global Challenges, and Implications for Small States" (unpublished paper, Aalborg University, 2005), 14.

15. Hedetoft, "Sovereignty Revisited," 23.

16. Thomas Risse, "A European Identity? Europeanization and the Evolution of Nation-State Identities," in *Transforming Europe: Europeanization and Domestic Change*, eds. Maria Green Cowles, James Caporaso, and Risse (Ithaca, NY: Cornell University Press, 2001), 203–4.

17. John Gillingham, *European Integration, 1950–2003: Superstate or New Market Economy?* (Cambridge: Cambridge University Press, 2003), 335.

18. Ronald Tiersky, ed., *Euroskepticism: A Reader* (Lanham, MD: Rowman & Littlefield, 2001).

19. For official information on EU institutions, see the EU's web site, http://europa.eu.

20. Fondation Robert Schuman, "The Lisbon Treaty: 10 Easy-to-Read Fact Sheets" (Paris: Fondation Robert Schuman, December 2007), fact sheet 2, www.robert-schuman.eu.

21. Amato quoted in Attila Melegh, *On the East-West Slope: Globalization, Nationalism, Racism and Discourses on Central and Eastern Europe* (Budapest: Central European University Press, 2006), 9.

22. Étienne Balibar, *We, the People of Europe? Reflections on Transnational Citizenship* (Princeton, NJ: Princeton University Press, 2004), 89.

23. Samuel P. Huntington, *The Third Wave* (Norman: University of Oklahoma Press, 1993).

24. Jacques Rupnik, "Europe's New Frontiers: Remapping Europe," in *Boundaries and Place: European Borderlands in Geographical Context*, eds. David H. Kaplan and Jouni Häkli (Lanham, MD: Rowman & Littlefield, 2002), 6, 9.

25. Therborn, *European Modernity and Beyond*, 243

2

Quarreling over Institutions in an Enlarging EU

Throughout the 1990s, eastern European countries put into place, step by step, the various pieces making up a democratic system and market economy. At around the same time, the EU was deepening integration with the adoption of the Maastricht Treaty. The obvious question arose as to whether these two processes, occurring independently of each other in the two parts of Europe, should somehow be fused. After all, European integration and democratic consolidation could be turned into complementary processes serving the interests of both parts of Europe. Should, then, eastern European countries be given membership in the EU as quickly as possible, or should they apprentice for a time?

The question assumes that enlargement was EU-driven rather than shaped by the national politics of applicant states. This view is best described as an *external incentives model* where the EU dangles rewards (assistance and institutional ties) and sanctions (exclusion from the club) before a state that is a prospective rule adopter. Examples of rules that are to be adopted range from Maastricht-set limits on the budgetary deficit to treatment of minority groups.

The EU insisted that new members had to comply with the 80,000-page *acquis*, thereby making accession conditional on its legal, political, economic, and social criteria. The process of rule adoption in the applicant states was inextricably tied to harmonizing their national legislation with the *acquis*, though occasional progress reports from the European Commission (described later) appeared at times to suggest that embracing the

39

acquis was not enough. The image the EU wished to project was of its rigorous application of membership conditionality.

On the other hand lay the fact—attentively grasped by western European publics skeptical about enlargement—that "the EU has not been very vigorous in enforcing its conditionality in some policy areas." For example, requiring EU-wide open markets for the purchase and sale of land was not pushed very aggressively in the first years of accession negotiations. In particular, the EU was willing to accept asymmetrical arrangements for new states to cover transitional periods of various lengths.

The EU's role as principal agent in the enlargement process is questionable because of another consideration. "While the EU might demand adjustment and actively promote the adoption of its rules in a particular issue area, its actions might merely coincide—and possibly reinforce—a process of rule adoption that a state has embarked on independently."[1] If we accept these arguments, then it is hard to depict the enlargement process as engineered exclusively by the EU.

A more nuanced approach is to recognize that instead of being lured merely by external incentives, "A government adopts EU rules if it is persuaded of the appropriateness of EU rules" either by the EU or by the rules' resonance at home. Such a *social learning model*, as it has been called, underscores the autonomy of applicants in making up their minds whether what are clearly externally formulated rules should be transferred to their countries. A key factor is whether an applicant state "regards EU rules and its demands for rule adoption as appropriate in terms of the collective identity, values, and norms."[2]

Finally, there is the *lesson-drawing model*. "A government adopts EU rules if it expects these rules to solve domestic policy problems effectively." Communism had failed eastern European societies, whereas the EU stood as a model of promoting prosperity and peace. Comparisons were regularly made; for example, Poland compared itself to Spain: a Catholic society of similar size with a recent experience of authoritarianism. While Spain's economy took off with membership in the Community, Poland's languished in the CMEA. For Poland and other eastern European states, the transferability of EU rules became attractive when "A key condition for a state to draw a 'positive' lesson from scanning rules in operation elsewhere is the perception that these rules are successful in solving policy challenges similar to those at home."[3] The fact that the lesson-drawing process often involves rule adaptation rather than pure rule adoption by an applicant state made it even more appealing to new Europe.

Prospective rule adopters may become frustrated, however, by the slower pace of gaining admission when their input into shaping the rules—illustrated by the social learning and lesson-drawing models—is given importance. Being an EU apprentice for a time because of the need to match national rules with EU ones was interpreted by some as deliberate delaying tactics. This critique was seized upon by Eurosceptics in eastern Europe before accession to achieve electoral gains. But anti-EU forces would also not have welcomed a faster track to membership, among other reasons because it would have imposed unmodified external rules, for example, fully open markets for property transactions. It is also plausible that the EU's enlargement process involved use of *both* external incentives *and* an extended apprenticeship with little real opportunity for applicant states to modify existing rules.

The EU's terms of apprenticeship for applicants were set in Copenhagen in 1993 while Denmark held the presidency of the EU Council. Membership conditionality for applicant states entailed three criteria:

1. a functioning market economy with the capacity to cope with competitive pressures and market forces within the EU;
2. stable political institutions guaranteeing democracy, the rule of law, and respect for human rights and minority rights;
3. ability to take on the obligations of EU membership, including the *acquis communitaire*—the EU's legislative corpus.

An additional condition that seemed ominous at the time concerned the EU's integrative capacity—the ability of the existing EU to absorb new members and maintain its momentum for integration.[4] This potentially significant caveat gives the EU the right to slam the door on applicants should difficulties arise within the EU. But it was not invoked, even after September 11, when security concerns could easily have justified sealing existing EU borders. Old Europe was serious about incorporating new Europe into its organization.

New Europe leaders had enough reasons, however, to be anxious about their membership bids. From 1997, the European Commission had begun to issue regular progress reports on applicant countries. Commission president Prodi's 1999 report, for example, deflated hopes of immediate EU accession for Poland, Hungary, and the Czech Republic. Central European candidates had recorded little improvement since the Commission had issued its encouraging initial opinion in 1997. Prodi's 1999 finding was that candidates had "not progressed significantly" in adapting laws and structures to EU criteria. Some eastern European countries had been slow to implement reforms in such key areas as reducing government aid for ailing industries, restructuring their steel industry, and modernizing their agricultural sector, fisheries, and infrastructure (especially highways). In short, while the countries had fulfilled the first two conditions for membership—a market economy and political stability—they had work to do in harmonizing national laws with the *acquis*.

Prodi announced that from then on two procedural considerations would be given greater importance. First, the accession timetable would be based exclusively on merit rather than politics. Successful democratization was not in itself a reason to accelerate the accession timetable if economic and social progress was unsatisfactory. Second, the Commission would now itself monitor applicants' claims about progress rather than trusting their self-reporting.

As the new millennium neared, other potential problems with membership bids surfaced. The third Copenhagen condition had made reference to the need for protection of minority rights. The Commission's 2001 report recognized the stability of political institutions and the existence of a functioning free market in central Europe, but it emphasized that protection of minorities had become problematic. The Czech Republic was given the lowest rating because of its discriminatory practices against its Roma population. In addition, it had never rescinded the Beneš decree (named after president Edvard Beneš) of 1945, which had expelled Czechoslovakia's German and Hungarian minorities. It remained in effect when the Czech Republic had applied for EU membership.

The Commission also cited Slovakia's discriminatory laws on its Hungarian minority and Hungary's nationalist and irredentist rhetoric in aspiring for a greater Hungary of all Magyars as alarming developments.

For their part, applicant states were frustrated with taking aim at what they saw as a moving target. What was perceived as a capricious use by the EU of membership conditionality aroused Euroscepticism across the region. Nationalist anti-EU right-wing parties started to make gains in elections to national parliaments. It came as a relief to supporters of EU accession when the Commission's 2002 report offered grounds for optimism. In the case of the largest applicant, twenty-seven of the thirty chapters of the accession negotiations with Poland had been successfully completed; only agriculture, fisheries, and the environment needed further harmonization. The report did point out that "corruption remains a cause for serious concern" across the region. Nevertheless, it forecast that ten states were on track to be admitted before the 2004 European Parliament elections.[5] For accession to become a reality, a final round of bargaining had to be conducted.

Denmark was again at the head of the rotating presidency of the EU Council when the summit of EU member and applicant states' leaders was convened in December 2002. The Danes had become known as the "norm entrepreneurs" of the EU, and under their EU presidency the enlargement criteria of human rights and democracy were reinforced.[6] Still, it came as a surprise that the Copenhagen summit, instead of tying up loose ends, was shaken by the Polish government's demand for more concessions on the preliminary terms of accession. Their counterparts from the nine other applicant states were, by contrast, eager to sign the accession terms.

The most significant concession that the Poles obtained was an advance payment in 2005–2006 of €1 billion from the EU structural fund for urgent state expenditures. Originally, Poland was to have received this sum after 2007 and then only to finance infrastructural projects. Another concession that Poland gained was an additional €108 million for securing the country's eastern borders, above and beyond the €172 million earmarked for this purpose earlier.

The EU's Common Agricultural Policy (CAF) proved the most serious stumbling block in Copenhagen. With its price and income support for farmers, it is costly to maintain. Enlargement was certain to raise its costs by increasing the pool of eligible recipients in the large eastern European agrarian sectors. The compromise reached in Copenhagen was that Polish farmers would be eligible to receive "topping up" amounts ranging from 50 to 60 percent of the farm subsidies given to their counterparts in existing EU member states. The rural development package of €5 billion from 2004 to 2006 for the ten accession countries also proved attractive to their agrarian sectors.

Probably the most emotional issue in joining the EU for average Poles was the sale of land to foreigners. The specter of Germans, in particular, buying land in their ancestral homes in Silesia and Pomerania (provinces that reverted to Polish rule after World War II) was worrying.[7] As one analysis concluded, because of repeated invasions and border changes, "To Polish patriots, land is not so much a good as a heritage never to be betrayed."[8] Land has, of course, more than symbolic value: two-thirds of Poles still live in the countryside and one-quarter make a living from agriculture. A major negotiating coup for the Polish government was, therefore, the agreement with the EU for a twelve-year transition period—five years longer than any other candidate country—for restricting land sales to EU nationals.

The Copenhagen agreement finalized the terms of accession of the ten applicants and scheduled formal enlargement for May 1, 2004. Only a year after the agreement was concluded, however, another divisive issue confronted the enlarging EU—the status of the Common Foreign and Security Policy. In 2003, the EU published its European Security Strategy, which pointed out political problems in eastern Europe. The document observed: "the integration of acceding states increases our security but also brings the EU closer to troubled areas."[9] The way to address security challenges in the east was to "promote well governed countries to the east of the EU with whom we can enjoy close and cooperative relations." At the time that President Vladimir Putin seemed to be rolling back Russia's democratization gains, the EU claimed that "the best protection for our security is a world of well-governed democratic states."

This policy document constituted a pragmatic approach to dealing with two interrelated phenomena in eastern Europe: accession states' Russophobia and, conversely, Russia's NATO-phobia. For the CFSP really to become a common EU policy, ex-communist states' fear of Russia had to be mitigated. At the same time, the Russian Federation could not be allowed to gain politically from western Europe's willingness to be more conciliatory towards it. The tension between new Europe and Russia had to be relaxed if CFSP was to take hold. But it was to persist for years, as eastern Europeans could not comprehend why the west did not seem very Russophobic.

CONFLICT OVER A CONSTITUTION

EU enlargement was set for May 1, 2004. Some of new Europe's more radical Eurosceptics and anti-communists—the two often were the same people, nationalists hostile to any type of external interference in their countries—pounced on the May Day accession. Eastern Europe, they claimed, was trading in domination by Moscow for domination by Brussels.

Their suspicions were further raised by the start of discussions about an EU constitution. These talks began even before the EU was formally enlarged. In 2002–2003 the European Convention, headed by former French president Valéry Giscard d'Éstaing, began to review a number of different constitutional drafts. An EU summit in 2003 in Porto Carras, Greece, approved a number of key clauses for a draft constitution.[10] Proposed Article 10 asserted that "The constitution and law adopted by the Union's institutions shall have primacy over the law of the Member States."[11] The EU was to have its own foreign minister, though heads of national governments would retain a veto over the making of EU foreign policy and would maintain control of their own armed forces. The EU was to have a legal personality, allowing it to sign treaties in its own right that would bind all members. It was even suggested that at some point the EU might have a seat on the UN Security Council in place of Britain and France.

A number of the provisions of the 2007 Lisbon Treaty originated in a constitutional draft approved by the Porto Carras summit. The EU Council was to have a president with a longer term than the six months the hitherto rotating incumbent enjoyed. Though it was not formally included in the draft, there was an unstated assumption that at some time in the future the two EU presidencies—of the Council and the Commission—could be merged into a single "President of Europe." The smaller EU states—and many of the ten accession countries, which had not been invited to the summit—expressed concern that the Franco-German alliance anchoring the EU was conspiring to ensure that such a European president would either be chosen from either country or at the least would do its bidding. In turn, states with larger populations welcomed the proposal for the European Parliament to enact legislation by majority vote.

In addition, the constitutional draft enshrined such values as human dignity, freedom, democracy, equality, the rule of law, and human rights. It also codified European citizens' rights in a Charter of Fundamental Rights, which was to become legally binding on all members.

In fall 2003, an Intergovernmental Conference convened in Rome to finalize the Constitutional Treaty. The timing of the Rome summit was significant: six months later ten new members were joining the EU. It appeared the EU was prepared to take another step towards federalism even though two basic powers—raising taxes and going to war—still eluded it.

When the final version of the constitution was presented to a summit of all twenty-five member states, held again in Rome in October 2004, it bore all the appearances of a *fait accompli*. Indeed, the document was formally approved by all national leaders and was scheduled to come into force in November 2006, after ratification—by referendum or vote in parliament—by all twenty-five states. The process seemed to be on track when nine states quickly signaled their approval. But then voters in France and Holland voted down the document in summer 2005. The constitution had been torpedoed.

In France, the concern was that enlargement would weaken the country's influence within the EU. French and Dutch nationalists opposed their countries' surrendering so much sovereignty to the EU. Many French and Dutch voters on the left were hostile to the creation of an enormous free market that the constitution would sanction. Fears of massive immigration of cheap labor from the east were heightened by a constitution perceived as transferring social protection policy to the EU. Individual states would no longer be able to decide how "welcoming" a policy they should adopt for immigrants. If the EU were to rigorously enforce border controls and restrict the movement of labor and the influx of immigrants, it would receive the backing of members, which would drop their concern about the centralization of power. But an EU taking over labor and immigration policies from member states and liberalizing them would lead to vehement opposition to such usurpation of power. Finally, start-up talks about membership for Turkey became another grievance that voters had about the EU at a time of growing Islamophobia.

Though not a major reason for the referendum defeats, the rise in the influence of Germany at the heart of the EU must be noted. Germany was seen to be pushing the constitutional project hardest. As two British academics wrote, "The trend towards a stronger constitutional and more federal EU is a direct consequence of German power. The consolidation and Europeanization of central Europe and to a lesser extent of the further eastern countries is to a considerable extent the result of German influence."[12]

The "no" votes in France and Holland derailed the constitutional process, but EU elites were not ready to give up. By early 2007, another nine member states had ratified the document. Calling themselves the "constitution bloc," they emphasized that 270 million EU citizens were now in their camp. The eighteen states supporting the draft constitution met in Madrid in early 2007 and proposed that the draft—already a lengthy document—should be further expanded to address citizen concerns in such sensitive spheres as immigration, EU expansion, energy, and climate change.

Two large EU states—Britain and Poland—along with the Czech Republic (none of which had ratified the draft or attended the Madrid meeting) proposed just the opposite—a new, slimmed-down mini-treaty. Their opposition to the constitution stemmed in part from a concern that the Franco-German core of the EU would be strengthened at their expense.

The UK's exceptionalism in the EU has always stood out. It is usually explained away by the fact that it is not on the continent. There is more to it than that. Britain has jealously guarded its right to determine its domestic and foreign policies. As a permanent member of the UN Security Council, partner in the Anglo-American special relationship, and effective head of the far-flung British Commonwealth, it feels that it can afford to give a lower priority to EU integration processes. This has regularly provoked rancor within the EU.

The cases of Poland and the Czech Republic—and a number of the other ex–Soviet bloc nations—cannot be reduced to geography. A political science explanation would stress how eastern European politics is "out of phase" with the west. "Fundamentally, the East European states are still in a 'state-building' and 'nation-building' phase, whereas most West European states have long since completed (or exhausted) their state-building and nation-building projects and have moved essentially into the post-nationalist era."[13]

Poland's special role in blocking a constitutional agreement derives from a number of factors. It was by far the largest of the eastern accession states. It had been in the front line in opposing Sovietization and in bringing down the communist system. It remained absorbed in the myth of *antemurale Christianitatis*—serving as the easternmost bulwark of Western Christianity. The Catholic Church, a powerful institution in the country, raised concerns about the EU's secularism. Poland's governments at this time were prickly, unstable, fickle, and stridently independent-minded. In short, the country felt that it was "owed" something by the West. The last thing it was prepared to do was to allow an externally created constitution to be imposed on it.

In summary, we can agree that "the debate and framing of the European Constitution is a good example of the social construction of the European polity in a process of contestation, negotiation, persuasion, and power in which multiple actors are involved."[14] Cultural factors in large measure have driven this contestation. They help explain the schism that undermined the constitutional project. How, then, was an agreement on the Reform Treaty forged in 2007?

HAMMERING OUT THE 2007 LISBON TREATY

The specter that had been haunting nationalist movements in Europe was that the EU would become a superstate led by France and Germany that would steadily erode the national powers of other member states, whether in the west or the east. The EU summit held in Brussels in June 2007 and chaired by German chancellor Angela Merkel had to make decisions that would allay such fears. Symbolic politics was the natural place with which to begin this process.

At the summit, leaders agreed to drop the term constitution, which had become associated with the superstate idea, and to describe the proposed new set of institutional arrangements as a reform treaty, highlighting the part played by the sovereign nation-state in the process. Furthermore, the status of this treaty, drafted by an Intergovernmental Conference the following month, was that it was the latest in a series of EU treaties and did not supplant the others. Terms associated with superstate construction such as frameworks and European law were removed and the less presumptuous EU lexicon of regulations, directives, and decisions was embraced. Unlike the constitutional draft, the Reform Treaty contained no references to such statist symbols as the EU flag, the anthem ("Ode to Joy"), and the motto ("Strength in Diversity"). These ceased to have any legal standing—from one perspective a step back from constructing a more integrated Europe. The Reform Treaty became known as the Lisbon Treaty in December 2007 when all twenty-seven leaders of EU member states signed the accord in the Portuguese capital.

Box 2.1. No Poetry Here

"When we started this summit I said that the goal was to find the right arrangements to improve and to guarantee our capacity to act, the new treaty architecture does it. Last night was the entrée, tonight was certainly the main course, there was a lot on the plate and I have to admit that at times it was not easy to digest. And I have to say honestly that maybe it is not the most beautiful lyrics the text we have adopted but I am sure it will be efficient prose."

Source: José Manuel Barroso, "European Council: Extracts from the Presidency's Press Conference," June 23, 2007, http://ec.europa.eu/avservices/services/showShotlist.do?filmRef=52676&out=HTML&lg=en&src=1.

Setting aside the symbolic politics, in most other respects the Reform Treaty was a thinly disguised version of the constitution. Before it could take effect, it had to be approved by all twenty-seven member states. At the time Irish voters rejeced the Treaty in 2008 by a vote of 53 to 47 percent (with 53 percent turnout), eighteen states had approved the agreement in their parliaments with the remaining eight set to follow the same course.

Let us recall some of the main provisions of the Treaty as described in chapter 1. There would be a full-time president of the EU Council, which consists of the regular meetings of heads of government and state. This office could be parlayed in the future into a directly elected President of Europe. European Commission membership would be reduced in size. More powers would be granted to the European Parliament at the same time that national veto power would be curtailed in many areas. The EU would appoint a new High Representative for Foreign Affairs and Security Policy who would have an enhanced budget and discretionary powers. At the same time, the intergovernmental character of the CFSC was underscored. These measures were to come into force in mid 2009.

Nevertheless, a few substantive aspects of the failed constitution were not incorporated into the Reform Treaty. The most publicized one was the clause in the constitution that had asserted that the EU "shall have an internal market where competition is free and undistorted."[15] The intent of the clause had been to emphasize that free competition was one of the EU's principal objectives. Its status as a clause in the constitution had been an upgrade from its place as a subclause in the Treaty of Rome.

At the EU summit in Brussels in 2007, French president Nicolas Sarkozy persuaded German chancellor Merkel to redraft the clause and omit the phrase "where competition is free and undistorted." Sarkozy's recent election to the French presidency had in part been attributable to his campaigning against allegedly unfair competition from low-cost nations inside and outside of Europe. Nevertheless, deleting the competition phrase appeared to alter one of the EU's fundamental principles. It could affect EU competition policy, which was regulated by a Competition Commissioner whose activities were aimed at combating cartels and illegal state aid that could distort fair trade. Sarkozy's coup—which also pleased left-wing critics who branded the EU as a vast capitalist market insensitive to citizens' interests—was partially undone by EC president José Barroso's insistence that a protocol to the treaty restating EU competition policy had to be added.

The constitutional draft had referred to the EU as having its own legal personality, empowering it to sign international treaties and join international organizations in its own right. The Reform Treaty affirmed that the EU had the status of a legal person. But it also added a caveat: that having such a legal personality "will not in any way authorize the Union to legislate or to act beyond the competences conferred upon it by the member states in the treaties."[16]

Box 2.2. What England Can Expect from the 2007 Treaty
"Just to recap, what this will mean is that under the new Constitution there will be the likelihood of a European Public law offical, The European Public Prosecutor, who will be able to order British police to arrest somebody in Britain for a crime (such as the thought crimes of racism and xenophobia), which is not a crime in Britain.

Then under the European Arrest Warrant the individual can be extradited to a European country where they can be held without charge at the judge's pleasure (remember the plane spotters in Greece), and then flung into a foreign jail."

Source: "The Devil's Kitchen, More EU Reform Treaty Fun," August 5, 2007, http://devilskitchen.me.uk/2007/08/more-eu-constitution-reform-treaty-fun.html.

One other principal change effected by the Treaty on the constitution draft involved the status of the fifty-article Charter of Fundamental Rights. The Charter provides a comprehensive list of well-established rights ranging from freedom of speech and religion to the right to shelter, education, and fair working conditions. The Charter was not made an integral part of the Treaty, though there is a reference to it. Concerned about the Charter's possible effect on its own legal system, Britain was allowed to opt out of the Charter altogether. Poland also stayed out—even with a change of government in 2007 that brought a more pro-European coalition to power—because of the felt need to protect its Catholic moral system.

Giscard d'Éstaing, the former French leader who had headed the initial convention commissioned to write a constitution for Europe, viewed the changes from his draft to the agreement that was approved in Lisbon as insignificant and triggered only by tactical considerations. The new treaty was not going to be put to popular vote and possibly suffer a humiliating defeat, as had happened earlier in France and the Netherlands. "Above all, it is to avoid having referendum thanks to the fact that the articles are spread out and constitutional vocabulary has been removed," he claimed, rather persuasively.[17]

SETTING STANDARDS OR DOUBLE STANDARDS?

The constitutional and treaty processes involved not just power relations within the EU but also EU standard setting. What has been the Union's record on standard setting? Has it been consistent, and are standards set for applicants standards that longtime EU members are able themselves to meet? More generally, has enlargement made standardization more difficult?

The issue of respect for minority rights is a case in point. The very definition of minorities is contested by some EU states, above all France. Some countries have put the onus of defining who constitutes a minority not on the minority group itself but on the people who constitute the majority group in the state. By this logic, the identification of the majority people serves as the starting point. Thus the present Russian Federation constitution refers to titular nationality—the people or ethnicity embodying a republic. Traditional German constitutional law referred to *Staatsvolk*—the people making up the state. Such constitutional or legal distinctions about who *really* belongs to a state provide validation for labeling remaining groups as minorities or outsiders.

The rise of anti-immigrant parties in western Europe has illustrated the increasing political salience of minority and immigration issues. For some time one of the region's greatest fears has been of large-scale immigration. It has become an emotional issue and has developed into an electoral hot potato. It spawned robust far-right parties in a number of countries: the electoral success of Jörg Haider's far-right Freedom Party in Austria in 2000; Jean-Marie Le Pen's qualification for the second round of the French presidential elections in 2002; and the 2002 second-place finish in Holland of the Pim Fortuyn List (a party named after the Dutch populist murdered on the eve of a general election).

The anti-immigrant movement has put into question whether EU minority rights standards are really fixed and nonnegotiable in the west. Three Norwegian specialists, observing the EU from a critical if close distance, inferred from this that "There is a risk that on the day of enlargement the applicant states will have a 'higher' standard of rights than the existing EU."[18]

Just as evocative an example of possible EU double standards was the practical question of ceilings on government budget deficits. Under the Stability and Growth Pact agreed upon at the EU Council in 1997 in Amsterdam, the Commission had established a set of rules at Germany's behest intended to more rigorously monitor budget deficits in the poorer Eurozone member states such as Greece and Portugal. An excessive deficit procedure was put into place to enforce fiscal discipline in Eurozone states. Budgetary deficits were limited to no more than three percent of GDP. In practice the larger EU economies—Germany, France, and Italy—were more often guilty of profligate spending and deficits above this ceiling. It was particularly incongruous that just weeks after agreeing to enlarge to twenty-five members, the EU Commission had to warn Germany to bring down its deficit, which had reached 3.9 percent (the Eurozone average was 2.2 percent). A number of EU leaders criticized the pact as inflexible and unsuited to current economic conditions. Germany's larger deficit was blamed, for example, on the costs of German unification. Commission president Prodi called the excessive deficit procedure "stupid, because rigid."[19]

These were not the type of criticisms that the new accession members were in a position to make. If they were to entertain hopes of joining the Eurozone any time soon, they had to follow the path leading to fiscal convergence that the Stability and Growth Pact had sketched out. Some wiggle room was created in 2005 when EU finance ministers enacted some modifications to the pact. While maintaining existing threshold values, they proposed different ways of accounting for budget deficits. In particular, "exceptional conditions" in a country could justify higher budget deficits.

Few leaders in existing EU states thought it "stupid" to apply the excessive deficit procedure to prospective Eurozone members in eastern Europe. Not surprisingly, one Polish finance minister proposed an ingenious, if self-serving, solution to the deficit problem. The government budgets of a bloc of countries—for example, central Europe—should be pooled so that one country's excessive deficit could be balanced out by others' smaller or nonexistent deficits.[20] The formula was modeled on the Kyoto environmental treaty's concept of transferable pollution rights. This idea was never going to fly, however. While Poland, with a deficit in 2003 slightly higher than Germany's, would stand to gain from such "transferable deficits," those central European states which had adhered to strict budgetary discipline would have gone unrewarded.

The first former communist nation to be admitted to the Eurozone was Slovenia at the start of 2007. It had satisfied EU finance ministers that it had attained required low levels for the budget deficit, public debt, interest rates, and inflation. Other states in new Europe had some way to go before gaining admission. Lithuania's application was turned down because of its high rate of inflation while Hungary put back its date for entry because of a huge budget deficit. Estonia, whose economy has been favorably described as "the New Zealand of eastern Europe," had to deal with high inflation and was unlikely to make a serious bid for Eurozone membership before 2011. High public spending levels and excessive budgetary deficits in Poland and Romania pointed to their not gaining admission until around 2013 if not later. This slower-than-anticipated process of Eurozone entry demonstrated that fiscal convergence did seem to be taken very seriously by EU finance leaders. Only Slovakia, scheduled to enter the Eurozone in 2009, proved an exception.

Standards for securing national borders have been another important subject confronting the EU. One of its recurring visions, articulated in the 1997 Amsterdam Treaty, is of a common area of freedom, security, and justice. Earlier, the 1986 Single European Act had defined the Community's market as an area without internal frontiers. A year earlier in Schengen, a

Luxembourg town bordering on France and Germany, these three states, together with Belgium and Holland, had reached an agreement—outside EU structures—on border controls for people. Except at airports, there would not be any routine passport checks within this newly established Schengen zone. More rigorous controls would be conducted on the zone's external frontiers. There would be greater standardization of rules among the countries to deal with asylum and immigration issues and increased cooperation in combating crime would also be institutionalized. The Schengen concept caught on and by the 2007 enlargement phase thirty countries—all twenty-seven EU members plus Norway, Iceland, and Switzerland—had signed the agreement.

Signing and implementing the Schengen agreement are two different things, however. Britain and Ireland, which have reached a bilateral immigration control agreement, have not taken part in a control-free border with other EU states. Neither have the twelve new accession states. It does not automatically follow that border controls are dismantled upon EU accession. Greece, for example, joined the EU in 1981 but was admitted into the Schengen zone only in 1999.

Before allowing them to implement the Schengen agreement, the EU undertook a review of accession countries' border preparedness in four areas—air space, visas, police cooperation, and personal data collection. The planned date for incorporating the new EU states into the Schengen zone was 2008. A series of "logistical" problems seemed to make that target date unrealistic. For example, the EU's border agency Frontex, whose headquarters are in Warsaw—the first EU agency to be based in one of the accession states—had trouble finding suitable job candidates. Lower salary levels in Poland, even for EU employees, made recruitment difficult, thereby threatening to undermine efforts to curb illegal immigration. These problems sparked concerns among some eastern Europeans that they were being treated unequally by their western counterparts and that a two-tier Europe of border controls was coming into existence.

To be sure, the need to ensure uniform standards of public security within the Union was brought home by the 2001 terrorist attacks in the United States, which were planned in Hamburg and other parts of the EU. Even before accession, the eight eastern European applicants were wrestling with the problem of stopping the flow of illegal migrants from Belarus, Russia, and Ukraine. They also were screening for drugs, weapons, and human smugglers from Central Asia and elsewhere looking for a back door into western Europe. The challenge has been to balance the interests of freedom of movement *within* the EU against secure EU borders with non-Schengen states, which include several former Soviet republics—Belarus, the Russian enclave of Trans-Dniester in Moldova, and Ukraine—all of which may have had nuclear warheads on their territory, some of which may not have been accounted for. The border control challenge for new Europe is made more difficult because these countries have catch-up economies.

It was with much fanfare, therefore, that in late December 2007 nine new countries formally joined the Schengen zone. All but Malta were from new Europe: Estonia, Latvia, Lithuania, Poland, Slovakia, the Czech Republic, Hungary, and Slovenia. Presiding at the removal of a barrier with Austria, Slovak prime minister Robert Fico proclaimed: "From midnight tonight you can travel 4,000 kilometers (2,485 miles) from Tallinn in Estonia to Lisbon in Portugal without any border controls."[21] The European Commission estimated that it had spent one billion euros on securing the EU's new extended frontiers. Internal controls have been dropped at all land, sea, and air borders in these twenty-four states. While EU citizens can enjoy passport-free travel, some countries still require other types of travel documents. For non-EU nationals, a Schengen visa is needed to travel in all the participating countries.

New Europe has mixed feeling about applying strict and secure border controls to non-Schengen states. The curtain can be politically costly, possibly creating rifts between the new accession states and their less stable eastern neighbors. At the level of the individual, the Schengen regime may close off borders to families living on either side as well as to legal, profitable cross-border trade. The hyperbole of a "new iron curtain" dividing Europe has been invoked to attack Schengen arrangements. Poland faces the greatest challenge in having to bring down the Schengen curtain on Belarus, Russia, and Ukraine. In order not to slam the door on these fellow Slavs, it has negotiated reciprocal facilitated border-crossing arrangements with their non-EU eastern neighbors for citizens living near the frontier.

Europe is far more complex than a simple division into EU states and *excommunitari* (those outside of the Community), into old and new, into euro and Schengen zones and those outside them. A simultaneous process of regionalization promoted by the EU's Committee of the Regions and European Regional Development Fund makes mapping Europe elusive. Regional political parties have emerged from Scotland and Belgium to the Basque country and northern Italy. To cite Rupnik, "A 'Europe of Regions' has fed the dreams of borderland denizens—the Sami, the Catalans, the Basques, the Tyroleans, the Galicians."[22] Geographer Donald McNeill has referred to a process of reterritorialization marking "a shift from the one-dimensional map of Europe as having fixed borders to one in which city-based, regional, national, and European scales of action are fluid."[23]

Europe's appearance of institutional unity is, therefore, deceptive. Bringing down borders and reconfiguring regions mean that its political geography is being unmade. Whether in this process an organic geographic unity will eventually arise remains unclear. As we explore in the next chapter, the discourse of Europe's political elites may also mask fault lines even as it proclaims unity.

NOTES

1. Frank Schimmelfennig and Ulrich Sedelmeier, "Introduction: Conceptualizing the Europeanization of Central and Eastern Europe," in *The Europeanization of Central and Eastern Europe*, eds. Schimmelfennig and Sedelmeier (Ithaca, NY: Cornell University Press, 2005), 9.

2. Schimmelfennig and Sedelmeier, *The Europeanization of Central and Eastern Europe*, 18.

3. Schimmelfennig and Sedelmeier, *The Europeanization of Central and Eastern Europe*, 22–23.

4. "Conclusions of the Presidency," (Copenhagen: European Council, June 21–23, 1993), SN/180/93, 13.

5. Commission of the European Communities, "2002 Regular Report on Poland's Progress Towards Accession," (Brussels, October 9, 2002), 135, http://europa .eu.int/comm/enlargement.

6. Christine Ingebritsen, *Scandinavia in World Politics* (Lanham, MD: Rowman & Littlefield, 2006), 51.

7. Poles and central Europeans generally were not the only ones fearing a wave of German second-home hunters. Denmark had earlier negotiated a deal with the EU making it difficult for other EU nationals—in particular Germans—to purchase summer homes along the Danish coast.

8. "Polish Land: A Most Emotional Issue," *The Economist*, March 23–29, 2002, 48.

9. "A Secure Europe in a Better World" (Paris: EU, Institute for Security Studies, December 2003).

10. "Your darkest fears addressed, your hardest questions answered—Europe's constitution," *The Economist*, June 21, 2003, 23–28.

11. Quoted in "Your darkest fears addressed, your hardest questions answered—Europe's constitution," *The Economist*, June 21, 2003, 23–28.

12. Gerard Delanty and Chris Rumford, *Rethinking Europe: Social Theory and the Implications of Europeanization* (London: Routledge, 2005), 43.

13. Robert Bideleux and Richard Taylor, *European Integration and Disintegration East and West* (London: Routledge, 1996), 285.

14. Delanty and Rumford, *Rethinking Europe*, 19.

15. "A Constitution for Europe," prepared by Brit Helle Aarskog, member of the Text Technologies Research Group, Department of Language, Culture and Information Technology, http://gandalf.aksis.uib.no/~brit/EU-CONST-EN-cc/TITLEI-DEFI-NITIONANDOBJECTIVESOFTHEUNION.html.

16. "The Impact of the Lisbon Treaty on CFSP and ESDP," *European Security Review* 37 (March 2008), 3n7, www.isis-europe.org/pdf/2008_artrel_150_esr37tol-mar 08.pdf.

17. "Lisbon Treaty made to avoid referendum, says Giscard," quoted by euobserver.com, November 29, 2007, http://euobserver.com/9/25052/?rk=1.

18. Erik Oddvar Eriksen, John Erik Fossum, and Helene Sjursen, "Widening or reconstituting the EU? Enlargement and Democratic Governance in Europe" (paper presented at the 43rd Annual International Studies Association Convention, New Orleans, Louisiana, March 24–27, 2002), 20.

19. "The End of the Stability and Growth Pact?" *International Economics and Economic Policy* March 2004, http://goliath.ecnext.com/coms2/gi_0198-328415/The-end-of-the-Stability.html#abstract.

20. The finance minister was Grzegorz Kołodko, who served in Poland's social democratic–led government until 2003.

21. "Fanfare for Bigger Border-free EU," BBC News, December 20, 2007, http://news.bbc.co.uk/go/pr/fr/-/2/hi/europe/7153490.stm.

22. Jacques Rupnik, "Europe's New Frontiers: Remapping Europe," in *Boundaries and Place: European Borderlands in Geographical Context*, eds. David H. Kaplan and Jouni Häkli (Lanham, MD: Rowman & Littlefield, 2002), 12.

23. Donald McNeill, *New Europe: Imagined Spaces* (London: Arnold, 2004), 89.

3

Metacultural Presumptions of European Elites

CONSTRUCTIONS OF EUROPE

Since the 1957 Treaty of Rome, European leaders have been making statements seeking to explain the relationship between unity in Europe and the diversity found in it. Their discursive practices have led to greater confusion about what European identity entails. Frustrated by differing constructions of Europe, in a speech made in 1994 to the European Parliament then–Czech president Václav Havel called for a "charter of European identity." He wanted it to make clear what it meant to be a European.

One of the most important contributors to the debate on the nature of the European Union has been Romano Prodi. As former EU Commission president and two-time Italian prime minister—in addition to being a bureaucrat, politician, and professor—Prodi was well-positioned to assay the question of Europeanness. "Europe's destiny is not inherently Eurocentric, but one of universality," he asserted. He did not *a priori* assume the existence of a common European culture. Universalism must aspire to "a new cultural unity" while giving "mutual acceptance among Europeans of their cultural diversity."[1]

If there is a hint of doublespeak in Prodi's discourse on Europe, it has not gone without criticism. For academic John Gillingham, "When Prodi talks, almost no one listens. The same thing happens when he shouts."[2] If there is any truth in this statement, it derives from the fact that Prodi honed "Orwellian" Eurospeak (in the words of Havel's successor as Czech president, Václav Klaus) to a fine art.

This chapter reviews the public discourse of European political and intellectual elites on political and cultural integration in the EU.[3] We want to

57

gain a sense of how different these discursive practices may be. Whether European citizens are listening to any of them is the subject of subsequent chapters.

The Europe of the EU has been construed as having an underlying unity, of embracing a moral universalism, of constituting a *demos* rather than an *ethnos*, of being held together by a decentered culture, of representing a network of differences, and of being little more than a thin discursive identity anchored only in dialogic structures. At its most simplistic, elites refer to the EU's unity in diversity—hardly a groundbreaking idea. The European right is less divided on the issue of unity versus diversity since it posits that national cultures are separate and cannot in any way be reconciled with unity.

One school of thought emphasizes the communitarian nature of Europe—the existence of a people unified by a basic cultural foundation. Another school points to republican roots—a civil society or *demos* that transcends class, ethnic, and party divisions and is willing to take on mutual responsibility for a shared future. This introduces the Kantian notion of a people defined by the civic consciousness of a *demos* rather than of a state.

Europe is also constructed as an *ethos*—a morally superior European system that transcends parochial or illiberal national values. In this view, the EU is fundamentally a "Moral Union." This understanding was reflected in the EU's Millennium Declaration of 1999, which described the "ties that bind" in these terms: "The Union's citizens are bound together by common values such as freedom, tolerance, equality, solidarity and cultural diversity." Historian Tony Judt took this objective at face value when he praised Europe's twenty-first century normative regime as a model for all to emulate.[4]

Franco-Bulgarian philosopher Tzvetan Todorov, whose professional career spans old and new Europe, also asserts that the continent possesses a set of distinctly European values. These values—not practices—include rationality, justice, and democracy.[5] Very typical of European discourse on what makes the continent unique, it is nevertheless hard to see—given twentieth-century European history—how Todorov's values mark Europe off from other civilizations.

In turn, Italian writer Umberto Eco has highlighted the centrality of "the practice of translation." It is similar to what French philosopher Balibar described as Europe's tradition-bound praxis of learning cultural and linguistic idioms, of speaking and listening, of teaching and learning, of understanding and making oneself understood. In short, such praxis entails translation from the linguistic to the cultural level.[6]

Other interpretations of the EU's *raison d'être* aim at greater concreteness and realism. The EU has been conceptualized in terms of *governance*. Whereas government entails centralized rule over a territory, governance brings together a combination of state, nonstate, public, private, national, and international actors. Business, labor, interest groups, civil society, epistemic communities (groups with specialized knowledge), public-private partnerships, and various agencies and networks all are increasingly brought into the process of EU governance. Governance has been expanded not just horizontally but also vertically, through multilevel governance involving interlocking regional, national, and supranational institutions. The publication of the European Commission's white paper on governance in 2001 inspired the strengthening of a number of independent regulatory authorities in such areas as environmental issues, health and safety at work, food and aviation safety, and racism and xenophobia issues.

Let us briefly examine the regulatory agency dealing with racism and xenophobia. The origins of the European Commission against Racism and Intolerance (ECRI) lie in the Vienna Declaration adopted at the summit of leaders of Council of Europe states in 1993. In 2002, the Council approved a new statute for the ECRI, transforming it into an independent human rights–monitoring body. At the Warsaw summit of the Council of Europe in 2005, the ECRI was given additional powers and resources to carry out its work. It was also to cooperate with national authorities and institutions and civil society. One of its chief objectives is to combat the use of racist, anti-Semitic, and xenophobic terminology in political discourse.[7]

When not talking in moral terms, European elites will, at a minimum, advance an instrumentalist vision of Europe based on the market and efficiency. Here Europe is viewed merely as a postnational polity in which the process of integration has been replaced by one building on the specific features of a polity. This process can entail bottom-up self-constitution that produces a whole greater than a simple collection of states, or it can entail laying the foundations of a suprastate complex. Such polity building embraces a host of factors—citizenship, civil society, constitutional framework, institutions, and governance—that together promote Europeanization.

Some social psychologists believe that a process of "entitativity" in which perceptions of a common fate, proximity, and boundedness will lead to the reification of a group into an entity—of European nations transformed into Europe.[8] For identification with institutions to become pervasive, "the new political community needs to establish itself as a possible self-representation at the collective level for its citizens."[9]

Anthropologists have examined the emergence of contemporary Europe in terms of migration patterns, core and periphery, and cohesion at different levels of society (regional, national, and supranational).[10] They have focused on such anthropological phenomena as blood, soil, border crossings, national anxieties, cultural fundamentalisms, exile, and images of home.[11] Ethnographers have played an especially important role in bringing to light the diverse small communities of people that have long inhabited Europe.

At the core of much recent theorizing about European society—or its absence—has been a presumed nexus between supranational institutions, citizenship, and civil society.[12] This nexus may have a tangible quality to it, but it also involves a form of transformed social consciousness. Thus, "Europeanization is a process of social construction rather than one of state building and one in which globalization, in all its facets, plays a key role in creating its conditions."[13]

METACULTURAL DISCOURSES OF POLITICAL ELITES

Two general methodological approaches characterize the study of culture today. One proposes that culture fulfills peoples' desire for wholeness and coherence. It may best be understood as *metaculture*—"a discourse in which 'culture' addresses its own generality . . . and historical conditions of existence." Metaculture "has been the form in which culture dissolves the political and takes up the general labor proper to it, assuming the role of a valid social authority."[14]

The concept of metaculture is especially relevant to a multicultural state where citizens are located in differing ethnic and regional cultures but are nevertheless influenced by a unifying culture promoting a shared political home. It is also salient to a transnational project that attempts to create an identity such as Europeanness. In general, before recent enlargement, metacultural discourses were *de rigueur* among those liberal political elites who profess an ideology of transnationalism. To say that European elites hold metacultural perspectives is in a sense, therefore, tautological.

A second approach is the narrative view of culture. Cultures are "polyvocal, multilayered, decentered and fractured systems of action and signification."[15] Accordingly, extolling the particularist ideals embedded in a culture takes precedence over arriving at synthesizing metanarratives that homogenize. This approach is especially useful in examining minoritarian voices within a culture. Polyvocality is primarily the practice of the European public, which is conscious of its own particularities and differences. It is also largely the approach taken by its cultural producers, which generally resist homogenizing, reductionist, essentialist ideas about national identity. We consider polyvocal perspectives in chapters 7 and 8.

In analyzing the discourse of Europe's political elites, it is important to acknowledge a caveat. Like politicians anywhere in the world, they are not free of doublespeak. Most talk the EU talk on demand or when politically expedient. When speaking on behalf of the public's desires and interests, they perform the rituals of cultural symbolism and embrace a totalizing framework. What was in an early period described as national sacrality has in the EU today given way to supranational sacrality—a claim to the transcendence of the EU.[16]

Plentiful references to the civic, liberal, tolerant community that the EU is building are a sure way for a political leader to hold the moral high ground, establish cosmopolitan credentials (more on this below), and curry favor with established EU elites. There are times, however, when metacultural practices have to give way to old-fashioned nationalist rhetoric. Thus, "national policy makers routinely reify the nation-state in their dealings with Brussels. Whenever they can charge the EU with the responsibility for some tough decision at home, they adopt a populist rhetoric of conscious blame shifting ('Brussels made me do it') and construct EU institutions as remote bureaucracies that cannot be trusted (in contrast to national governments, of course)."[17] While leaders of all EU countries make recourse to this pragmatic discourse, what we wish to consider is whether those in new Europe do it more often—if only because their publics remain skeptical about political Euro-packaging.

In the first decades of integration, Europeanness—a metacultural proposition—was invoked as a key objective by European leaders to varying degrees. Expressed in the policies, actions, and statements of leaders such as Jean Monnet and Robert Schuman in the beginning and Jacques Delors, Romano Prodi, François Mitterrand, and Helmut Kohl in the 1980s and 1990s, the dominant values we "read" are of a single Europe being built out of diversity.

Box 3.1 Europe's First Metaculturalist
In anticipation of an era when "there are no more French, German, Spanish, even Englishmen whatever one says, there are only Europeans. They all have the same tastes, the same passions, and the same way of life."

Source: Jean-Jacques Rousseau, *Considerations on the Government of Poland and on its Proposed Reformation,* 1772 (Indianapolis, IN: Hackett, 1985).

As we noted in chapter 1, postwar Europe's founders were focused largely on piecemeal integration, even though some shared Rousseau's vision. However, Monnet attached relatively little importance to culture—even though he is supposed to have said subsequently that if he were going to start on the European project again, he would begin with culture. Probably he never did say this, because he knew that in that case he would have failed.[18]

A *caesura* in placing greater importance on integrating society took place when Delors served as Commission President from 1985 to 1994. A protégé of Mitterrand who once described Europe as a UPO (Unidentified Political Object), Delors proposed a European Social Model (ESM) that sought to balance economic integration with social harmonization and the single market with social protection.

The ESM comprised four principles: 1) the inviolability of human rights, 2) culture as the means of emancipation, 3) sustainable development, and 4) peace in the international order. Delors' ESM represented an effort to link European integration to freedom rather than simply to markets. The EU agenda was now not to be purely economistic but was also to be concerned with social problems such as inequality, poverty, and unemployment. The novelty of the ESM was in proposing that not just markets but also welfare were transnational. In sum, the ESM asserted that economic policy is social policy.

It was German chancellor Kohl, however, who championed the role of *Kultur* in the EU. "Europe is more than just politics and the economy," he stated. "Above all, it represents a magnificent cultural heritage: classical antiquity, humanism, the Enlightenment and Christianity."[19] This was a metacultural thesis. Kohl employed more nationalist discourse at home and was attacked for *Renationalisierung*—a return to the vocabulary of nationhood that was taboo in Germany after World War II.

We have seen how culture is viewed as integrative and consensual. But it can also be seen as fluid, negotiable, not anchored in immutable principles, and not defined by reference to a territory, state, religion, or political party. Different "national" understandings of culture's importance can be identified. For Germany's postwar leadership, European identity is a surrogate for a German identity scarred by the World War II experience. French and Italian elites often seem to imagine that European culture and identity are largely replicas of their own. By contrast, the English elite has generally believed that the continent's political, legal, and cultural pathways are alien.

What is clear is that as European integration has progressed, so the significance of culture in its making has grown. This may in part be attributable to the multiple meanings culture has today. Culture has been understood as praxis, as performative, as a mode of communication, and as evaluation.[20] Common culture can be tied to the success of common institutions. The notion of an essential European unity is associated with a Eurofederalist project resting on a civilization whose highest expression is culture. This is seen in the declaration of article 151 of the Treaty of Amsterdam: "The Community shall contribute to the flowering of the cultures of the Member States, while respecting their national and regional diversity and at the same time bringing the common cultural heritage to the fore."

But is metaculture really as important to European elites as it is to the European public? It may be the case that citizens are more culturally attached to Europe and elites are more institutionally grounded. "Europeans distinguish between cultural and civic aspects of their Europeanness, with the former attached to 'Europe' as a whole and the latter to the EU in particular."[21]

Europeanness refers to any of the social, cultural, symbolic, economic, political, and philosophical processes promoting integration. Spanning so many spheres, it is no surprise that "Europe is no longer a residual category in contemporary conceptions of the nation; it has a huge presence in all societies."[22]

For clarity's sake, let us assume for a moment that the idea of Europe is dichotomous—it is either present or absent in a given society. It follows that "nation-building is often a matter of positioning the nation in a larger cultural-geographical context and whereby 'Europe' is used as a stereotype in the construction of both 'Us' and 'They,' of self-identification and of distinction of 'the Other.' Such auto-stereotypes and xeno-stereotypes reinforce each other."[23] This has been the experience of new Europe in the run-up to EU accession. To join, the eastern countries had to accept that they had not really been European until then. Such a conceptualization—even though intended to be transitional—split Europe into new and old. In many ways, it was a retooling of the historical division of Europe into eastern and western parts. This is a cultural grievance expressed by writers from new Europe that will be examined later in the book.

MANY EUROPES

Social theorists Delanty and Rumford have pointedly asked: "If there are several 'Europes'—western, Nordic, central and eastern—does this mean there is no such thing as Europe?"[24] If we answer that Europe *qua* Europe does exist, it becomes even more important to know what its western, Nordic, central, and eastern components have in common and in what ways they differ.

Delanty and Rumford claim that Europe is "in a process of becoming and in which peoples are seeking to orientate themselves in a post-western, post-national, and post-welfare state configuration of societies dominated to a large degree by, but ultimately not answerable to, the European Union." Enlargement directed Europe in a post-western direction and has brought about "the transformation of Europe, the relativization of western Europe, and an awareness of many Europes shaped by multiple modernities." Most importantly for our purposes, "the postcommunist era has not led to the erasure of the East but its reconfiguration."[25]

Some eastern Europeans have presented a radically different perspective on enlargement. Several studies conducted by academics from the region examined whether the EU is a reformulated empire in which eastern enlargement was a straightforward imperialistic arrangement.[26] In one volume, the contributing authors applied the conceptual tools of postcolonial

studies to eastern European cases. They also analyzed the discursive practices of exclusion as found in certain official EU documents and in speeches
by leading EU politicians. It may be difficult for us to see in what way old
Europe has established an imperial relationship with the new member
states. Undoubtedly, inequalities exist between western and eastern Europe,
many of them originating in contrasting pre-enlargement processes shaping
the two parts. The current institutions of the EU, especially as modified by
the Lisbon Treaty, are designed to democratize all of Europe. Nevertheless,
fearing a loss of identity and control over the making of their own destinies,
some eastern Europeans are drawn to the conclusion that they are being
colonized by the west.

The division of Europe into west and east raises the obvious question of
where the dividing line is drawn. Delanty and Rumford answer that "There
is no clearly defined eastern border and it can be argued that in fact it is the
constantly changing eastern border that has been the defining feature of Europe's geopolitics."[27]

It has been said, half-facetiously, that Europe and civilization end on
most countries' eastern border. One writer tried to be less stark about it and
introduced the idea of east-west slopes, "based on the idea of gradually di-
minishing civilization toward the 'East.'"[28] There is some folk wisdom that
would support such perspectives. The British imperial belief of their superior civilization to that on the continent lying to the east is mirrored by
Dutch feelings about Germany, of Germany about Poland, of Poland about
Ukraine, of Ukraine about Russia, and, further south, of France about Italy,
Italy about Greece, and Greece about Turkey. A notable exception to the rule
is on the Iberian Peninsula, where Portugal is largely free of a condescending view of Spain.

One academic has coined the idea of nesting orientalisms to describe the
pecking order prevailing among eastern societies. Thus Asia is more Oriental, or eastern, than eastern Europe. But in eastern Europe it is the nations
that made up former Yugoslavia that are the most Oriental.[29]

Playful speculation about what is east and what is west reflects a deeper
conviction that Europe is not an organic whole. If there are "many" Europes, one we cannot overlook is what has been termed the EU's "twenty-
eighth member state"—the foreign population living in the twenty-seven
countries. As much as the real or imagined divide between west and east,
the division of people living in Europe into nationals on the one hand and
immigrants or minorities on the other shapes popular understandings of
who belongs to Europe.

Balibar has suggested that "European apartheid" exists on the basis of nationals and foreigners. Far from adopting a metacultural perspective on European identity, Balibar blames Europeans for adopting unofficial
apartheid: "The ethnicization of human groups and the correlative repre-

sentation of unbridgeable 'cultural differences' between individuals . . . is much more the doing of the societies of the North that organize the movement of immigrants than that of the immigrants themselves."[30]

Ingenious efforts have been made to address the phenomenon of many Europes. Prodi and others spoke of network Europe—a fluid interconnected Europe. Other discursive innovations have included proximity politics (integration through non-enlargement), wider or undivided Europe (extended political spaces), and borderlands (zones in place of dividing lines).

The European Neighborhood Policy originating in the 2001 Laeken summit was a pragmatic approach designed to blur Europe's external borders by helping create zones of prosperity. In 2003, the European Commission published "Wider Europe—Neighborhood: A New Framework for Relations with Eastern and Southern Neighbors." Employing officious Eurospeak, its objective was to promote a "ring of friends" with which the EU would develop peaceful cooperation. In return for opening markets and adopting EU norms of democracy, human rights, and the rule of law, non-EU countries could participate in core areas of EU activity.

Targeted countries included former Soviet republics as far away as Armenia (Russia was placed beyond the ENP initiative) and Maghreb states and Egypt across the Mediterranean. Under the ENP, the EU and its neighbors could share everything but institutions, in effect producing integration without enlargement. The spatial reconceptualization of Europe would facilitate and legitimate an expansive area of Europeanization. ENP seemed a lot like old-fashioned buffer zones, though the choice of soft (the politics of inclusion) or hard (the politics of exclusion) borders was yet to be made.[31]

Even leaving out EU neighbors, the integration of the EU calls for a progressively more common pan-European consciousness and set of values. But what canon of values can be agreed upon to represent not only Christians—Protestants and Catholics—but also the Orthodox and Muslim populations that live inside the EU?

Table 3.1 provides data on the size and makeup of these religious communities in various parts of Europe. Adopting an explanatory framework similar to Huntington's civilizational one, Dieter Fuchs and Hans-Dieter Klingemann examined the extent to which systematic differences between western, central, and eastern Europe existed and where cultural borders lay. Using religious affiliations, they subdivided Europe into different clusters, each supposedly having a different cultural heritage. Their empirical research, carried out in 2000 before the EU's eastern enlargement, concluded that "As far as the liberal community is concerned, the major cultural dividing line suggested by Huntington does exist, separating the Western-Christian civilization (including Central Europe) from the Orthodox-Muslim civilization in Eastern Europe," which is more communitarian and less law-abiding.[32]

The authors also found that "Between the countries of Europe there is little difference in the political values and behaviors that are essential to a democracy. The potential for Europeans in Western, Central, and Eastern Europe to consider each other as democrats, and to integrate this
understanding in their collective identity is thus considerable." However,
"The Slavic successor nations to the Soviet Union (Russia, Ukraine, Belarus,
and Moldova) together with Albania are the exception."[33]

Finally, Fuchs and Klingemann determined that differing conceptions of
a democratic community constituted the dividing line between western and
central Europe (roughly coterminous with the 2004 postcommunist accession states). The two parts attached somewhat different importance to such
factors as self-responsibility, solidarity, trust, and especially civic engagement (which was lower in central Europe). To be sure, the authors recognized that "no threshold can be identified between West and East, only a
continuous decline in the extent of a democratic community," with the west
more solidly democratic. This was enough, however, to signify that "Every
eastward enlargement poses integration problems and increases the difficulty of constituting a European *demos*."[34]

Referring to civilizational clashes may miss the point. But these findings
lend support to the assertion that a continental divide in Europe between
west and east does exist. There may be apartheid in Europe based primarily
on ethnic categories. But even within "the west," cultural differences may be
significant. Such intracivilizational fault lines may also shape European
politics.

A good example is former British prime minister Margaret Thatcher's
views on foreigners. Implying a clash of civilizations, in the 1979 election
campaign she warned that Britain was being "rather swamped" by immigrants.[35] This discourse helped catapult Thatcher to 10 Downing Street for
the first time. But in her memoirs, she also made much of an intra-
European schism:

> This desire among modern German politicians to merge their national identity
> in a wider European one is understandable enough, but it presents great diffi-
> culties to self-conscious nation-states in Europe. In effect, the Germans, be-
> cause they are nervous of governing themselves, want to establish a European
> system in which no nation will govern itself. Such a system could only be un-
> stable in the long term and, because of Germany's size and preponderance, is
> bound to be lop-sided. Obsession with a European Germany risks producing
> a German Europe.[36]

Or, to say the unsayable about the Germans—as Thatcher's trade and industry secretary Nicholas Ridley did immediately after resigning from his
post—if you give sovereignty to the European Commission, you may as
well give it to Adolf Hitler.[37]

Table 3.1. Cultural Heritage: A Classification of Countries by Denomination

Countries	P %	C %	PC %	O %	M %	OM %	S %	T %	CL
Anglo-American Countries									
USA	36	25	61	0	0	1	18	80	P
Australia	48	26	74	1	1	2	3	79	P
New Zealand	60	14	74	0	0	0	4	78	P
Western European Countries									
Norway	82	1	83	1	1	2	4	89	P
Sweden	81	5	86	1	4	5	1	92	P
Finland	80	3	83	2	0	2	1	86	P
West Germany	39	33	72	0	1	1	1	74	C
Spain	1	82	83	0	0	0	1	84	T
Central European Countries									
East Germany	18	5	23	0	0	0	1	24	T
Czech Republic	2	39	40	0	0	0	3	43	C
Slovakia	10	73	83	0	0	0	3	86	C
Hungary	17	55	72	2	0	2	1	75	C
Slovenia	2	69	71	2	1	3	1	75	C
Croatia	0	82	82	1	1	1	1	85	C
Baltic Countries									
Estonia	10	0	10	16	0	16	2	28	T
Latvia	19	18	37	18	0	18	5	60	P
Lithuania	2	77	79	4	0	4	2	85	C
South-Eastern European Countries (Mainly Orthodox)									
Yugoslavia	1	6	7	64	8	72	2	81	O
Romania	2	5	6	87	0	87	3	96	O
Bulgaria	1	1	2	53	12	64	1	67	O
South-Eastern European Countries (Mixed-Muslim)									
Macedonia	0	1	1	45	24	69	0	70	O
Bosnia-Herzegovina	2	14	16	26	27	53	1	70	M
Albania	0	6	6	20	67	87	0	93	M
Eastern European Countries									
Russia	0	0	0	48	5	53	1	54	O
Ukraine	0	6	6	56	0	56	1	63	O
Belarus	0	8	8	54	0	54	0	62	O
Moldova	0	0	0	83	0	83	1	84	O

P = Protestant; C = Catholic; PC = sum of Protestant + Catholic; O = Orthodox; M = Muslim; OM = sum of Orthodox + Muslim; S = Sects; T = proportion of respondents mentioning a denominational affiliation; CL = generalized denominational classification. Cell entries are data generated by the World Values Survey 1995–1999.

Source: Dieter Fuchs and Hans-Dieter Klingemann, "Eastward Enlargement of the European Union and the Identity of Europe" (Berlin: Veröffentlichungsreihe der Abteilung Institutionen und sozialer Wandel des Forschungsschwerpunkts Sozialer Wandel, Institutionen und Vermittlungsprozesse des Wissenschaftszentrums Berlin für Sozialforschung, September 2000), 13.

The debate within Germany on the role of Europe after World War II may have given Thatcher—and Ridley—grounds for Germanophobia. In June 1945, the draft CDU Program referred to Germany's greatness embodied in "the Christian western values which once held sway among the German people who therefore were held in high regard by the other European nations." Theologian Walter Künneth argued for a European return to belief in God, or as Romano Guardini put it, "Europe will either become Christian, or it will simply cease to exist." Political journalist Eugen Kogon referred to the long-concealed "gold of true German qualities" that after "uncovering the historical and spiritual roots of our guilt," would "reemerge cleansed and purified to fulfill the true task allotted to the Germans in Europe and the world."[38]

Liberal discourse, in its turn, acknowledged Germany's central mission in constructing a democratic Europe. Europe, especially its German center, had to be built on free democratic foundations. Konrad Adenauer's discourses described true democrats as the best Europeans. Socialist leader Kurt Schumacher emphasized the need for a "united Germany in a socialist Europe." These various constructions reflected an "instrumentalized and selective historical consciousness which attempts to correct people's real experience of what they are actually experiencing."[39]

The formal unification of Germany in 1990 aroused the type of suspicions that Thatcher had harbored while Prime Minister, Chancellor Kohl tried to be reassuring but in repeatedly invoking the historical responsibility and special vocation Germany had for European unification, he only deepened mistrust among entrenched Germanophobes. "With our rewon (*wiedergewonnen*) national unity our country wants to . . . expedite European unification: that is the task of the Basic Law, our tested constitution."[40]

OVERCOMING MANY EUROPES: TRANSNATIONALISM, EUROPEANNESS, AND COSMOPOLITANISM AS IDEALS

Suspicion of a nation's universalist pretensions, whether those of Germany or some other European state, triggered opposition to a seemingly benign project like an EU constitution enshrining transnationalism. Constitutionally affirming the paramount goal of a supranational European identity has been a matter for serious disagreement within the EU since the turn of the new century. The force behind the adoption of such a provision is a group of secular-oriented and, simultaneously, older and wealthier EU states which are pressing for a de-denominationalized Europe; that is, one where religious affiliations have no salience. On the other hand, newer, economically less-advanced EU countries do not see the need to prioritize such a metacultural objective.

The first fifteen articles of the EU's draft constitution, published in 2003, contained references to national identities, the need for human rights, the commitment to social justice, and the importance of environmental protection. But they made no mention of a deity or religion. Italian, Polish, Slovak, and even German delegates initially lobbied for inclusion of a reference to God and to Europe's Christian heritage. The Polish primate went so far as to say he supported EU entry "but only with God," while the Roman Catholic primate of Hungary observed that "without Christianity, the heart of Europe would be missing."[41]

More secular nations, like France and Holland, opposed these proposals. They largely had their way. The final draft of the Preamble stated that Europe's leaders were

> Drawing inspiration from the cultural, religious and humanist inheritance of Europe, from which have developed the universal values of the inviolable and inalienable rights of the human person, freedom, democracy, equality and the rule of law,
> Convinced that, while remaining proud of their own national identities and history, the peoples of Europe are determined to transcend their former divisions and, united ever more closely, to forge a common destiny,
> Convinced that, thus 'United in diversity', Europe offers them the best chance of pursuing, with due regard for the rights of each individual and in awareness of their responsibilities towards future generations and the Earth, the great venture which makes of it a special area of human hope. . . .

Ironically, the secular nations of France and Holland caused the draft constitution to fail. While religion was an insignificant issue in the referendum defeats of the constitutional project in these countries, national identity was not. In addition, the fear of a weakened France and a less-protected Netherlands in the EU and the corollary—a more influential Germany—demonstrated how national interests won the day over the EU's "united in diversity" mantra.

Yet *transnationalism*—a condition where national interests are subordinated to wider ones involving promotion of a notional common good—is a term that meets with widespread approval in the EU. Much of the recent theorizing on transnationalism originates in western Europe, where issues of integration, identity, and belonging have represented integral parts of the EU's unifying project. The assumption in most theories of transnationalism is that citizens have multiple, nested, situational, and fluid identities—not a single fixed one. Moreover, transformative political processes have challenged traditional, restrictive notions of national citizenship. Economic and cultural globalization has further weakened citizens' exclusive attachment to the nation-state.

The European nation-state itself is not what it used to be. With the immigration of millions of non-Europeans, host societies have been transformed.

The term integration does not fully capture the processes taking place within them: "Successful integration is a two-way process, a process of mutual recognition, which has nothing to do with assimilation. Rather than using the term 'integration,'" one European institution suggests it is more accurate "to refer to an 'integrated society,' which is equally inclusive of majority and minority groups."[42]

Many people are also increasingly involved in transnational politics through their discourse, networks, commerce, and organizations. In the process, they have developed identities of a supranational kind. Some have even become cosmopolitans.

The paradigmatic form of transnationalism today is Europeanness. Theorists of transnationalism hold that for lifelong or longtime residents of EU member states, Europe has become the main locus of their political orientations and identifications. A similar orientation is emerging, it is being argued, in eastern Europe—both in the EU accession states and, to a lesser degree, in those left out.

Transnationalism involves transcending boundaries. This is a more contentious idea than it first appears because boundaries are "physical demarcations between territories, linear representations on maps, and ideas rooted in social practices." Transnationalism would remove all these classic demarcations.[43]

Box 3.2. Measuring Success in the EU
"Fathoms, inches, feet, yards, miles, acres, ounces, gallons, pounds, therms—all will be banished by a diktat of the European Commission."

Source: Neil Hamilton, "Do We Really Want 0.454 kg of Apples and Not 1 lb?" *Daily Mail*, February 26, 1995.

Transnationalism goes hand in hand with *postnationality*. The first presumes the erosion of nationally anchored identity. Postnationality seems conceivable only in circumstances under which transnational identity has spread. Balibar put it this way: "if we are justified in speaking of an end of the nation or a decline in its importance, this phenomenon would have to be illustrated in specific, concrete situations. Particular nations or groups of nations, for example, would have to be crossing the 'threshold' of postnationality together; certain societies would have to be becoming progressively 'denationalized' or 'transnationalized.'"[44] The French philosopher was persuaded that this was indeed happening in western Europe, but he reserved judgment on its progress in eastern Europe.

European transnationalism was largely the product of a Christian Democratic vision of Europe. Catholic France (represented by Schuman) and Italy (represented by Alcide de Gasperi, postwar prime minister at the head of eight governments over eight years) reached out to Catholic German chancellor Adenauer (who governed from 1949 to 1963) to promote a pan-European ecumenism. A social model for Europe was to take the place of Europe's long-held obsession with power politics. It was particularly aimed at Germany's Nazi experience, which habitually functioned as the European Community's "Other."

By contrast, European social democracy was wrong-footed by its need to establish credentials as defender of the nation-state, thereby distinguishing itself from its leftist brethren in the internationalist camp spearheaded by the communists. Social democracy supported Christian democracy's conceptualization of the social state and extended it farther with advocacy of full employment, welfarism, and social inclusion.

As we discussed in the first chapter, communism's collapse added further momentum for European enlargement and integration. In France, "many intellectuals—with the decline of Marxism, of universalism and of general ideologies promising a future paradise on earth—came back to a more realistic cause, and a democratic one: Europe."[45] After 1989, Europe became a democratic horizon for "the other Europe."

Despite transnational trends, Europe has yet to embrace *supranationalism*, which challenges the *raison d'être* of the nation-state while borrowing and expanding on its ideology. Euronationalism is an example of a feeble supranationalism that seeks to be inclusionary and, simultaneously, territorially bounded. It is largely limited to a kind of normative supranationalism that is anchored in the European Convention on Human Rights. Thus, while an issue like minority rights may still be managed by an EU nation-state, it is regulated and standardized according to a supranational normative regime.

In a number of respects, the development of supranationalism "pushes states to imagine themselves as nonstate transnational actors, coordinating their interests and their strategies beyond their territory."[46] Euronationalism has not reached that point and instead represents a form of "non-national nationalism" which is modeled on postwar Germany and is characterized by reflexivity and self-critique. Euronationalism is therefore more like *transnational nationalism* than supranationalism: "At the level of collective identity formation, the growth of so-called transnational nationalisms, national but 'de-territorialized' forms of identification that straddle political boundaries in multiple ways, is an obvious manifestation of the impact of globalization."[47]

In theory, *Euronationalism* as transnationalism describes the emergence of a European identity based on liberal European values as most recently enumerated in the Lisbon Treaty—democracy, tolerance, inclusion, and respect for human and minority rights—but also globalization and even the rights of multinational corporations. Since about the time of Maastricht, however, Euronationalism has in practice developed into a kind of banal nationalism—cliché-ridden, self-regarding, even intolerant and, some would say, Islamophobic.[48] It has involved process, negotiation, and long-term goal-setting more than representing an empirical reality. Banal Euronationalism is more and more contested even in societies where it has roots and is given the generic name of *Euroscepticism*.

Euroscepticism can be found in countries across the continent. Some single-issue political parties have been founded to capitalize on this attitude. In Britain, Euroscepticism is encapsulated by use of such politically pejorative keywords as federalism, superstate, bureaucracy, and unaccountability.[49]

The term transnationalism is occasionally used in a different context—the reach of diaspora group activity. The defining characteristic of a *diaspora* is sustained long-term economic, political, and sociocultural activities across borders, in this way making it a transnational actor. For diasporas, key issues are citizenship (single or dual) and the nature of belonging ("belonging" for the homeland while "belonging" to the host society). In theory, members of diaspora groups can build civic allegiances to the country they live in while remaining "ethnically" tied to their country of origin; that, too, is transnationalism.

The transnationalism inherent in diaspora groups can signify two things. First, it describes the existence of affective links between minorities in a host society and their homelands, for example, Turks resident in Germany for Turkey. Second, it relates the ethnic harmony that exists between majority and minority groups within a country, for example, between ethnic Germans and Turks in Germany.

Those most successful at negotiating borders and boundaries have earned the designation of cosmopolitan. *Cosmopolitans* are the finished product of transnationalism. They constitute a privileged group whose material circumstances—money, celebrity status, a politically correct passport, indeed, passport shopping for just the right one to suit any circumstances—enable them to embrace a cosmopolitan consciousness.[50] They can include privileged members of diaspora groups as well as well-traveled and well-to-do citizens of economically advanced states. Of course, Europe's leaders bear most of the characteristics of cosmopolitans. With their established social and educational hierarchies, polyglot speakers, and imperial heritages, European countries—above all, those in the west—are a greenhouse for the cultivation of cosmopolitans.

A cosmopolitan social identity manifests itself as postnational self-understanding both within and beyond national cultures. As Craig Calhoun put it, "Today, cosmopolitanism has considerable rhetorical advantage. It seems hard not to want to be a 'citizen of the world.'"[51] Part of the difficulty in criticizing European integration is that it seems to be an attack on the notion of transnational citizenship.

Cosmopolitanism and its close cousin, transnationalism, have some unsavory origins. As Calhoun makes clear, they often were the project of empires and particularly flourished in imperial capitals and trading cities, for instance, in London and Liverpool, Paris and Marseilles, and Moscow and Odessa. The multiple citizenships that cosmopolitans aspire to frequently are enabled by the existence of far-flung empires.

More recently, cosmopolitans have held themselves up as paragons of multicultural modernity—in self-conscious and self-righteous opposition to those rooted in monocultural traditions. They espouse the firm belief that cosmopolitan, postnational politics is the surest road to democracy. In the economic sphere, the ideology of neoliberalism can be viewed as the cosmopolitan dimension of finance capital.

Similar to Europeanness, "Cosmopolitanism seems to be more about transcending cultural specificity and differences of local institutions than about defending them . . . . Cosmopolitan thought has a hard time with cultural particularity, local commitments, and even emotional attachments."[52] In practice, it reflects an elite perspective on the world. That is the precise critique that sections of the European public have leveled at Eurocrats.

For Ulf Hedetoft, therefore, cosmopolitanism represents a "harder" stage of transnationalism. Proficiency in a number of languages and the ability to move and work in different countries characterize cosmopolitan behavior. Intellectual, business, and political elites in western Europe furnish good examples.[53]

At the end of the day, transnationalism and cosmopolitanism may be more about economics than culture. That has been the position of most antiglobalization critics, who believe that supranational economic interests are the hidden agenda giving rise to the transnational and the cosmopolitan. One of these economic interests, imputed to multinational corporations, is the effort to create a division of labor so as to keep labor costs to a minimum. In the case of the enlarged EU, a hierarchy based on a division of labor seems to have unfolded. Eastern Europe's part in transnationalism has been construed by antiglobalization and nationalist critics as primarily economic in nature: the region serves as a sweatshop for western member states.

This is a provocative claim to make. According to Naomi Klein, "Poland, Bulgaria, Hungary, and the Czech Republic are the postmodern serfs, providing low-wage labor for the factories where clothes, electronics, and cars are produced for 20–25 per cent of the cost of making them in Western Europe." This is a cheap-labor substitution economy. As she asked about the

EU, "How do you stay open to business and closed to people? Easy: First you expand the perimeter. Then you lock down."[54]

A division of labor invariably entails some group doing the dirty work no others want to do. The dirty jobs new Europe has undertaken to do include responsibilities related to security and military tasks. Among the dirty military work it has accepted that western European states proffer horror at are secret rendition camps for terrorism suspects, antimissile bases for the U.S. military, and cannon fodder in Iraq and Afghanistan. That was before the "Coalition of the Willing" metamorphosed into the "Coalition of the Leaving" toward the end of the Bush presidency.

Oddly, Britain under New Labor shares many of the characteristics of new Europe. Under Blair and Gordon Brown, his long-serving chancellor of the exchequer and successor as prime minister, wage costs in the UK have been among the lowest in the EU. British workers had a forty-five-hour work week compared to the EU average of forty. Written employment contracts were not required in Britain as they were elsewhere in the EU. To be sure, Britain's low-wage, low-labor-protection workforce was still significantly better off than the workforce in eastern Europe. Consequently, after enlargement Britain lured hundreds of thousands of workers from Poland and several of its neighbors. In another way, too, Britain was new Europe: it formed part of the "Coalition Forces"—alongside U.S. troops—in Iraq.

EUROPE AT FIFTY

The events held in March 2007 to mark the fiftieth anniversary of the signing of the Treaties of Rome lend insight into the discursive, metacultural assumptions of the EU's political leadership. As president of the EU Council at the time, German chancellor Angela Merkel presided over the official ceremony in Berlin. She stated, "The source of Europe's identity are our shared, fundamental values. They are what holds Europe together. Let us not forget: For centuries Europe had been an idea, no more than a hope of peace and understanding. Today we, the citizens of Europe, know that hope has been fulfilled."[55]

Given the rise of xenophobia in Europe, Merkel added defensively:

This dream could come true because we let ourselves be guided by that quality which for me gives Europe its true soul, that quality which made the Treaties of Rome possible. That quality is tolerance. We have taken centuries to learn this. On the way to tolerance we had to endure cataclysms. We persecuted and destroyed one another. We ravaged our homeland. We jeopardized the things we revered. Not even one generation has passed since the worst period of hate, devastation and destruction.[56]

Box 3.3. The Original Scepticism about European Integration
"A Belgian newspaper, *La libre belgique*, wrote at the time of the negotiations on the Treaties of Rome that the Germans were all important doctors and well-organized; the French were well bred, loved
plans and theories. The Italians wore wonderful ties and stockings and
even statistics exploded like fireworks in their country. Yes, ladies and
gentlemen, we are all of this and much, much more. That is Europe.
Scepticism, contradictions, diversity, even some much loved clichés,
but not least—courage. Europe is all of that."

Source: Angela Merkel (speech at at the official ceremony to celebrate the 50th anniversary of the signing of the Treaties of Rome, March 25, 2007), http://www.eu2007
.de/en/News/Speeches_Interviews/March/0325BKBerliner.html.

This familiar unity-out-of-diversity discourse may exemplify what a former German minister of justice called "empty tolerance"—an uninterested
acceptance of oddities in others that has a patronizing and discriminatory
tone to it. The consigning of religion to private life is an example. "A climate
in which the different religious communities get to know one another better, and inspire each other in mutual respect, will not arise in such a way."[57]

Different symbolism accompanied European Commission president José
Manuel Barroso's speech to the Lithuanian parliament, titled "We Are All
New Europeans Now." He declared, "The division between old Europe and
new Europe is a fallacy. There is now only a new Europe. The new Europe
is a global Europe, a Europe of true solidarity, and a Europe which engages
with its peoples and parliaments."[58]

The Berlin Declaration of March 25, 2007, was a typical EU compromise
that allowed all twenty-seven member states to sign despite various objections a few harbored. It outlined the EU's main goals: "We, the citizens of
the European Union, have united for the better . . . . We are striving for
peace and freedom, for democracy and the rule of law, for mutual respect
and shared responsibility, for prosperity and security, for tolerance and participation, for justice and solidarity."[59]

No official mention was made of Christianity—an omission that Pope
Benedict XVI condemned as nothing short of an act of apostasy. To be sure,
in her speech Merkel had added the "personal comment" that it was Europe's Jewish-Christian heritage that made possible the paramount importance of the dignity of the individual. The declaration also did not mention
a European constitution, which gave satisfaction to the Czech Republic and
other states opposing it such as Britain and Holland.

In his speech in Vilnius, Barroso listed six guiding principles for the Union that were embedded, if not explicitly stated, in the Berlin declaration: 1) economic growth and competitiveness in an era of globalization, 2) solidarity through strengthened economic and social cohesion, 3) sustainability through the fight against climate change and a proper European energy policy, 4) accountability: a citizen's right and European institutions' obligation to greater transparency and access to information, 5) security—a commitment to protect EU peoples while preserving fundamental freedoms, and 6) global outreach—promoting Europe's values in the world. While economic growth, the promotion of liberal values and, above all, security were principles that had long been the hallmark of the Bush administration, EU discourse was distinctive in its stress on solidarity, sustainability, and accountability.

The voices of the discontented on Europe's fiftieth anniversary were primarily those of political leaders in new Europe. Czech president Klaus complained that he had been given twenty-four hours to review the preliminary draft of the Berlin Declaration. He did not mention that the draft consisted of fewer than seven hundred words. The Czech leader had called his country's entry into the EU "the end of our national sovereignty," cautioning that "we mustn't allow ourselves to dissolve in Europe like a sugar cube in a cup of tea."[60] He called the Berlin Declaration signing process "a classic example of a lack of democracy" within the EU and the document itself "Orwellian Eurospeak." Klaus only agreed to sign it and not be a troublemaker after chancellor Merkel had called him personally to assure him the word "constitution" would not appear in the final declaration. However, another of Klaus's objections—that there should be no reference to 2009 as the target date for a constitution or "renewed common basis" (the euphemism agreed upon)—was not met.

Polish president Lech Kaczyński grudgingly agreed to sign the Declaration, but hardly for noble reasons: "We have reservations concerning some parts of the declaration, but if Poland does not sign it, we would be the only country in the EU not to do so."[61] His brother Jarosław, the country's prime minister, also objected to the draft because it did not contain a direct reference to God or Christianity. On this momentous occasion, however, the Poles did not hold out for concessions.

The last word on Europe's birthday celebrations goes to a non-European. Some of the most trenchant criticism of the EU anniversary came in an editorial written by former right-wing U.S. presidential candidate Patrick Buchanan. "The EU birthday party was further proof, were any needed, that no transnational institution can elicit the love and loyalty of a country. World Government is a vision of elites no patriot will ever embrace. Men have died in the millions for Poland, France, Italy, England and Germany. Who would walk through fire for the European Union?"[62]

Buchanan concluded, "Dry documents, no matter how eloquent, and abstract ideas, no matter how beautiful, do not a nation make. What makes a people and a nation is a unique history and heritage, language and literature, songs and stories, traditions and customs, blood, soil and the mystic chords of memory. The EU is a thing of paper, an intellectual construct. Unlike a nation, it has no heart and no soul."

Box 3.4. Europe's Mission in the World

"The world needs the European method of putting together different national practices. The world needs the European principles of open societies and open economies. The world needs the European way of linking the imperative of freedom to the idea of solidarity and justice. The world needs the European priority in tackling climate change and promoting sustainable development with respect for our planet. By promoting its values and its interests, the Union not only delivers to its citizens but also helps the world to be a better place."

Source: José Manuel Durão Barroso, "The European Union after the Lisbon Treaty" (speech given at the 4th Joint Parliamentary Meeting on the Future of Europe, Brussels, December 4, 2007), http://europa.eu/rapid/pressReleasesAction.do?reference=SPEECH/07/793&format=HTML&aged=0&language=EN&guiLanguage=en.

Such pessimism about the EU was replaced with barely suppressed euphoria in Lisbon when the Reform Treaty was signed by European heads of state and government. EU commissioner Barroso emphasized how the EU was entering a more democratic as well as politicized era that would make it more salient for its citizens. He also highlighted how out of necessity the EU was becoming an external unified actor in international affairs: "it is crucial to defend and to promote the European interest in the age of globalization. 'Offensive openness' is the key idea to protect the European interest without falling into a protectionist agenda: openness without naiveté. . . . An open European Union in an open world has been at the heart of our policy agenda, and will continue to be a top priority."[63]

Compared to the frantic eleventh-hour efforts by German chancellor Merkel to achieve a semblance of harmony at the Berlin summit earlier in the year, the Lisbon signing went off smoothly. Only British prime minister Brown's late arrival—due to domestic factors rather than reservations about the treaty—tarnished the ceremony. As a sign of the turnaround in mood, the leadership of formerly recalcitrant Poland pledged that it would try to be the very first country to ratify the agreement. The vanguard state of new Europe was becoming mainstream European.

Our focus so far has been on Europe's institution builders and integration ideologues. We have also reviewed the key concepts related to con-
structing an integrated EU and have considered the views of the Eurosceptic elites. The next chapter will focus on the European public's views of the
EU and of its quest for unity, and of the attitudes citizens have towards each
other as well as towards those perceived as outsiders. Differences between
western and eastern publics will also be identified.

NOTES

1. Romano Prodi, *Europe As I See It* (Cambridge: Polity Press, 2000), 46–47.
2. John Gillingham, *European Integration 1950–2003: Superstate or New Market
Economy?* (Cambridge: Cambridge University Press, 2003), 482.
3. For an introduction to the method, see Véronique Mottier, "Discourse Analysis and the Politics of Identity/Difference," *European Political Science* 2, no. 1 (Autumn 2002), 57–60, www.essex.ac.uk/ecpr/publications/eps/onlineissues/
autumn2002/research/mottier.htm.
4. Tony Judt, *Postwar: A History of Europe Since 1945* (New York: Penguin, 2005).
5. Tzvetan Todorov, *Le nouveau désordre mondial* (Paris: Robert Laffont, 2003),
87ff.
6. See Umberto Eco, *La recherche de la langue parfaite dans la culture européenne*
(Paris: Seuil, 1994). Étienne Balibar, "Europe: Vanishing Mediator," *Constellations* 3
(2003), 312–38.
7. See European Commission against Racism and Intolerance, "The Use of Racist,
Anti-Semitic and Xenophobic Elements in Political Discourse" (high-level panel meeting on the occasion of the International Day for the Elimination of Racial Discrimination, Paris, March 21, 2005), www.coe.int/T/e/human_rights/ecri/4-Publications/.
8. Richard Herrmann and Marilynn Brewer, "Identities and Institutions: Becoming European in the EU," in *Transnational Identities: Becoming European in the EU,*
eds. Herrmann, Thomas Risse, and Brewer (Lanham, MD: Rowman & Littlefield,
2004), 7. See also in the same volume Emanuele Castano, "European Identity: A
Social-Psychological Perspective," 40–58.
9. Castano, "European Identity," 43.
10. Susan Parman, ed., *Europe in the Anthropological Imagination* (New York: Prentice Hall, 1997).
11. Ulf Hedetoft and Mette Hjort, eds., *The Postnational Self: Belonging and Identity* (Minneapolis: University of Minnesota Press, 2002).
12. Yasemin Nuhoglu Soysal, *Limits of Citizenship: Migrants and Postnational Membership in Europe* (Chicago: University of Chicago Press, 1995).
13. Gerard Delanty and Chris Rumford, *Rethinking Europe: Social Theory and the
Implications of Europeanization* (London: Routledge, 2005), 6.
14. Francis Mulhern, *Culture/Metaculture (The New Critical Idiom)* (London: Routledge, 2000), 181, 166.
15. Seyla Benhabib, *The Claims of Culture: Equality and Diversity in the Global Era*
(Princeton, NJ: Princeton University Press, 2002), 26.

16. See Michael Herzfeld, *The Social Production of Indifference: Exploring the Symbolic Roots of Western Bureaucracy* (Chicago: University of Chicago Press, 1992), 6.

17. Thomas Risse, "European Institutions and Identity Change: What Have We Learned?" in *Transnational Identities: Becoming European in the EU*, eds. Richard Herrmann, Risse, and Marilynn Brewer (Lanham, MD: Rowman & Littlefield, 2004), 262.

18. Bronisław Geremek, "Thinking about Europe as a Community" (speech delivered at the conference "Quelles valeurs pour quelle Europe?" organized by the République des Idées, Paris, June 19, 2003), http://myeurope.eun.org/ww/en/pub/myeurope/home/activities/citizenship/geremek.htm.

19. Helmut Kohl, *Bulletin*, June 21, 1996, quoted in Colin Good, "The European Debate in and between Germany and Great Britain," in *Attitudes Towards Europe: Language in the Unification Process*, eds. Andreas Musolff, Good, Petra Points, and Ruth Wittlinger (Aldershot, UK: Ashgate, 2001), 156.

20. See Jost Hermand and James Steakley, eds., *Heimat, Nation, Fatherland: The German Sense of Belonging* (New York: Peter Lang, 1996).

21. Risse, "European Institutions and Identity Change," 257.

22. Gerard Delanty, "Conceptions of Europe: A Review of Recent Trends," *European Journal of Social Theory* 6, no. 4 (November 2003), 472.

23. Mikael af Malmborg and Bo Stråth, "Introduction: The National Meanings of Europe," in *The Meaning of Europe*, eds. af Malmborg and Stråth (Oxford: Berg, 2002), 23.

24. Delanty and Rumford, *Rethinking Europe*, 36.

25. Delanty and Rumford, *Rethinking Europe*, 24, 25, 30.

26. József Böröcz and Melinda Kovács, eds., *Empire's New Clothes: Unveiling EU Enlargement* (Budapest: Central Europe Review, 2001), e-book. Jan Zielonka, *Europe As Empire: The Nature of the Enlarged European Union* (New York: Oxford University Press, 2006).

27. Delanty and Rumford, *Rethinking Europe*, 32.

28. Attila Melegh, *On the East-West Slope: Globalization, Nationalism, Racism and Discourses on Central and Eastern Europe* (Budapest: Central European University Press, 2006), 2.

29. Milica Bakić-Hayden, "Nesting Orientalisms: The Case of Former Yugoslavia," *Slavic Review* 54, no. 4 (Winter 1995), 918.

30. Étienne Balibar, *We, the People of Europe? Reflections on Transnational Citizenship* (Princeton, NJ: Princeton University Press, 2004), 42.

31. See Joan DeBardeleben, ed., *Soft or Hard Borders? Managing the Divide in an Enlarged Europe* (London: Ashgate, 2005).

32. Dieter Fuchs and Hans-Dieter Klingemann, "Eastward Enlargement of the European Union and the Identity of Europe" (Berlin: Veröffentlichungsreihe der Abteilung Institutionen und sozialer Wandel des Forschungsschwerpunkts Sozialer Wandel, Institutionen und Vermittlungsprozesse des Wissenschaftszentrums Berlin für Sozialforschung, September 2000), 29.

33. Fuchs and Klingemann, "Eastward Enlargement," 35–36.

34. Fuchs and Klingemann, "Eastward Enlargement," 35.

35. Thatcher quoted in Teresa Hayter, "Thatcher's Toll on the Empire," *Multicultural Monitor* 7, no. 15 and 8, no. 1 (December/January 1986–1987), http://multinationalmonitor.org/hyper/issues/1986/12/hayter.html.

36. Margaret Thatcher, *The Downing Street Years* (London: HarperCollins, 1995), 748.

37. Interview with Nicholas Ridley, "Saying the Unsayable About the Germans," *The Spectator* ca. 1990, quoted in Timothy Garton Ash, "The Chequers Affair," *New York Review of Books* 37, no. 14 (September 27, 1990), 65.

38. These quotations are taken from Heidrun Kämper, "Words, Phrases and Argumentational Structures in the German Debate on Europe in the Early Post-War Period," in *Attitudes Towards Europe: Language in the Unification Process,* eds. Andreas Musolff, Colin Good, Petra Points, and Ruth Wittlinger (Aldershot: Ashgate, 2001), 102–7.

39. Kämper, "Words, Phrases and Argumentational Structures," 102–7.

40. Kohl quoted in Jonathan P. G. Bach, *Between Sovereignty and Integration: German Foreign Policy and National Identity after 1989* (New York: St. Martin's Press, 1999), 133.

41. Quoted in ReligiousTolerance.org, "Do 'God' and 'Christianity' have a Place in the European Union Constitution?" www.religioustolerance.org/const_eu.htm.

42. European Commission against Racism and Intolerance, "Annual report on ECRI's activities covering the period from 1 January to 31 December 2006," CRI(2007)21 (Strasbourg: ECRI, May 2007), www.coe.int/t/e/human_rights/ecri/1-ECRI/1-Presentation_of_ECRI/4-Annual_Report_2006/Annual_Report_2006.asp.

43. Jacques Rupnik,"Europe's New Frontiers: Remapping Europe," in *Boundaries and Place: European Borderlands in Geographical Context,* eds. David H. Kaplan and Jouni Häkli (Lanham, MD: Rowman & Littlefield, 2002), 6.

44. Balibar, *We, the People of Europe?* 13.

45. Robert Frank, "The Meanings of Europe in French National Discourse: A French Europe or an Europeanized France?" in *The Meaning of Europe,* eds. Mikael af Malmborg and Bo Stråth (Oxford: Berg, 2002), 324.

46. Riva Kastoryano, "Transnational Networks and Political Participation: The Place of Immigrants in the European Union," in *Europe Without Borders: Remapping Territory, Citizenship, and Identity in a Transnational Age,* eds. Mabel Berezin and Martin Schain (Baltimore, MD: Johns Hopkins University Press, 1999), 84.

47. Ulf Hedetoft, *The Global Turn: National Encounters with the World* (Aalborg, Denmark: Aalborg University Press, 2003), 5.

48. See Michael Billig, *Banal Nationalism* (London: Sage, 1997).

49. Wolfgang Teubert, "A Province of a Federal Superstate, Ruled by an Unelected Bureaucracy—Keywords of the Euro-Sceptic Discourse in Britain," in *Attitudes Towards Europe: Language in the Unification Process,* eds. Andreas Musolff, Colin Good, Petra Points, and Ruth Wittlinger (Aldershot: Ashgate, 2001), 45–86.

50. See Craig Calhoun, "The Class Consciousness of Frequent Travelers: Toward a Critique of Actually Existing Cosmopolitanism," *South Atlantic Quarterly* 101, no. 4 (2002). For a different perspective, see Seyla Benhabib, *Another Cosmopolitanism* (New York: Oxford University Press, 2006).

51. Calhoun, "The Class Consciousness," 872–73.

52. Calhoun, "The Class Consciousness," 885.

53. Hedetoft, *The Global Turn,* 5.

54. Naomi Klein, "The Rise of the Fortress Continent," *The Nation,* February 3, 2003.

55. Angela Merkel (speech at at the official ceremony to celebrate the 50th anniversary of the signing of the Treaties of Rome, March 25, 2007), www.eu2007.de/en/News/Speeches_Interviews/March/0325BKBerliner.html.

56. Merkel, speech.

57. Ernst Hirsch Ballin, "European Identity and Interreligious Dialogue," in *The Cultural Diversity of European Unity: Findings, Explanations and Reflections from the European Values Study*, eds. Wil Arts, Jacques Hagenaars, and Loek Halman (Leiden: Brill, 2003), 429.

58. José Manuel Barroso, "We Are All New Europeans Now" (speech at Lithuanian Parliament (Seimas) Vilnius, March 29, 2007), http://europa.eu/rapid/pressReleasesAction.do?reference=SPEECH/07/211&format=HTML&aged=0&language=EN&guiLanguage=en.

59. European Union, "Declaration on the Occasion of the Fiftieth Anniversary of the Signature of the Treaties of Rome" (Berlin Declaration), March 25, 2007, www.eu2007.de/en/About_the_EU/Constitutional_Treaty/BerlinerErklaerung.html.

60. Vaclav Klaus, quoted in "The EU: Love it or Leave it," *Time*, October 13, 2002. On eastern European leaders' views of the enlargement process see the special issue edited by David Lane, "European Union: Enlargement and After," *Journal of Communist Studies and Transition Politics* 23, no. 4 (December 2007).

61. Lech Kaczyński, quoted in Euractiv.com, "Germany Wins Poland Backing for EU Birthday Text," March 19, 2007, www.euractiv.com/en/future-eu/germany-wins-poland-backing-eu-birthday-text/article-162565.

62. Patrick Buchanan, "The EU at 50: Can it Survive Midlife Crisis?" *Investor's Business Daily*, April 2, 2007, www.ibdeditorials.com/IBDArticles.aspx?id=260406436848534&type=right.

63. José Manuel Durão Barroso, "The European Union after the Lisbon Treaty" (speech to the 4th Joint Parliamentary meeting on the Future of Europe, Brussels, December 4, 2007), http://europa.eu/rapid/pressReleasesAction.do?reference=SPEECH/07/793&format=HTML&aged=0&language=EN&guiLanguage=en.

4

The Politics of Phobias

IMMIGRATION AND XENOPHOBIA: THE FORMATIVE YEARS

Welcoming attitudes towards foreigners may represent the most important litmus test of democratic progress today. As Balibar put it, "more and more, the modalities in which political programs of *struggle against exclusions and discriminations* are defined and put to work constitute the touchstone of democracy in a world in which self-sufficient nationality has disappeared."[1]

Xenophobia is, literally, a fear of foreigners. Xenophobes are considered to be those people who harbor negative attitudes to foreigners, motivated specifically by a fear of them. An enormous literature studying the psychological basis of xenophobia has pointed to how external threats increase group solidarity and ethnocentrism while, as a corollary, promoting intolerance and closed-mindedness.[2]

A pioneering study of xenophobia in the EU unwrapped the dynamics of xenophobia:

> Foreigners are seen as carriers of a different culture with the potential to threaten the integrity of one's own nation. The assumption that the nation embodies culture comes from a belief that the nation is the arena in which critical values and beliefs are transmitted to developing members. Since each culture consists of a unique mix of orientations, foreigners inevitably threaten to alter the domestic culture through the introduction of new orientations.
>
> Because membership in a nation is often equated with an ethnic heritage, cultures may appear relatively fixed and distinct in character from each other. This national cultural identity contributes to the xenophobic perception of stark, irreconcilable differences between cultural groups.[3]

In its annual report for 2005, the European Commission against Racism and Intolerance (ECRI) identified a specific form of xenophobia, cultural racism, as "increasingly worrying. Today, the idea of 'culture' appears to increasingly replace the idea of 'race,' and take on the role it used to play in the field of racism and discrimination. According to this new form of racism, cultures make up predefined entities that are homogenous, rigid, and above all, incompatible with one another. Groups of persons are therefore defined by their culture, with some cultures being 'superior' to others."[4]

Beginning in the 1950s, Europe underwent a transformative political process that made a fear of foreigners salient. European modernity, as it had developed over the first half of the twentieth century, had been *emigrant* in nature. Out-migration, primarily to North America, had kept western European states homogeneous and eased their social conflicts. There were differences among these states, of course. Whereas France was one of the few European countries that did not have sizeable out-migration, Italy had sent wave after wave of its sons and daughters abroad.[5] Migration *into* Europe, though not new, caught the European public by surprise.

By the turn of the 1960s, the accelerating disintegration of the British Empire caused the U.K. to begin granting citizenship to its colonials, a process that had started on the Indian subcontinent after partition in 1947. At about the same time a labor shortage, largely resulting from Germany's economic boom, fuelled that country's need for immigrants. Swedish academic Therborn highlighted the unprecedented nature of these developments: "The shift from emigration to immigration represents an epochal change in European social history. Ethnic—and largely continental ethnic—conflict has substituted for intra-European nationalist rivalry. The socio-political effect has been to weaken class cleavages and politics in favor of ethnic and other non-class ones."[6]

After a brief interlude following the end of World War II, xenophobic and even racist politics began to make waves—again—in Europe.[7] The flow of refugees from Hungary after its failed 1956 anticommunist revolution; from Czechoslovakia after Soviet tanks crushed the 1968 reforms; and from Poland during the tense years of Solidarity's tenuous existence in 1980–1981, ending with the imposition of martial law, offered previews of east-to-west population movements. But anxiety about massive migration from eastern Europe to the west reached a high point after the Iron Curtain came down in 1989.[8] It helped put xenophobia on the agenda of some political parties.

By far the most important factor stimulating xenophobic attitudes from the 1960s on was the foreigner from the Third World—not the foreigner who was a national of another European state. Granted, "non-Europeans" had been settling on the continent for centuries. But the difference now was in the sheer numbers arriving in Europe in a brief time span. Though they appeared to be able to accommodate and absorb the new arrivals in practical ways—providing jobs, housing, schools, and health care—host societies were unprepared psychologically to adapt to the multiculturalizing impetus stemming from large-scale in-migration.

The standard retort to hostility towards new immigrants is that we are all—one way or another—descendants of immigrants. Immigration has defined and shaped most societies in the world, so why should people today view it as an aberration and threatening? Historian Walter Laqueur ventured an answer by suggesting that there was something quantitatively and qualitatively different about migration patterns of the last half century:

> There is, to begin with, the scale of immigration. Only tens of thousands came to Western Europe 100 years ago, not millions. They made great efforts to integrate socially and culturally. Above all, they wanted to give their children a good secular education at almost any price. The rate of intermarriage was high within one generation, and even higher within two. No one helped them: There were no social workers or advisors, no one gave them housing at low or no rent, and programs such as Sure Start (a British equivalent of Head Start) and 'positive discrimination' had not yet been invented. There were no free health-service or unemployment benefits. There were no government committees analyzing Judeophobia and how to combat it.[9]

The perception by sections of a host society that their state was laying out welfare and benefits to immigrants caused resentment. The political effects of this sentiment took some years to surface. Xenophobic attitudes were also hardened by the *demographics* of immigration, which, as noted earlier, were different from the past. Instead of migration from one part of a continent to another, the new wave of immigrants came from distant—and

---

Box 4.1. No Going Home

"There had been guest workers, millions of them, who played a vital role in the economic miracle of the 1950s. But those had been mainly Europeans: Italians, Spaniards, Portuguese, and Yugoslavs who eventually returned to their countries of origin. They were replaced by millions of new immigrants from Asia, the Middle East, and Africa; many of those had come as political-asylum seekers but had, in fact, been in search of a better life for themselves and their children. Unlike earlier guest workers, they had no intention of returning to their homelands."

Source: Walter Laqueur, "So Much for the New European Century," *The Chronicle of Higher Education*, May 11, 2007, B8.

poor—continents. As one French demographer put it, this wave represented the revenge of the Third World.[10]

Then there was the issue of how immigrants would integrate, assimilate, and acculturate into a host society. Their developmental trajectories could not be reduced to dichotomous categories like the adoption of positive or negative, liberal or illiberal, and democratic or nondemocratic collective identities. Given the existence of group-specific moralities, the relevant questions to ask were: "What kinds of *special* obligations, loyalties, solidarities among the members of some collectivity could be justified? And how should conflicts between competing loyalties be resolved?"[11]

Bernhard Peters identified six sets of concepts—both descriptive and normative in content—related to collective identity. Such an identity could be: 1) deep or shallow, depending on strength of group solidarity and time span; 2) coherent or fragmented, shaped by the degree of unity in a group; 3) genuine or manipulated, depending in part on whether it is created from below or imposed from above; 4) inclusive or exclusive, determined by the type of gatekeeping applied towards potential new members; 5) open or closed, a cognitive dimension related to reflexivity or dogmatism; and 6) cooperative or aggressive in negotiating group interests with outsiders.[12]

It is a truism that immigrant groups are transformed in the process of taking up residence in new host societies. Peters' typology is useful in determining the different ways that immigrant groups strive to maintain a collective identity. They may, for example, decide on an identity-maintenance strategy that does not prioritize coherence or gatekeeping and instead adopts open—even negotiable—and cooperative values. Clearly, this strategy is what host societies—even those championing multiculturalism—would prefer from their immigrant communities. The typology can also suggest what type of collective identity embraced by immigrants is likely to be viewed as antagonistic by host society members—thereby contributing to the scope and intensity of xenophobic attitudes.

IMMIGRANT ASSERTIVENESS AND ITS BACKLASH

A secondary factor—but a significant one nonetheless—in engendering increased xenophobia directed at new and established immigrant communities is the political and cultural demands made by immigrants themselves. For starters, immigrant group leaders have asserted the right to be different as a universal human right. Their logic is this: "While nation-states and their boundaries are reified through assertions of border controls and appeals to nationhood, a new mode of membership, anchored in the universalistic rights of personhood, transgresses the national order of things."[13] Being taught in one's mother tongue is considered by many immigrants as a human right. Given their long presence in that country, Turkish organizations in Germany have represented the vanguard of this immigrants' rights movement.

The dynamics internal to immigrant groups may also serve as a flashpoint setting off hostility towards them. Benedict Anderson, one of the most respected experts on nationalism, warned about the "radically unaccountable form of politics" practiced by some immigrant groups. It did not help their cause that some were involved in the transnational trafficking of drugs, arms, and money.[14] From financially supporting nationalist causes back home to simply projecting oneself as a success story in a new land, for the adherent of "long-distance nationalism," Anderson bitingly noted, "That same metropole that marginalizes and stigmatizes him simultaneously enables him to play, in a flash, on the other side of the planet, national hero."[15] In short, "Portable nationality, read under the sign of 'identity,' is on the rapid rise as people everywhere are on the move."[16] Formulating this theoretically, one conclusion is that "Ethnicity has no existence apart from interethnic relations."[17]

In their host societies, immigrants and their children come to learn about, enjoy, and demand rights that had been unavailable to preceding generations of newcomers to "immigrant societies." Writing about the United States but applicable elsewhere, too, Samuel Huntington noted ruefully how "Previously immigrants felt discriminated against if they were not permitted to join the mainstream. Now it appears that some groups feel discriminated against if they are not allowed to remain apart from the mainstream."[18] This has followed on from the more general phenomenon of "multiethnic chic": "The commodification of Otherness has been so successful because it is offered as a new delight, more intense, more satisfying than normal ways of doing and feeling. Within commodity culture, ethnicity becomes spice, seasoning that can liven up the dull dish that is mainstream white culture."[19]

The result has been that in place of the immigrant groups of the past, which wished to integrate into host societies, a new breed of diaspora groups has emerged which "forge and sustain multiple social relations that link their societies of origin and settlement."[20] These have "recently experienced an unprecedented range of linguistic, religious, cultural, and even political choice."[21] It has led one writer to speak of immigrant groups' "postnational membership" based on the presumption that nothing less than the international normative regime on human rights—not the venial domestic laws of the host society—is held to govern citizenship rights.[22]

The anti-immigrant backlash is only exacerbated when official discourse comes down hard on any questioning of newcomers' status. For example, it seems unfair that any risqué ethnic joke is treated as offensive, but bland politically correct ones are regarded as a model of good humor. Here is an

example of the latter. After the success of the Austrian right in the 2006 legislative elections, comedian Dirk Stermann suggested it was time to set up
a foreigners' party that hates Austrian nationals.

Such "jest" is—though perhaps unintentionally—polarizing, and it becomes the fuel of xenophobia. It leads directly to a backlash against politically correct ideologues almost as much as to newcomers themselves. In the
French-speaking Canadian province of Québec, a government-sponsored
commission headed by academics Charles Taylor and Gérard Bouchard had
to be set up to decide what precisely "reasonable accommodation" for newcomers should entail. This was after a controversy broke out involving
whether veiled women—who therefore could not be identified as registered
voters—should be allowed to vote in the 2007 provincial election. Politicians and courts went back and forth on whether this represented reasonable accommodation or not.

The Québec town of Hérouxvile did not wait for the commission's recommendations. In early 2007, its mayor and six town council members
published a code of conduct that people here had traditionally adhered to.
One was that "killing women in public beatings, or burning them alive are
not part of our standards of life." No female circumcision was to be allowed. Other norms included a ban on kids bringing weapons to school—
Sikhs would not be allowed to wear ceremonial daggers. Boys and girls
could swim together in the same pool. Female police officers were empowered to arrest people. The general admonition issued to newcomers was
this: "We would especially like to inform the new arrivals that the lifestyle
they left behind in their birth country cannot be brought here with them
and they would have to adapt to their new social identity."[23] While the
town's contrarian discourse caught the imagination of many Quebeckers
who believed that their identity was being undermined through unreason-
able accommodation of foreign cultural practices, its leaders backtracked
on some of these provisions after entering into a dialogue with a delegation
of Muslim women. Canada was experiencing the same dynamics shaping
integration and acculturation of Muslim immigrants that Europe experienced.

Arguments over accommodating immigrants took a more strident turn in
Italy in late 2007. An Italian woman was brutally killed by a Roma from Romania, one of a series of violent crimes committed by Romanian citizens.
More than half a million Romanian citizens had come to Italy since it had
eased visa restrictions for eastern Europeans in 2002. An emergency session
of Prodi's government enacted a decree that empowered regional prefects—
who are the representatives of the interior ministry—to summarily expel citizens of other EU states if they are judged a threat to public security. The
prologue to the decree made it explicit that it was aimed at Romanians: "In
the last few years the proportion of crime committed by foreigners has in-

creased, and those who commit most crime are the Romanians."[24] Instead of debating accommodation, many Italians had decided it was time to debate conditions for exclusion and even expulsion of immigrants. If, as Adam Luedtke asserts, "immigration is a strong test of supranational influence" in the EU,[25] then member states like Italy were finding compelling reasons to keep control of immigration policy.

Box 4.2. East-West Intercultural Encounter: Fiasco—or Success?

"Croatia rose to the occasion in their crucial Euro 2008 defeat of England—after an apparent X-rated gaffe by an English opera singer at Wembley. Tony Henry belted out a version of the Croat anthem before the 80,000 crowd, but made a blunder at the end. He should have sung *Mila kuda si planina* (which roughly means 'You know my dear how we love your mountains'). But he instead sang *Mila kura si planina* which can be interpreted as 'My dear, my penis is a mountain.'

Now Henry could be one of the few Englishmen at the Euro 2008 finals in Austria and Switzerland as Croatian fans adopt him as a lucky omen. They believe his mistake relaxed their chuckling players, who scored an early goal in the 3-2 win that put Croatia top of the group and knocked out England."

Source: Frank Keogh, "Anthem Gaffe 'Lifted Croatia,'" BBC News, November 23, 2007, http://news.bbc.co.uk/sport2/hi/football/7109058.stm.

The negative reception given in receiving societies—Austria, France, Germany, and others—to calls for expansive immigrant rights has resulted in a turn to "corporate nationalism" whose obverse side is an anti-immigration agenda. "Today, the increasing power and visibility of ethnic minorities and the accompanying social problems which growing migration is producing, have raised concerns over what has been described as 'cultural pollution,' 'overforeignization,' or 'minorization.'"[26] More practical concerns deal with the economic costs of receiving immigrants, the fraudulence occurring in refugee and asylum claims, and the perceived lukewarm commitment of newcomers to their host societies.

As Laqueur wrote, therefore, recent immigrants are qualitatively different. It is not just their numbers and places of origin that distinguish them from earlier waves, but the demands they make. Predictably, their assertiveness is equated with chutzpah by anti-immigrant groups. Krishan Kumar cautioned, therefore, that minority and immigrant groups in the EU "would be wise to wait for supranational institutions to realize their promise before they abandon the strategy of seeking to make the nation-state live up to its own ideals."[27]

MAPPING XENOPHOBIA AND TRANSNATIONALISM

Figure 4.1 illustrates the context in which xenophobia and transnationalism, discussed in the previous chapter, can be viewed.[28] An identity that is supranational but that espouses illiberal values—a claim to racial, religious, or civilizational superiority—is associated with the era of European empires. It can also apply to radical immigrant group leaders who claim that both as supranationals and as originating in a "higher" civilization (oftentimes religiously defined), their groups are entitled to special rights above and beyond those Europeans enjoy.

Liberal values can exist at both the national and transnational levels. The distinction between transnational and national liberalisms is the focus of identity—on a political community extending beyond the nation, such as the EU, or on only the national community, such as Britain or Germany.

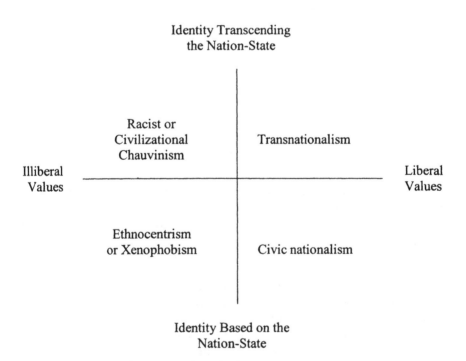

Fig 4.1.   Identities, Values, and Orientations.

Very few Western societies or regional organizations would admit to being anything other than liberal. Yet they are occasionally accused of being illiberal in their restrictive asylum, immigration, and minority rights policies.

When nation-state nationalism is combined with illiberal values, ethnocentrism and xenophobia result. The purported Islamophobia of old Europe, as well as the anti-Semitism and other phobias of new Europe (discussed later), can be said to exemplify this variant.

Cultural values are one of the most important factors shaping attitudes towards foreigners. Thus, "Immigration remains tinged with cultural or societal considerations that correlate with more affective than instrumental evaluations of policy preferences." Indeed, "The primacy of cultural values is particularly pertinent to issues related to identity, such as immigration, asylum, and citizenship."[29] As one academic put it, "identity is the dangerous area where the [integration] project can destruct if it challenges the nations in an overly confrontational manner."[30] Highlighting the power of culture is consistent with Ronald Inglehart's finding that culture ultimately underpins those societies that have achieved freedom and modernization.[31]

The cultural dilemma that the EU faces in trying to reconcile European integration with national identities and continued in-migration was summed up by Gallya Lahav: "Should the European public succumb to the threat of losing their unique cultures and identities for a viable European Union to exist or should the potential of this supranational force be dismissed for the preservation of national identity?"[32] For many citizens of Europe, EU integration and the centralized decision-making structures it fostered went hand in hand with a lax approach to managed immigration. After all, ephemeral European identity would not be impacted to the same extent as individual national identities.

XENOPHOBIA, ITS OFFSHOOTS, AND INTEGRATION

Is the proposition that xenophobia has become rife in Europe accurate? Eurobarometer survey results from 1988 to 1997 did not find high levels of xenophobia among Europeans. No more than 15 percent of respondents asserted that the presence of people of other nationalities was disturbing on a personal basis. However, a pecking order of desirable immigrant groups existed. Of all migrant groups, respondents were most favorably disposed to north and south Europeans in that order. The groups viewed most unfavorably were Turks followed by North Africans and Asians.[33] A survey of Members of the European Parliament (MEPs) found that they, too, regarded the latter three groups as the least desirable. There were some national variations, however: German MEPs identified eastern Europeans as least desirable while Greek MEPs named Turks as least desirable.[34]

Explaining these survey results, Lahav noted that "Elites in general preferred the more economically competitive, yet culturally more similar Eastern European immigrants to those from developing countries." Those that
did favor decreased immigration from eastern Europe were more concerned
with the issue of unemployment, whereas those who believed immigration
from the Third World should be restricted were more alarmed by racial
problems.[35] A counterintuitive finding of another Eurobarometer survey
was that there was no significant correlation between being oneself unem-
ployed and harboring xenophobic or racist attitudes.[36]

Where xenophobia ends and *misoxenia*—outright hostility towards and
hatred of foreigners—begins is difficult to determine. No doubt misoxenia
may be a more appropriate term to use to describe some of the attitudes we
encounter in this book. The word is rarely employed and does not appear
in dictionaries. One of its first scholarly appearances was in a book published in 1982 that identified racist and antiblack popular music traditions
in the United States.[37] Misoxenic attitudes are usually associated with right-
wing anti-immigrant and racist movements that have tapped the majority
ethnic group's resentment over never being consulted or asked about the
desirability of uncontrolled immigration. Such movements stress how the
majority only gradually becomes aware that its members are becoming
strangers in their own homeland. To be sure, various surveys have been
publicizing the fact that by about 2020 a number of cities in Britain will no
longer have a majority of any ethnic kind.

Xenophilia is a strong bias favoring foreigners. The term has not entered the
European political lexicon, but is sometimes found in cultural narratives. For
instance, it was used in French by novelist Andreï Makine to deplore the erosion of French national identity as a result of what he viewed as an overly liberal immigration policy. In his campaign for the presidency in 2007, conservative candidate Nicolas Sarkozy echoed Makine's sentiment and criticized
xenophilic attitudes without actually using this esoteric word.

Misoxenia and xenophilia are dialectically linked—one is the antithesis
of the other. In public attitudes, the embrace of one of these orientations is
likely to trigger a backlash against it and a show of support for the opposite
orientation. Let us consider an example. An improbable coalition of the political establishment, major corporations seeking to keep labor costs down,
and intellectuals on the left has for some time viewed the influx of foreign
workers as about as harmful as apple pie (or *charlotte russe*). Yet much of the
European public has grown steadily suspicious of the "unquestioned value"
of the unmanaged in-migration of foreigners. Indeed, much of the public
seems to have engaged in a kind of balancing behavior, seeking to offset the
xenophilic bias of elites.

Why citizens come to fear and even hate foreigners has been the subject
of considerable research. Often, the fear of foreigners is less self-induced

than incited by those in authority to serve their interests. Even defining a group as foreign can be an insidious act leading to xenophobic attitudes towards it. This understanding resembles Russian literary critic Mikhail Bakhtin's idea of "official fear"—an offshoot of the cosmic fear felt by impotent humanity in the face of Nature.[38] Political elites everywhere know the power of spreading fear among their citizens.

Research has pointed to the association of national levels of xenophobia with the number of immigrants in a country. Lahav found that "52 percent of the variability in the European public's perception that immigrants are a big problem by nation is explained by the percentage of non-EU foreigners per nation. As the percentage of non-EU foreigners resident in a country increases by 1 percent, those saying immigration is a big problem increases, on average by 9.9 percent." Going further, comparing public attitudes towards EU versus non-EU foreigners "points to the greater resistance Europeans have toward accepting immigrants least like themselves."[39] MEPs were slightly less committed to restricting immigration, though there were national anomalies. For example, in both Denmark and Greece, where the foreign population was small (3 percent and 1 percent respectively), twice as many of their MEPs and their general publics wanted decreased immigration in 1992.[40]

To sum up, in western Europe the rise of xenophobia is nearly synonymous with the anti-immigrant backlash. Xenophobes see immigrants as people coming from foreign, especially non-European, lands and people who are not racially Caucasian or religiously Judeo-Christian.[41] An ECRI report catalogued the problems that parts of the European public associate with newcomers: "Immigrants, and particularly foreigners, are presented as the persons responsible for the deterioration of security conditions, terrorism, unemployment and increased public expenditure. This process of stigmatization and criminalization provides a breeding ground for racial discrimination towards this part of Europe's population."[42]

In western Europe, immigrants have, over the years, faced a process leading, surprisingly, from inclusion to exclusion based on three metamorphoses: from status as foreigners to status as resident aliens, from being subjects of protection to discrimination, and from recognition of cultural difference to racial stigmatization.[43] Put differently, the real bias against non-Europeans increases the longer they live in Europe. The last two metamorphoses cited roughly parallel the process that converts xenophobia into misoxenia.

In the former Soviet bloc, which includes new Europe, xenophobia has been more closely linked to historical interethnic rivalries and hatreds such as anti-Semitism. As Balibar contended, all of Europe suffers from phobias "profoundly buried in the collective unconscious that trace back to centuries of religious and colonial conflicts."[44] But for a long time, there was no anti-immigrant bias to speak of in the countries making up the Soviet bloc because they were not permitted to become immigrant societies. Paradoxically, this did not prevent the emergence of antipathetic attitudes to outside groups, as we discover in the next chapter. Recent influxes of immigrants from the poorer countries of Eurasia and the far East, together with economic dislocations at home, have exacerbated ethnic competition and xenophobia in eastern Europe.

Zygmunt Bauman associated the rise of xenophobia with the replacement of structures of solidarity by competition: "Xenophobia, the growing suspicion of a foreign plot and resentment of 'strangers' (mostly of emigrants, those vivid and highly visible reminders that walls can be pierced and borders effaced, natural effigies, asking to be burned, of mysterious globalizing forces running out of control), can be seen as a perverse reflection of desperate attempts to salvage whatever remains of local solidarity."[45] When the line in a given society between the included and excluded begins to disappear, and when natives and citizens by bloodlines become marginalized at the time that foreigners are being included, xenophobic attitudes become heightened. Michel Wieviorka emphasized the big picture: "racism, in its links with modernity, cannot be reduced to a single logic."[46]

New Europe's inclusion in an EU actively promoting processes of integration can be viewed, in Bauman's terms, as the replacement of a structure of solidarity with one of competition. Processes of integration may generate increased fear of the foreign in the following way:

> If xenophobic individuals perceive the inviolability of the nation and hence culture to be protected by a political institution, they are less likely to exhibit visible xenophobia. While they may still fear the foreign as represented by other people or institutions, the security provided by the nation-state mitigates the necessity of expressing that fear. Should the sovereignty of the nation-state be threatened, active xenophobia may rise in response to the perceived danger to the nation and culture. European integration could present such a threat if seen as an attempt to subsume nation-states into a larger entity that forces individuals from multiple nations with conflicting cultures into close proximity. Hence the expression of xenophobia in member states of the European Union may represent a response to integration as a form of political transformation threatening the sovereignty of the nation-state.[47]

Introducing the concept of *far-away locals* into the analysis of xenophobia can help us better understand who the xenophobes are targeting. The term was coined by Bauman to describe people in distant countries who we learn about from the global-oriented media. What we learn about them, the author laments, is the "murder, epidemic and looting" that occur in "their" countries—nothing else. As a result, we "cannot but thank God for making them what they are—the far-away locals, and pray that they stay that way."[48] Bauman cited British prime minister Blair's proposal to unload would-be economic immigrants to temporary camps close to their home countries. These "safe havens" would ensure that "local problems of local peoples remained local—that is, faraway."[49]

Far-away locals can also be used to refer to minority groups in a country. "International boundaries create minorities as much as they create nations," Rupnik stated,[50] and for all practical purposes an ethnic minority or diaspora "beached" (to use David Laitin's term)[51] in another state represents one group of far-away locals.

The term *minority* contains several ambiguities. It can refer to officially recognized minorities (Catalans in Spain), officially recognized immigrant communities (Moluccans in Holland), and ethnic kin returning to the homeland (German-speaking groups in Germany who originate from outside the country, for example, Volga Germans). The European Convention on Human Rights' definition of a minority is straightforward: "a group inferior in number to the rest of the population and whose members share in their will to hold on to their culture, traditions, religion, or language."[52]

Before Bauman's use of the term far-away locals, Jacques Derrida had theorized about the politics of hospitality offered to strangers. It was contingent in nature because it invariably involved legal and judicial systems grounded in the host society, above all, reflected in its immigration laws. These systems suspended and conditioned the immediate, infinite, and unconditional welcoming of the Other.[53] As elaborated by sociologist Meyda Yeğenoğlu, "conditional hospitality is offered at the owner's place, home, nation, state, or city—that is, at a place where one is defined as the master and where unconditional hospitality or unconditional trespassing of the door is not possible."

In short, "The *law of hospitality* is the *law of oikonomia*, the law of one's home. Offered as the law of place, legal-juridical hospitality lays down the limits of a place and retains the authority over that place, thus limiting the gift that is offered. . . . In this way, the foreigner is allowed to enter the host's space under conditions determined by the host."[54] No wonder that far-away locals are reminded of their status as strangers regularly.

Having the status of stranger frequently invites hostile reactions. As Georg Simmel contended, "a stranger is not one who comes today and goes tomorrow, but rather is the person who comes today and stays tomorrow."[55] It follows that, as Bauman believed, strangers are "always uninvited guests" violating the basis of the host-guest relationship.[56] Yeğenoğlu added:

> it is not simply the crossing of territorial borders that turns migrants into strangers. Rather it was due to transgressing the dividing line between remoteness and nearness, between temporariness and settlement, inside and outside, that migrants became strangers in Germany. Because they trespass over the allowed borders of guest status, migrants engender uncertainty and ambivalence. By refusing to accept the termination of their allowed period of stay and

thereby turning their temporary status into an unexpected permanency, they remain 'stubbornly and infuriatingly indeterminate,' to use a phrase from Bauman.[57]

Our use of "far-away locals" is thus in keeping with Bauman's original conceptualization. The term offers a better way to capture the idea of "not belonging" to a host society. It also offers insight into the mindset of the majority ethnic group.

To summarize, the term far-away locals can apply to diverse groups—immigrants, guests, settlers, sojourners, strangers, and stranded diasporas—that live in a host society but are viewed by it as outsiders. Far-away locals are all those viewed as not really belonging, regardless of their citizenship status or length of residence in a country. One author cites the example of Chechens and other Caucasian nationalities in Moscow who "proved" to Muscovites that "the frightening far-away locals had arrived."[58] In the case of much of eastern Europe, Jews, Roma populations, peoples from the Caucasus, and other "undesirable foreigners" living in the country are accorded the status of far-away locals.

As for western Europe, Muslims constitute above all these far-away locals. Most have unquestionably "local" credentials: anywhere from one-quarter to one-third of the inhabitants of the inner quarters of many European cities consists of newcomers. In Brussels, 55 percent of children born in the city in 2004 were born of immigrant parents. The public fixation with kids from the periphery—*les jeunes des banlieues* or *Verlan*—underscores the local sites that these far-away people have occupied.

Related to far-away locals are non-national groups—those that identify with either a subnational or supranational community and do not regard the present state as their real home.[59] Non-national groups tend to be defined on the basis of ideological rather than ethnic or civic criteria. For example, those Russians still attached to the Soviet state have become a non-national group in the Russian Federation. Similarly, Croatians still attached to the former Yugoslavia have been treated as virtual non-nationals in Croatia; the case of writer Dubravka Ugrešic (considered in chapter 7) is illustrative. Attributing cosmopolitanism to Jews, as has happened in various European countries, is equivalent to treating them as a non-national group. If far-away locals face low-intensity hostility in their host societies, non-national groups face the threat of total exclusion—and much worse—if the right political circumstances arise.

XENOPHOBIA IN EUROPE COMPARED

A comparative study of eastern and western European xenophobia published in 2003 found a higher rate in the east. But it appeared to "be related more to recent structural changes than to more profound understandings of how 'us/we' is conceptualized."[60] If we also take into account recent in-migration to eastern Europe of refugees and job seekers from Southeast Asia, some Arab states, and Africa, then the result may be the type of anti-immigrant xenophobia found in the west.[61] The distinction between a sup-posed western "civic" xenophobia and an eastern "ethnic" one seems spurious.

Another comparative study—though it did not include eastern European cases—focused on how political parties exploited voters' xenophobic atti-tudes for electoral gain. However, the authors' conclusions, which were based on empirical data from the United States, Britain, Denmark, and France, may have wider applicability.

From the 1970s on, right-wing politicians capitalized on voter resentment of ethnic minorities to win legislative seats and, with that, were able to limit government aid to the poor. Voters' attitudes about race and immigration shaped political parties' policies on income distribution. By appealing to vot-ers who have conservative views on race and immigration but are otherwise liberal on economic issues, conservative parties exploited social issues to ad-vance their economic agenda. The authors estimated that if all voters held non-racist views, liberal and conservative parties alike would have pushed for levels of income redistribution 10 to 20 percent higher than they did.[62]

This raises the question of how xenophobic contagion can spread from single-issue right-wing parties to established, mainstream ones. The ECRI warned that xenophobia as a "type of argument is no longer confined to the sphere of extremist political parties, but is increasingly contaminating mainstream political parties."[63]

In a pioneering study of racist extremism in central and eastern Europe (CEE), differences in levels of such extremism seemed to be more profound within the region than between it and western Europe. According to Cas Mudde, author of the study, "If one compares the state of racist extremism in Central and Eastern Europe to that in Western Europe, the differences seem less striking than is often assumed."[64]

Table 4.1 indicates that the least troublesome areas in CEE are the Baltic states. The racist trouble spots are Poland and Slovakia, with the Czech Re-public and Romania close behind. The latter had the only extremist *political party* in CEE—the Greater Romania Party (PRM)—that became an estab-lished opposition party. Active *extremist organizations* exist in Poland (the League of Polish Families and its influential radio station Radio Maryja), Slovakia (*Matica Slovenská* and the National Movement), and Romania (*Liga Mareşal Antonescu*). Racist and violent subcultures made up of skin-heads are palpable in Poland and Slovakia as well as the Czech Republic. Fi-nally, in terms of the frequency of racist incidents, often perpetrated by skinheads with Roma as the chief target, Poland, Slovakia, and the Czech Republic again lead the way.

Table 4.1. Strength of Racist Extremism within Central and Eastern Europe

	Political Parties	Extremist Organizations	Racist Subcultures	Racist Incidents
Weak or Few	Bulgaria, Baltic states	Bulgaria, Baltic states, Czech Rep., Slovenia	Latvia, Romania	Baltic states
Moderate	Czech Rep., Slovakia, Hungary, Slovenia, Poland	Hungary	Bulgaria, Estonia, Lithuania, Hungary, Slovenia	Romania, Slovenia
Strong or Many	Romania	Poland, Slovakia, Romania	Czech Rep., Poland, Slovakia	Bulgaria, Czech Rep., Hungary, Poland, Slovakia

Source: Adapted from Cas Mudde "Central and Eastern Europe," in *Racist Extremism in Central and Eastern Europe, ed. Mudde* (London: Routledge, 2005), 268–71.

We can draw eight tentative conclusions from Mudde's comparison of the ten CEE cases with western Europe:

1. Racist extremist parties were not really a major force in CEE and look "pathetic" when compared to their western European counterparts.
2. Extremist organizations are not as completely marginalized from mainstream politics in CEE as they are in western Europe.
3. Skinheads had their heyday in the west in the 1980s and 1990s while in CEE—and Germany—they persist.
4. Racist extremist violence in CEE is on average higher than in the west.
5. The international community has largely ignored nonviolent racist extremism in CEE (not to mention Russia), while being more concerned with its manifestations in old Europe.
6. Anti-Semitism and Holocaust denial are more common phenomena among the political elites of CEE than among their western counterparts
7. Mainstream political parties in CEE are less willing to denounce racist extremism than their western counterparts.
8. Religious organizations in CEE are less willing to take on racist extremism than in the west.[65]

Fear of spreading racist-motivated politics led to the EU's adoption of appropriate legislation in 2007. Following six years of negotiations, EU justice and interior ministers reached a compromise on new rules to combat racism and hate crimes.[66] The centerpiece of the agreement, which had to be ratified by all the national parliaments, was to treat as a crime any "incitement to hatred and violence and publicly condoning, denying or grossly trivializing crimes of genocide, crimes against humanity and war crimes." Cross-border law enforcement would be put into place for acts of xenophobia alongside terrorism and 30 other crimes.

In contrast to the 2001 first draft, the 2007 rules set only minimum standards for combating racism and xenophobia. Prison sentences would be handed down on Holocaust deniers, but only when they were "likely to incite to violence or hatred." The mass extermination of Jews during World War II was the only genocide referred to within the new rules. Efforts by the Baltic states to include Stalinist atrocities as genocidal were rebuffed. However, a public debate was promised on the issue of genocide and other hate crimes currently not included in the draft rules. Finally, the new legislation punished incitements to hatred towards a *religious* group only when they were linked to incitements to hatred of *national, ethnic, or racial* groups.

Criticism was leveled at the timidity of the EU's legislation. The human rights group European Network Against Racism (ENAR) claimed, "The protracted discussions have resulted in a weak text, which will not require substantive changes to the legal orders of many member states."[67] EU states can choose to limit punishment to only those cases likely to disturb public order. Moreover, an EU country's rules on freedom of expression can always take precedence over the EU rules. Member states would also not be obliged to cooperate in judicial investigations. Nordic countries such as Denmark and Sweden came down in defense of freedom of expression. Others such as France and Germany took tougher positions on punishing racist statements. Britain supported an EU-wide ban limited to incitements to religious hatred.

Racism is a broadly defined term with a sting to it. It can be bandied about loosely in order to stigmatize opponents. An illustrative case was the diplomatic row between Cuba and Sweden in 2007. It began when Swedish foreign minister Carl Bildt criticized Cuba's human rights record at the UN Human Rights Council. Cuba's delegate, Rodolfo Reyes Rodriguez, retorted that "Cuba, unlike Sweden, does not persecute migrants or carry out ethnic cleansing that only allows those whose skin and hair color fit with the racial patterns of former Viking conquerors to remain in the country." Going further, the Cuban diplomat insinuated that Bildt's comments evoked "the not-so-glorious days of Swedish imperialism, which filled with blood and pain their neighboring countries."[68]

Taken off guard by the racist accusations, Bildt scolded the Cuban for employing "completely unacceptable language." The former Swedish prime minister condemned the "furious outburst from the Cuban ambassador about Sweden's blood, colonialism, imperialism, Vikings and oppression, and so on." He reassured the public that "The Viking days are gone. This is one of the most open countries in Europe in terms of immigration."

If "even" Sweden can be accused of racism, that left Switzerland as one of a few European countries that enjoyed a relatively wholesome image as a society devoid of racism. Its record has been impressive: over the past fifty years, the Swiss refused to pass thirteen proposed immigration reforms, including the 18 percent initiative in 2000 which would have limited the foreign-born resident population to this figure. But the image of an idyllic Swiss multicultural home came to grief in 2007 when an anti-immigrant nationalist party—the Swiss People's Party (*Schweizerische Volkspartei* or SVP)—repeated its 2003 breakthrough and won the most number of seats to parliament (62 of 200), subsequently forming a coalition government. What caught the EU's attention—though the country is not a member state—was an election poster the party displayed depicting three white sheep standing on the Swiss flag. Under the banner line "Bringing Security," one of the three is shown kicking a black sheep off the flag. The ratio of white to black sheep mirrors the composition of the country's workforce, in which one in four is not a nationalized Swiss.

In its election campaign, the SVP, whose leader was Christoph Blocher, also publicized its intention to submit a parliamentary bill that would allow the deportation of the entire family of a criminal aged under eighteen. Though it stood virtually no chance of being enacted, such a law invoked associations with the Nazi practice of *Sippenhaft*, or kin liability, under which criminals' relatives were held equally responsible and punished equally. Given that Switzerland arguably had Europe's toughest naturalization law—twelve years residence, evidence of paying taxes, no criminal record, irrelevance of being born on Swiss soil, and approval by a possibly finicky local commune where the foreigner lives—the country was at odds with the norms and practices of EU states. Not surprisingly, one British press report dubbed Switzerland "Europe's heart of darkness."[69]

The SVP has pledged to keep the country out of the EU. With its anti-immigrant policies, Switzerland's record would be carefully scrutinized were it ever to join. In 1998, the EU had established a separate agency entrusted with the task of documenting cases of racism in the EU. The Monitoring Center on Racism and Xenophobia, renamed the Fundamental Rights Agency in 2007 and located in Vienna, has published an annual report summarizing problems in the twenty-seven member states. In the next chapter, we examine popular attitudes in various European countries about race, nationality, ethnicity, and religion, including the much-publicized subject of Islamophobia.

PARANOIA IN THE WEST

EU enlargement has involved not just the near doubling of member states this century but also earlier, over a period of several decades, a steadily increasing influx of immigrants, refugees, and asylum seekers. Popular perceptions among a section of the European public have been that these various groups are motivated above all by the desire to take a share of Europe's wealth. The evidence that such is the case is mixed. One recent major study concluded that "refugees are not 'bogus' opportunists in search of better wages in wealthy countries."[70] Changing demographics have shaped changing attitudes about belonging and citizenship. In turn, these have given rise to new political movements that oppose or, less often, seek the support of immigrants and minorities.

The rise of the ultranationalists within the EU was demonstrated by the immediate effect of the 2007 accession of Bulgaria and Romania. European parliamentary elections in Romania resulted in five members of the Greater Romania Party—an anti-Roma, anti-Hungarian, anti-Semitic movement—being voted to the European Parliament. This pushed right-wing parties already in Strasbourg over the threshold needed to gain official recognition as a parliamentary bloc. Recognition guaranteed the bloc more speaking time, funding (up to €1 million), and political influence. The new bloc, calling itself "Identity, Tradition, Sovereignty" (ITS), claimed the backing of 23 million Europeans. However, internal disputes led to its quick disintegration.

The group's founding principles sounded innocent: recognition of national interests, sovereignties, identities, and differences and commitment to Christian values and the traditions of European civilization. But the personal background of the first head of this bloc exposed what the group's politics really were. Bruno Gollnisch was a member of France's National Front party and was awaiting a verdict on charges of Holocaust denial. Among incoming MEPs was a Bulgarian who had accused Roma parents of selling twelve-year-olds into prostitution.

Apart from the National Front and the Greater Romania Party, others in the bloc included the Austrian Freedom Party, *Vlaams Belang* (Flemish nationalists), the National Union Attack (Bulgaria), *Fiamma Tricolore* (Italy), and *Alternativa Sociale* (Italy), whose leader was Alessandra Mussolini, granddaughter of dictator Benito Mussolini.[71] Previous far-right groups in the European Parliament had faltered. France's National Front leader Le Pen had been at the head of a European Right alliance from 1984 to 1989. In turn, its successor, the Technical Group of the European Right, lasted from 1989 to 1994. The successes of the far right in this early period were converted subsequently into its greater political influence in individual European countries, if not within EU institutions.[72]

In Austria, Jörg Haider became leader of the Freedom Party in 1986 and led his party into a coalition government in 2000. The EU subsequently marginalized Austria until Haider was removed. His successor, H. C. Strache, a charismatic and xenophobic figure—the two often complement each other—helped his party gain 15 percent of the vote in Vienna in the 2006 national elections.

Austria is the best-known case of the success of xenophobic politics, but there are others. In Denmark, the ultra-right Danish People's Party led by Pia Kjærsgaard kept its place as the third-largest party after the 2007 parliamentary elections and became an unofficial partner in the governing coalition. Its popular appeal increased significantly following the publication of controversial cartoons of the prophet Muhammad by a major Danish newspaper in 2005. The following year, the nationalist Northern League entered into a right-wing coalition in Italy with Silvio Berlusconi's government. In Belgium, far-right Flemish separatists gained support throughout the decade. In 2007, they produced a stalemate in which the country had no government for months. In the Netherlands, populist anti-immigration campaigner Pim Fortuyn was a growing influence until his assassination by a left-wing lawyer in 2002.

Since the 1980s, the rise of the far right has gone hand in hand with the increased size and heightened profile of the EU's Muslim communities. So long as Europe needed both guest workers and increasing populations, there was a convincing psychological explanation for the relaxed immigration regimes of the second half of the twentieth century. "A sense of guilt over Europe's colonial past and then World War II, when intolerance exploded into mass murder, allowed a large migration to occur without any uncomfortable debates over the real differences between migrant and host."[73]

After the terrorist attacks in the United States in 2001, in Madrid in 2004, and in London in 2005, Europe became more attentive to the threat posed by Muslim fundamentalists. One 2006 assessment put it starkly: "Europe appears to be crossing an invisible line regarding its Muslim minorities: more people in the political mainstream are arguing that Islam cannot be reconciled with European values." Political leaders seemed to be taking their cue from public attitudes. "For years those who raised their voices were mostly on the far right. Now those normally seen as moderates—ordinary people as well as politicians—are asking whether once unquestioned values of tolerance and multiculturalism should have limits."[74]

Muslims living in Europe seemed to have solid grounds for believing that Islamophobic attitudes were spreading from the grassroots to the elites. In 2005, a Danish newspaper published cartoons of the prophet Muhammad that were regarded by many devout Muslims as blasphemous. For example, one of these depicted a bomb placed in a turban. Particularly galling for

Muslims was that three years earlier the same newspaper had refused to print cartoons satirizing the resurrection of Jesus on the grounds that it would produce an outcry.[75] Invoking freedom of speech, the Danish press reprinted the cartoons in 2008. The head of the world's Roman Catholics was also implicated in a purportedly Islamophobic event. In 2006, Pope Benedict XVI quoted a fourteenth-century Byzantine emperor who had condemned Islam for having brought about "things only evil and inhuman."[76] Even the arts in Europe seemed to be shaped on occasion by alleged anti-Islamic populist content. A production of Mozart's opera *Idomeneo* had to be called off in Germany that year for security reasons because it included a scene showing Muhammad's severed head. Chancellor Merkel subsequently complained that "Self-censorship does not help us against people who want to practice violence in the name of Islam."[77] In 2008, a stage adaptation of Salman Rushdie's novel *Satanic Verses* in the east German city of Potsdam was seen as a provocative act by some Muslim groups in the country. Shortly after it had been published in 1988, the supposedly blasphemous novel had evoked a *fatwah* (religious directive) issued by Iranian leader Ayatollah Khomeini calling for the author's assassination. The play was put on stage just as the controversy had seemed to be forgotten.

In Britain, home secretary John Reid called on Muslim parents to keep a close watch on their children. "There's no nice way of saying this," he told a group of Muslims in London. "These fanatics are looking to groom and brainwash children, including your children, for suicide bombing, grooming them to kill themselves to murder others."[78] Former British foreign secretary Jack Straw wrote that he felt uncomfortable addressing women whose faces were covered with a veil—a "visible statement of separation and difference."[79]

Even the mythic Dutch reputation for tolerance was tested with the murder of filmmaker Theo van Gogh in 2004 by a Dutch-born Moroccan. Attacks on mosques followed, but mainstream Dutch politicians shied from using the anti-Islamic discourse of Fortuyn. Van Gogh had made a film critical of the social practices of Islam, which he had described as a "primitive religion."[80]

As his film collaborator, the Islamophobic van Gogh had chosen a Somali woman who had herself become stridently anti-Muslim while in Holland—though earlier in her life she had supported the *fatwah* issued against Rushdie for *The Satanic Verses*. Ayaan Hirsi Ali was the daughter of a prominent Somali politician and obtained asylum status in Holland on the basis of a story she later admitted to having made up—that she had spent time in refugee camps in the Horn of Africa. In the Netherlands, her outspoken critique of Islam, even calling the prophet Muhammad a pedophile, helped her win a parliamentary seat. Dutch voters seemed keen to overlook Islamophobia so long as the Muslim bashing was conducted by a lapsed Muslim. Following a TV exposé, which revealed that she had lied about her name, birth date, and reason for asylum on her Dutch application, Hirsi Ali lost her Dutch citizenship as well as parliamentary seat and moved to Washington.

All of this led to growing skepticism about the practical effects of Holland's liberalism. The Netherlands had chosen an original way to accommodate its growing Muslim population. Rather than France's assimilationalist republican model or Britain and Germany's multicultural models, Dutch political leaders—especially Christian Democrats—decided to extend the "pillarization" model designed for Dutch Catholics and Protestants to Muslims. According to the formula, Muslims were granted the right to organize their own schools with state support.[81]

The murders of Islamophobic public figures Fortuyn and van Gogh and the scandal surrounding Hirsi Ali raised questions about the Dutch approach to accommodating Muslims.[82] Novelist Leon de Winter began to articulate the resentments rising in Dutch society. Fearing Muslim intolerance of Holland's society and value system, the Dutch government produced a film for prospective residents. They had to purchase and study it, then take a general test about Holland. The film included scenes of a topless woman strolling on a beach and of two gay men kissing in a park. The objective was to teach tolerance and liberalism to *certain* groups of immigrants—EU nationals and citizens of the United States, Australia, New Zealand, Canada, Japan, and Switzerland were exempt from taking the test, and therefore watching the film. In practice, the DVD was offensive to most religious people, not just Muslims, and a prominent Dutch theologian spoke out against it.

The Dutch "film wars" continued into 2008 when Geert Wilders, the leader of an anti-immigrant bloc in parliament, released a video called *Fitnah* (or "strife" in Arabic) containing scenes of a burning Qur'an and graphic executions. It sparked demonstrations in many Muslim-majority countries before the web site it had been posted on was shut down. Wishing to express solidarity with the Muslim community, a prominent Jewish leader in Holland placed an ad in a national newspaper that raised questions for all of Europe to reflect upon: "if Wilders were to say about Jews what he is saying about Muslims—in other words, if he advocated that temples be closed and rabbis deported—the entire country would rise in retaliation over such an anti-Semitic act."[83]

NEW EUROPE'S NEW MORAL COMPASS?

Enlargement has brought political differences to the surface—and amplified them. As Balibar observed, "A veritable fracture has thus arisen, a sort of cold war after the Cold War . . . but one which is both plural and mobile, and which is hidden under a thick mythology about 'clashes of civilizations' between Eastern and Western Europe, supposedly inherited from religious tradition or from the form of state building, when not simply from the ethnic character of the nations involved."[84] Balibar sketches a system of concentric circles leading from the "true" Europe (the advanced western states) to an "outer" one asking to be Europeanized (the eastern part).[85]

One plausible example of a need to be Europeanized comes from the Czech Republic. In 2005, riot police broke up a techno rave using tear gas and water cannon that left close to 100 people injured. "CzechTek" had been staged since 1994, but this time the Czech prime minister publicly vilified techno fans as "not dancing children but dangerous people." They were made up of "obsessed people with anarchist proclivities and international links" who "provoke massive violent demonstrations, fuelled by alcohol and drugs, against the peaceful society." He rejected comparisons with crackdowns on students by the communist authorities in 1989: "Any analogy drawn with the current savagery of young anarchists is absolutely wrong and expedient."[86]

Similar socially conservative policies surfaced that same year in Warsaw when its mayor, Lech Kaczyński (who was soon to become Poland's president) banned a gay pride parade in the city. When it went ahead anyway, Kaczyński condemned the police for not using force to stop the march and for arresting people who had tried to disrupt it.

Ethnic tensions in the Baltic rose in 2007 after the Estonian government ordered the removal of a bronze statue of a Soviet soldier—commemorating the defeat of Nazi Germany—from a square in Tallinn. Protests by members of the country's Russian minority led to one death and dozens of injuries. Estonia's president claimed that "the common denominator of last night's criminals was not their nationality, but their desire to riot, vandalize and plunder."[87] The "Bronze Soldier" statue was moved to a cemetery on the outskirts of the capital but the Kremlin sharply attacked what it regarded as a Russophobic action.

Some of new Europe's leaders brought attention to themselves in other ways, including when taking part in the EU's core institutions. In 2005, Polish MEPs from a right-wing Catholic party (The League of Polish Families) set up an antiabortion display in a parliamentary corridor in Strasbourg. It showed children in a concentration camp, in this way linking abortion with Nazi crimes. "We want to see Europe based on a Christian ethic," said one of the party leaders.[88] When guards in Parliament, acting on a request from socialist MEPs, tried to remove the display, the Poles resisted and a scuffle ensued. The use of force was immediately pounced upon by one of the MEPs: "It reminds us of what we had in Poland before 1989."[89]

Balibar's notion of an outer Europe seems particularly applicable to Poland under the Kaczyńskis. Celebrated Polish intellectual Adam Michnik—a vigorous critic of the communist regime—turned his sights on

Poland's nationalist turn under the twins: "Rather than seize on its European Union membership to catapult the country forward, Poland's coalition government finds itself looking, and moving, backward. In a speech in the European Parliament, a politician from one of the coalition parties praised the dictatorships of António Salazar of Portugal and Francisco Franco of Spain; he also published an openly anti-Semitic booklet. During a dry summer, a group of coalition legislators called upon the Parliament to pray for rain. A similar group proposed that the Parliament vote to declare Jesus Christ the King of Poland."

Michnik attacked the anti-communist witch hunt launched under the Kaczyńskis: "The latest idea of the Polish governing coalition is 'lustration,' which means looking for and eventually barring from public life all people found to have been secret collaborators with the security services between 1944 and 1990. The search will last as long as 17 years and will affect approximately 700,000 people."[90]

For Michnik, then, Poland's "governing coalition employs a peculiar mix of the conservative rhetoric of George W. Bush and the political practice of Vladimir Putin."[91] If anything qualifies as a characteristic of an outer Europe, this combination certainly does.

Box 4.3. Populism's Spread Across New Europe:
"Everywhere, the phenomenon of populism has appeared. Slovakia is ruled by an ethnic populist coalition every bit as exotic as the Polish government, including a party that proposed expelling the Hungarian minority. In Hungary, the prime minister admitted that in order to respond to demands the government could not fulfill, "We lied day and night." The right-wing populist opposition replied, "Traitor, Communist pig!" In Lithuania, the former president, impeached for corruption, has made himself increasingly popular with an abundance of empty promises in his campaign for mayor of Vilnius. The president of the Czech Republic has made declaration after declaration against the European Union. Populism can assume the shape of nostalgic post-Communism or anti-Communism with a Bolshevik face."

Source: Adam Michnik, "Waiting for Freedom, Messing it Up," *New York Times*, March 25, 2007.

PARANOIA IN NEW EUROPE: THE SPECIAL CASE OF POLAND

The clash in the European Parliament over the abortion exhibit was not an isolated confrontation between MEPs from eastern and western Europe. It represented "an incipient culture war in the heart of Europe, a clash of values that has intensified since countries from Central and Eastern Europe that are experiencing an increase in the influence of the Roman Catholic Church joined the European Union." Issues related to women's rights, homosexuality, and other "family" issues have been turned into deep cleavages. One MEP from Britain described how "New groups have come in from Poland, the Czech Republic, Latvia, and Catholicism is certainly becoming a very angry voice against what it sees as a liberal EU." A gay rights activist, he added: "On women's rights and gay equality, we are fighting battles that we thought we had won years ago."[92]

As the largest accession country, Poland began to flex its muscles already in the 2002 Copenhagen summit finalizing EU enlargement. The country's Catholic conservatism—inspired loosely, at best, by John Paul II's papacy—came into play during the drafting of the European constitution in 2003. Initially supported by Spain and several other Catholic nations, Poland argued for the inclusion of a reference to Europe's Christian heritage. In the end, the idea was rejected partly because Spain—its own culture a mix of Catholic and Islamic heritage—lost its enthusiasm. The following year Poland tried to save the candidacy of Rocco Buttiglione, an Italian nominee for the European Commission whose remarks about women and homosexuality at a European Parliament hearing were widely regarded as offensive. The Poles lost this battle, too.

In 2005, national elections in Poland brought a conservative Catholic, Lech Kaczyński, to the presidency. Simultaneously, his twin brother Jarosław was leader of the party that won the most seats in the legislature and shortly afterwards he became prime minister. For the next two years, the Kaczyńskis turned Poland into Europe's lightning rod on any number of issues. They kickstarted their controversial administration by abolishing the post of minister for women's interests, making Poland a rare European country not having this portfolio. Gay pride marches were banned, not just in Warsaw but also in various Polish cities.

The exceptionalism of Poland was not confined to sociocultural issues—or to the Kaczyńskis' interlude. Standing in sharp relief to the EU's reticence and caution, Poland aggressively supported the Orange Revolution in Ukraine in 2005 and fought hard for the EU to enter into negotiations about eventual membership for that country. Earlier, Poland had given full support to the Bush administration's invasion of Iraq and, together with Britain, for a time administered one of its three sectors. Human Rights Watch identified Poland as a site of a secret CIA prison for terrorism suspects and as being involved in renditions. A Liberal MEP from Britain summarized concerns about the strong American influence on Poland: "We need to put a protective wing around some of our new countries that are quite unused to U.S. bullying."[93]

To be sure, Poland's support in the early 2000s for the Bush administration's foreign policy was not exceptional in central and eastern Europe; it seemed predetermined by the region's historical and cultural pathways. Two academics involved in the New European Democracies project reported that "In CEE countries, preemptive or preventive military action tends to be viewed more sympathetically, partly because of their own history with aggressive neighbors. To many western Europeans, however, U.S. preemption disregarded international norms, undermined state sovereignty, and set a disturbing precedent for aggressive action against independent states couched as defensive measures."[94] In addition, western European leaders regarded military action in Iraq as a failure of diplomacy—an approach that seemed held in less esteem in the CEE capitals.

In economic terms, Poland's fast-growth, low-wage, low-tax economy differs radically from those in Germany and France, which offer higher wages, more extensive social insurance programs, and, of course, higher taxation rates. Polish labor has migrated to those western European countries that have allowed it in. Since enlargement in 2004, as many as three million Poles went to Britain and up to 200,000 to Ireland in search of wages higher than at home but lower than those of British and Irish nationals. In a meeting with Prime Minister Blair in 2006, Polish president Kaczyński admitted that some "feckless" Poles working abroad were behaving badly.

Arguably the starkest evidence we have of the political elites of old and new Europe working at cross-purposes is the volatile relationship between Germany, the largest old European country, and Poland, the largest of the new member states. Perhaps we should credit Kant for having written a prescient preface to relations between the two nations. The advocate of a perpetual peace, in 1798 Kant noted: "Poland: that is a very strange country. . . . With them, there are no middle classes and, thus, they have little culture."[95]

Inevitably, bilateral relations deteriorated with the accession of the Kaczyńskis to power. One *cause célèbre* occurred in 2006, when the Polish president canceled an official visit to Germany after a Berlin newspaper, *Tagesspiegel*, mocked him as "a little potato" who wanted to rule the world. Polish officials demanded that the German government take legal action against the journalists, but it refused. The visit was to attend a meeting in Weimar on the fifteenth anniversary of the founding of the trilateral cooperation forum between Germany, Poland, and France. At the last minute, the Polish president announced his indisposition due to an alleged gastric ailment, which the media speculated was payback for the critical newspaper article.

Real Polish payback for the German newspaper story came in 2007, after the Berlin summit hosted by Merkel had approved the EU Reform Treaty. Poland had successfully won a reprieve for its overrepresentation in the European Commission, but it had caused much rancor. Shortly after the summit, a leading Polish newsmagazine published a photo of Merkel on its cover, superimposing the Kaczyńskis suckling on her bare breasts. The caption read: "Merkel: Europe's Sow."

To be sure, serious *substantive* disagreements affected Polish-German relations. In 2005, Germany and Russia decided to route a major gas pipeline under the Baltic Sea, therefore outside of Polish control. The Polish defense minister compared the decision to the secret agreement between Hitler and Stalin to carve up Poland in 1939. At subsequent EU summits, the Polish leadership emphasized the urgency of reaching a common energy security treaty for all EU states, which was made more difficult by Russia reaching special energy deals with Germany, Italy, France, and the Netherlands.

A second issue in German-Polish relations concerned recognition of minorities in each country. Adam Krzemiński, longtime editor of a leading Polish weekly, *Polityka*, asked: "Must mass immigration involve giving minority status to the new ethnic groups in the EU member states? This is currently a bone of contention between Germany and Poland. If hundreds of thousands of Poles live in Germany, why shouldn't they have minority status? Allocating such a status to Muslims has already been broached in debates in Germany. The joke is that until now no Polish National Catholic has demanded minority status for the one hundred thousand Poles living in the UK. What's really at stake in the case of Germany is the lack of symmetry. There is a long-established German minority in Poland, for that reason there should also be a Polish minority in Germany."[96]

In 2006, Prime Minister Kaczyński visited Berlin to discuss another controversial issue with Chancellor Merkel—a treaty that would rule out private German property claims on Poland stemming from World War II. The subject of restitution claims displaced from Poland at the end of World War II has been sensitive for both countries. The Potsdam Agreement transferred large parts of eastern Germany—East Prussia, Pomerania, and Silesia—to Poland. In total, some 12 million Germans were expelled from territories that are now part of Poland and other eastern European countries. Close to 700,000 Germans were forced to leave Poland after 1945 alone, leaving their property and possessions behind.

The Merkel government claimed that it was following the agreement reached in 2005 between then-chancellor Gerhard Schröder and his Polish counterpart that neither government would support restitution claims pursued by individuals in either country. But when the Kaczyńskis took power, they accused the Confederation of the Displaced (BDV) of becoming a highly influential lobby group enjoying close ties to Merkel's Christian Democratic Union (CDU). Prime Minister Kaczyński condemned an exhibition held in Berlin in 2006 on the fate of the expelled ethnic Germans on the grounds that it was "equating the victims with the persecutors."[97]

In late 2006, the restitution controversy was exacerbated when the *Preussiche Treuhand* (Prussian Claims Society), which represents a group of Germans expelled from Silesia, filed twenty-two claims with the European Court of Human Rights accusing Poland of violating the rights of those expelled from their prewar homes when borders were redrawn in 1945. "The expulsion of the German population, according to some international legal experts, amounted to genocide, or at least to crimes against humanity with the purpose of dispossessing them of property without any compensation," the Prussian Claims Society brief stated.[98] The suit demanded compensation for lost property.

Both Merkel's government and the BDV distanced themselves from this lawsuit, but Poland's foreign minister, Anna Fotyga, condemned the claims as "an attempt at reversing moral responsibility for the effects of World War II, which began with the German attack on Poland and caused irreparable losses and sufferings to the Polish state and nation."[99] She even called into question the 1990 treaty between the two countries, which confirmed the post–World War II border and excluded any claims of the German state on territory lost to Poland after the war. But the treaty did not deal with territorial claims made by individuals.

As an EU member, Poland would be subject to the decision handed down by the European court. But Prime Minister Kaczyński suggested that the Polish parliament should declare it would not respect any court verdict calling Poles' rights into question. In his turn, the Polish president warned that Poland could counter German lawsuits with its own multibillion-Euro claims for destruction suffered under the wartime Nazi occupation of Poland. He added how "obvious anti-Polish sentiment that is often racist"[100]—that term again—had increased in Germany.

The 2006 Weimar summit eased frictions in Polish-German relations. The main topic between President Kaczyński, Chancellor Merkel, and President Chirac was the energy security of Europe. Kaczyński argued that the fact that this subject was seen not simply as an economic but also a political matter was a success for Poland. The three leaders expressed hope that negotiations with Russia on energy issues and, more broadly, on a new EU-Russia partnership and cooperation agreement, would begin soon.

This represented a reversal of Poland's position at the EU's 2006 Helsinki summit, when it had vetoed the start of the partnership negotiations because of Russia's embargo on Polish meat and vegetable products. Russia had cited hygienic concerns for the ban, but the EU's enlargement commissioner, Olli Rehn, asserted that Russia's food safety concerns were part of "a political game" intended "to put pressure on the EU."[101] Indeed, the EU subsequently was emphatic about standing together in its dealings with Russia.

Merkel succeeded in getting the Polish leadership to sign the Berlin Declaration on the anniversary of the Treaty of Rome. But she was hard pressed to obtain its support for the Reform Treaty in June 2007 and had to threaten to exclude Poland altogether from negotiations—making the treaty an agreement of the other twenty-six EU states—before a compromise was reached. Rancor had increased on all sides. EC President Barroso had to issue a coded warning to Poland that newcomers had a responsibility to help bridge divides within the union. "It will be in their interest for them to show that their membership of the European Union is not making European Union life more difficult but, on the contrary, they are giving more impetus to the European Union." He added: "There is no plan B."[102]

It comes as no surprise, then, that citizen attitudes in Germany and Poland about each other reflect elite disagreements. When Germans were asked what they most associated with Poland, the top answers were "car theft and crime," "illegal workers," and "poverty, backwardness."[103] In turn, in a 2006 survey 49 percent of Poles questioned said they feared Germany could pose "an economic threat" to Poland in the future. The Kaczyńskis' Germanophobic policies were genuinely popular with a large part of the Polish electorate because they reflected a residual Germanophobia in Polish society that could be traced back centuries.

Poland's nationalist foreign policy added strain not just to bilateral relations with Germany but also to the EU's relations with Russia. Onetime Polish defense minister Radek Sikorski stated provocatively that "With Germany our relations are broad and deep, it is part of the family. But the relationship with the Russian Federation is different."[104]

The distrust of Russia—accurately captured by the term Russophobia—spilled over into foreign policy differences between eastern and western European states. "CEE representatives and their publics often perceive western European members of the EU as appeasers of Russia, while western Europeans view CEE members as too hostile toward Moscow."[105]

Poland had repeatedly warned old Europe about the dangers of dependence on Russian energy. It proposed establishing the equivalent of NATO for the energy area: member states would help each other if their energy supplies were endangered. Poland's Russophobia was affecting both EU policy towards the Kremlin and the Russian leadership's approach to Europe. Symbolically, President Putin added a new national holiday for Russia, which celebrated the expulsion of Polish armies from Moscow in 1612. In 2007, following Poland's and the Czech Republic's agreements to host U.S. missile interceptors and radar bases (respectively) in their countries, Russia withdrew from the 1990 Conventional Forces Europe Treaty, which had set limits on troop levels.

The Polish phobias that the Kaczyńskis had exploited were turning the country into a destabilizing force both within the EU and in eastern Europe—not to mention an embarrassment for more centrist and secular Poles. An unexpected development was to spare Europe of further Polish-induced headaches. A quarrel within Jarosław Kaczyński's government led to the holding of early elections in October 2007. Confident that his nationalistic policies were popular, he expected to emerge with a stronger electoral mandate. Instead, his party was squarely defeated by a more centrist pro-European one led by Donald Tusk, who succeeded Kaczyński as prime minister. The Polish electorate had shown that it had had enough of the politics of phobias. Tusk soon visited Chancellor Merkel in Berlin and proclaimed, "We are friends, and friends can't get themselves into a situation of not talking to one another."[106]

TRANSNATIONALISM IN THE EAST: UKRAINE?

Our case study of Poland may appear to substantiate the proposition that new Europe is beset with complexes that make it a troublesome counterpart to old Europe. That is not really the case. A country lying to Poland's east and not a member of the EU offers evidence that transnational values have spread beyond where Euro-discourse claims they have: among longstanding EU members and to a lesser extent the accession states. Ukraine may be illustrative of the emergence of transnational values among *excommunitari*, people living outside the EU. The country offers an important case study, symbolized by the fact that its name means "on the border"—not just with Russia (where the idea came from), but also now with the EU.

History may have accelerated Ukraine's embrace of transnationalism. Partitions and rule by powerful neighbors have left a multinational legacy—an advantage when nurturing transnational attitudes. The country's urban centers have long constituted multicultural meccas. Ukraine's linguistic and religious communities are diverse and do not seem to be at loggerheads with each other. There is little measurable hostility towards minorities such as Tatars, Jews, Moldovans, and Turks; they are not treated as far-away locals.[107] Simultaneously, Ukrainian identity is rooted in a traditional understanding of *sobornist* originating in Eastern Orthodoxy. Its focus is on the collective soul of the people—an inclusive and tolerant understanding of who belongs in Ukrainian society. That approach has been borrowed in the service of a new statist Ukrainian identity.

Circumstances dictated Ukraine's gravitation towards transnational values. The experience of forming part of the Soviet Union had some—possibly unintentional—positive consequences: the Ukrainian socialist republic unleashed strong multinationalizing and multiculturalizing forces. While they did not *ipso facto* lead to a dominant transnational orientation, they served as intervening variables that indirectly promoted transnationalism.

For Roman Szporluk, the European dimension is paramount in the formation of modern Ukraine. Complex interactions between Ukrainians and other European nations shaped the development of Ukraine. What is more, the Ukrainian factor was influential in the making of modern Europe.[108]

The Politics of Phobias

The "battle over European orientation" that in part triggered the Orange Revolution resurrected arguments made by past political and intellectual figures. Some of these claimed that Ukraine was an Austrian invention, others averred that Ukrainians were essentially southwestern Russians otherwise having no distinctive identity.

Ukrainian nation builders, Szporluk contended, "thought that in order to become European it was not necessary to be a Russian, or a Pole, or an 'Austrian' subject of His Imperial Majesty. They wanted to be Ukrainian Europeans or European Ukrainians." The transnational paradigm was crucial in the past and should be in the future: "the new generation of Ukraine's citizens need to be raised in a national spirit—that is, in a liberal, democratic, pro-Western spirit."[109]

The diplomatic way that Ukraine's elites and ethnolinguistic communities negotiated a series of political crises from the Orange Revolution on earned the praise of EU leaders. Successive Ukraine governments' policies on minorities, official languages, and citizenship have by and large emphasized inclusion rather than exclusion. While problems—especially corruption and economic development—remain, since independence in 1991 Ukraine has moved steadily towards a value system that bears a striking resemblance to Europeanness.

This account is not to suggest that Ukraine is a multicultural mecca, nor Poland a fearful theocracy. Popular prejudices and phobias about "foreigners," whether they be longtime settlers, sojourners, guests, immigrants, or stranded diasporas, may be hard to eradicate anywhere—as we learn over the next two chapters. But they become especially devastating when leaders make recourse to them for political gain. That has recently happened in Switzerland and Poland, but it has not in Spain or Ukraine.

NOTES

1. Balibar, *We, the People of Europe?* 24.

2. For a literature review, see Gallya Lahav, *Immigration and Politics in the New Europe: Reinventing Borders* (Cambridge: Cambridge University Press, 2004), 189–190.

3. Sara De Master and Michael K. Le Roy, "Xenophobia and the European Union," *Comparative Politics* 32, no. 4 (July 2000), 425.

4. European Commission against Racism and Intolerance, "Annual Report on ECRI'S Activities Covering the Period from 1 January to 31 December 2005," CRI(2006)32 (Strasbourg: ECRI, 2006), www.coe.int/t/e/human_rights/ecri/1-ECRI/1-Presentation_of_ECRI/4-Annual_Report_2005/Annual_Report_2005.asp#TopOfPage.

5. See Craig Parsons, *Immigration and the Transformation of Europe* (Cambridge: Cambridge University Press, 2006).

6. Therborn, *European Modernity and Beyond*, 51.

7. See Neil MacMaster, *Racism in Europe: 1870–2000* (London: Palgrave, 2001).

8. See Agata Górny and Paolo Ruspini, eds., *Migration in the New Europe: East-West Revisited* (London: Palgrave, 2004).

9. Walter Laqueur, "So Much for the New European Century," *The Chronicle of Higher Education*, May 11, 2007, B7. Excerpted from his *The Last Days of Europe: Epitaph for an Old Continent* (New York: Thomas Dunne Books, 2007).

10. Jean-Claude Chesnais, *La revanche du Tiers-Monde* (Paris: Robert Laffont, 1987). See also Alfred Sauvy, *La vieillesse des nations* (Paris: Gallimard, 2001).

11. Bernhard Peters, "Collective Identity, Cultural Difference and the Developmental Trajectories of Immigrant Groups," in *Identity and Integration: Migrants in Western Europe*, eds. Rosemarie Sackmann, Peters, and Thomas Faist (London: Ashgate, 2003), 29.

12. Peters, "Collective Identity," 30–31.

13. Yasemin Nuhoglu Soysal, *Limits of Citizenship: Migrants and Postnational Membership in Europe* (Chicago: University of Chicago Press, 1995).

14. Benedict Anderson, "Exodus," *Critical Enquiry* 20 (Winter 1994), 327.

15. Benedict Anderson, *The Spectre of Comparisons: Nationalism, Southeast Asia and the World* (London: Verso, 1998), 74.

16. Benedict Anderson, "Introduction," in *Mapping the Nation*, ed. Gopal Balakrishnan (London: Verso, 1996), 9.

17. Committee of International Relations, Group Advancement of Psychiatry, *Us and Them: The Psychology of Ethnonationalism* (New York: Mazel, 1987), 20. Cited in Vamik Volkan, *Blood Lines: From Ethnic Pride to Ethnic Terrorism* (New York: Farrar, Straus, and Giroux, 1997), 22.

18. Samuel Huntington, "The Erosion of American National Interest," *Foreign Affairs* 76, no. 5 (September–October 1997), 33.

19. Jan Nederveen Pieterse, "Varieties of Ethnic Politics and Ethnicity Discourse," in *The Politics of Difference: Ethnic Premises in a World of Power*, eds. Edwin N. Wilmsen and Patrick McAllisten (Chicago: University of Chicago Press, 1996), 35.

20. Nina Glick Schiller, Linda Basch, and Christina Szanton Blanc, "From Immigrant to Transmigrant: Theorizing Transnational Migration," *Anthropological Quarterly* 68, no. 1 (January 1995), 48. Quoted in Madeleine Demetriou, *Towards Post-Nationalism? Diasporic Identities and the Political Process*, Center for International Studies Discussion Paper No. 6/99 (Aalborg, Denmark: Center for International Studies, 1999), 2.

21. Khachig Toloyan, "Rethinking Diaspora(s): Stateless Power in the Transnational Moment," *Diaspora* 5, no. 1 (Spring 1996), 30. For a study that assumes that because they are by definition transnational, immigrants should enjoy transnational rights, including citizenship, voting, and so on in home and host societies, see Soysal, *Limits of Citizenship*.

22. Soysal, *Limits of Citizenship*, 143.

23. "Hérouxville: Cause Célèbre," *Montreal Gazette*, February 2, 2007.

24. John Hooper, "Italian Woman's Murder Prompts Expulsion Threat to Romanians," *The Guardian*, November 2, 2007.

25. Adam Luedtke, "The European Union Dimension: Supranational Integration, Free Movement of Persons, and Immigration Politics," in *Immigration and the Transformation of Europe*, eds. Craig A. Parsons and Timothy M. Smeeding (New York: Cambridge University Press, 2008), 439.

26. Demetriou, "Towards Post-Nationalism?" 9.

27. Krishnan Kumar, "The Idea of Europe: Cultural Legacies, Transnational Imaginings, and the Nation-State," in *Europe Without Borders: Remapping Territory, Citizenship, and Identity in a Transnational Age*, eds. Mabel Berezin and Martin Schain (Baltimore, MD: Johns Hopkins University Press, 1999), 50.

28. More on how I operationalize liberal and illiberal values can be found in Ray Taras, *Liberal and Illiberal Nationalisms* (London, Palgrave, 2002), chapter 7.

29. Lahav, *Immigration and Politics in the New Europe*, 224. For a comprehensive comparative study, see *Acquisition and Loss of Nationality: Policies and Trends in 15 European States*, 2 vols., eds. Rainer Bauböck, Eva Ersbøll, Kees Groenendijk, and Harald Waldrauch (Amsterdam: Amsterdam University Press, 2006). Data and additional analyses are available at www.imiscoe.org/natac.

30. Ole Wæver, "Identity, Integration and Security: Solving the Sovereignty Puzzle in EU Studies," *Journal of International Affairs* 48 (1995), 430.

31. Ronald Inglehart and Christian Welzel, *Modernization, Cultural Change, and Democracy: The Human Development Sequence* (New York: Cambridge University Press, 2005).

32. Lahav, *Immigration and Politics in the New Europe*, 104.

33. Standard Eurobarometer 30 (1988), 37 (1992), 39 (1993), and 48 (1998), http://ec.europa.eu/public_opinion/archives/eb_arch_en.htm.

34. Lahav, *Immigration and Politics in the New Europe*, 116.

35. Lahav, *Immigration and Politics in the New Europe*, 91–93.

36. Standard Eurobarometer 47 (Spring 1997), http://ec.europa.eu/public_opinion/archives/eb_arch_en.htm.

37. Sam Dennison, *Scandalize My Name: Black Imagery in American Popular Music* (New York: Garland, 1982). Morphologically, *misoxenic* is correct but the word does not appear in major dictionaries such as the Oxford English Dictionary and Webster's.

38. Mikhael Bakhtin, quoted by Zygmunt Bauman in *Wasted Lives: Modernity and its Outcasts* (New York: John Wiley, 2004), 46–53.

39. Lahav, *Immigration and Politics in the New Europe*, 118, 120.

40. Lahav, *Immigration and Politics in the New Europe*, 125.

41. Anti-immigrant attitudes may be on the increase in Ukraine, however, as migrants from Asia and Africa arrive. See Nataliya Panina and Yevgeniy Golovakha, *Tendencies in the Development of Ukrainian Society 1994–2001: Sociological Indicators* (Kiev: Institute of Sociology, National Academy of Sciences of Ukraine, 2001), tables B4 03–06.

42. European Commission against Racism and Intolerance, "Annual Report on ECRI'S Activities," CRI(2006)32.

43. Balibar, *We, the People of Europe?* 122.

44. Balibar, *We, the People of Europe?* 231.

45. Bauman, *Europe: An Unfinished Adventure* (New York: Polity Press, 2004), 99.

46. Michel Wieviorka, "Racism in Europe: Unity and Diversity," in *Racism, Modernity, and Identity: On the Western Front*, eds. Ali Rattansi and Sallie Westwood (Cambridge, MA: Polity Press, 1994), 174.

47. De Master and Le Roy, "Xenophobia and the European Union," 426.

48. Zygmunt Bauman, *Globalization: The Human Consequences* (New York: Columbia University Press, 1998), 76. On the success of the nation-state in making

ethnic unity more important than all other identities, see Zygmunt Bauman, *Liquid Modernity* (New York: Blackwell, 1999).

49. Bauman, *Europe*, 19.

50. Rupnik, "Europe's New Frontiers: Remapping Europe," *Daedelus* 123, no. 3 (Summer 1994), 12.

51. David D. Laitin, *Identity in Formation: The Russian-Speaking Populations in the Near Abroad* (Ithaca, NY: Cornell University Press, 1998).

52. European Convention on Human Rights, art. 29, para. 1. Cited by Riva Kastoryano, "Transnational Networks and Political Participation: The Place of Immigrants in the European Union," in *Europe Without Borders: Remapping Territory, Citizenship, and Identity in a Transnational Age*, eds. Mabel Berezin and Martin Schain (Baltimore, MD: Johns Hopkins University Press, 1999), 83.

53. Jacques Derrida, *Adieu to Emmanuel Levinas* (Stanford, CA: Stanford University Press, 1999).

54. Meyda Yeğenoğlu, "From Guest Worker to Hybrid Immigrant: Changing Themes of German-Turkish Literature," in *Migrant Cartographies: New Cultural and Literary Spaces in Post-Colonial Europe*, eds. Sandra Ponzanesi and Daniela Merolla (Lanham, MD: Lexington Books, 2005), 141–42.

55. Georg Simmel, "The Stranger," in *The Sociology of Georg Simmel* (New York: Free Press, 1964), 402.

56. Zygmunt Bauman, *Postmodernity and its Discontents* (Cambridge: Blackwell, 1997), 6.

57. Yeğenoğlu, "From Guest Worker," 143–44. Zygmunt Bauman, *Modernity and Ambivalence* (Ithaca, NY: Cornell University Press, 1991), 65.

58. Bo Petersson, "Combating Uncertainty, Combating the Global: Scapegoating, Xenophobia and the National-Local Nexus," in *Identity Dynamics and the Construction of Boundaries*, eds. Bo Petersson and Eric Clark (Lund, Sweden: Nordic Academic Press, 2003), 111.

59. Support for this can be found in Gwendolyn Sasse, "Conflict-Prevention in a Transition State: The Crimean Issue in Post-Soviet Ukraine," *Nationalism and Ethnic Politics* 8, no. 2 (Summer 2002), 1–26.

60. Mikael Hjerm, "National Sentiments in Eastern and Western Europe," *Nationalities Papers* 31, no. 4 (December 2003), 419.

61. For a study of in-migration to Ukraine's capital, see Blair A. Ruble, "Kyiv's Troeshchyna: An Emerging International Migrant Neighbourhood," *Nationalities Papers* 31, no. 2 (June 2003), 139–55.

62. John E. Roemer, Woojin Lee, and Karine Van der Straeten, *Racism, Xenophobia, and Distribution: Multi-Issue Politics in Advanced Democracies* (Cambridge, MA: Harvard University Press, 2007).

63. European Commission against Racism and Intolerance, "Annual Report on ECRI'S Activities," CRI (2006) 32.

64. Cas Mudde, "Central and Eastern Europe," in *Racist Extremism in Central and Eastern Europe*, ed. Cas Mudde (London: Routledge, 2005), 281.

65. Mudde, "Central and Eastern Europe," 267–82.

66. Council of the European Union, "Framework Decision on Racism and Xenophobia," October 9, 2007, www.legislationline.org/legislation.php?tid=218&lid=7975&less=false.

67. "EU to Agree Watered-down Anti-racism Law-diplomats," *The Scotsman*, April 18, 2007, http://news.scotsman.com/latest.cfm?id=598232007.

68. "Sweden and Cuba in Diplomatic Crisis," *Cubapolidata*, March 21, 2007, www.cubapolidata.com/category/international-relations/. See also "Cuba-Sweden Diplomatic Row Grows," BBC World Service, March 23, 2007, http://news.bbc.co.uk/2/hi/americas/6483699.stm.

69. Paul Vallely, "Switzerland: Europe's Heart of Darkness?" *The Independent*, September 7, 2007.

70. Will H. Moore and Stephen M. Shellman, "Whither Will They Go? A Global Study of Refugees' Destinations, 1965–1995," *International Studies Quarterly* 51, no. 4 (December 2007), 830.

71. See Stephen Castle, "Gypsy-haters, Holocaust-deniers, Xenophobes, Homophobes, Anti-Semites: the EU's New Political Force," *The Independent*, January 16, 2007.

72. For annual country-by-country accounts on manifestations of xenophobia, see the European Commission against Racism and Intolerance reports, www.coe.int/t/E/human_rights/ecri/.

73. Dan Bilefsky and Ian Fisher, "Across Europe, Worries on Islam Spread to Center," *New York Times*, October 11, 2006.

74. Bilefsky and Fisher, "Across Europe."

75. Peter Gottschalk and Gabriel Greenberg, *Islamophobia: Making Muslims the Enemy* (Boulder, CO: Rowman & Littlefield, 2008), 2.

76. "Pope's Speech at University of Regensburg," *Catholic World News*, September 20, 2006, www.cwnews.com/news/viewstory.cfm?recnum=46474.

77. Bilefsky and Fisher, "Across Europe."

78. "Reid Heckled During Muslim Speech," BBC News, September 20, 2006, http://news.bbc.co.uk/2/hi/uk_news/5362052.stm.

79. Bilefsky and Fisher, "Across Europe."

80. Bilefsky and Fisher, "Across Europe."

81. Mark Leon Goldberg, "The Death of van Gogh," *American Prospect*, December 3, 2004, www.prospect.org/web/page.ww?section=root&name=ViewWeb&articleId=8915.

82. For a debate among leading European intellectuals on monoculturalism versus multiculturalism, triggered by Hirsi Ali's attacks on Islam, see *Sign and Sight: Let's Talk European*, January 24, 2007, signandsight.com.

83. Robert Marquand, "'Fitna': Dutch Leader's Anti-Islam Film Brings Strife," *Christian Science Monitor*, March 26, 2008, www.csmonitor.com/2008/0326/p01s03-woeu.html.

84. Balibar, *We, the People of Europe?* 167.

85. Balibar, *We, the People of Europe?* 169.

86. "Czech PM Defends Rave Crackdown," BBC News, August 2, 2005, http://news.bbc.co.uk/go/pr/fr/-/2/hi/europe/4738371.stm.

87. Web site of the President of the Republic of Estonia. "President Ilves: I Invite Everyone to Exercise Level-Headed and Rational Thinking," April 27, 2007, www.president.ee/en/duties/press_releases.php?gid=92863.

88. Graham Bowley, "Poles on Ramparts of EU Culture War," *International Herald Tribune*, November 24, 2005

89. Graham Bowley, "Poles on Ramparts of EU Culture War."

90. Adam Michnik, "Waiting for Freedom, Messing It Up," *New York Times*, March 25, 2007.

91. Michnik, "Waiting for Freedom."

92. Michael Cashman, quoted in Bowley, "Poles on Ramparts."

93. Sarah Ludford, quoted in Bowley, "Poles on Ramparts."

94. Janusz Bugajski and Ilona Teleki, *Atlantic Bridges: America's New European Allies* (Lanham, MD: Rowman & Littlefield, 2007), 73.

95. Immanuel Kant, "The Contest of Faculties (1798)," in *Kant: Political Writings*, ed. Hans Resiss (Cambridge: Cambridge University Press, 1991), 182–83.

96. Adam Krzeminski, "The View from the Vistula," *Sign and Sight*, March 8, 2007, http://print.signandsight.com/features/1242.html.

97. Kaczyński quoted in *European Social Survey* 44, no. 1171 (October 2006), www.scp.nl/ess/events/r3/event.asp?id=1171.

98. Vanessa Gera, "Germans File WWII Claims Against Poland," *Washington Post*, December 15, 2006, www.washingtonpost.com/wp-dyn/content/article/2006/12/15/AR2006121501179.html.

99. Mark Landler, "German-Polish Relations Sink to New Low," *International Herald Tribune*, December 21, 2006.

100. Landler, "German-Polish Relations Sink to New Low."

101. Olli Rehn, quoted in "EU, Russia Play Down Discord after Polish Veto," Agence France Presse, November 24, 2006.

102. "Warning to EU Members over Treaty," BBC News, June 19, 2007.

103. Craig Whitlock, "Leaders Struggle to Repair Polish-German Ties," *Washington Post*, October 31, 2006, www.washingtonpost.com/wp-dyn/content/article/2006/10/30/AR2006103001175.html.

104. Jan Cienski, "Relations with Russia: Intent on Keeping Clear of the Bear's Embrace," *Financial Times*, December 20, 2006.

105. Bugajski and Teleki, *Atlantic Bridges*, 39.

106. "Tusk, Merkel Call for New Beginning for Polish-German Relations," *Deutsche Welle*, December 11, 2007, www.dw-world.de/dw/article/0,2144,2999634,00.html.

107. Ray Taras, Olga Filippova, and Nelly Pobeda, "Ukraine's Transnationals, Faraway Locals, and Xenophobes: The Prospects for Europeanness," *Europe-Asia Studies* 56, no. 6 (September 2004), 835–56.

108. Roman Szporluk, "The Making of Modern Ukraine: the European Dimension" (lecture, Cambridge University, February 28, 2003).

109. Szporluk, "The Making of Modern Ukraine."

5

European Publics
and Their Phobias

ATTITUDES AND PLATITUDES

Public attitudes about who belongs in a given society are markedly different from Euro-discourse about transnationalism. At the same time, public attitudes do differ from one EU country to another, though they cannot be reduced to a crude west-east divide.[1] What they do have in common is the use of ethnocentric norms as the primary way that citizens evaluate their worlds.

Ethnocentric norms are by definition discriminatory, focusing on one's own *ethnos* over others. They can be the basis for outright xenophobia and racism. In its annual report in 2006, the European Commission against Racism and Intolerance (ECRI) highlighted the part played by public opinion in enabling the strengthening and spreading of xenophobia. It noted that it

> is deeply concerned by the negative climate of opinion which plays a key role in the appearance of manifestations of racism or intolerance within society. This climate is fuelled by some media and also by the use of racist and xenophobic arguments in political discourse. Xenophobic discourse currently enjoys a free rein in countries where the transition to a multicultural society arouses fears which find an echo in a context of economic crisis and globalisation, raising for many citizens the issue of national identity. Once again, it is minority groups and different communities which are targeted, including by the traditional political parties of many countries.[2]

Preferring an ethnocentric to a multicultural approach does not *a priori* have to be reprehensible. Two psychologists concluded that "The struggle for the best Europe is likely to be biased by an ethnocentric view, with citizens generalizing some characteristics of their own nation as *pars pro toto* to the whole of Europe."[3] The example they cite is of German respondents who believed that other EU countries were mishandling the application of the Maastricht criteria—regarded primarily as a German creation.

In previous chapters we have seen that EU institutions are designed to foster a transnational form of decision making. Through their rhetoric, European elites, too, push hard for the transnational identification of citizens with the EU. The policies they pursue, however, often lapse into nationalist pathways. Dual identification—with Europe and with one's own nation—contributes to the persistence of intra-European cleavages. This seems particularly applicable to citizens in an old European state resenting how their counterparts in a new one are going about becoming Europeanized. Here we do not take up the vast subject of measuring the relative strength of European identification; the twice-yearly Eurobarometer surveys address the topic comprehensively. Instead we focus on public attitudes about who people feel belong in their country and the extent to which they outgroup the "other."

A team of psychologists carried out pioneering experimental research on processes of "ingroup prototypicality" and "outgroup derogation" within Europe. According to Amélie Mummendey, Sven Waldzus, and Michael Wenzel, when citizens adopt the standards of their own nation as a norm to hold others to, "different" does come to mean "worse."[4] In a separate study, the authors refer to the case of strained relations between Germans and Poles: "Germans who dislike Poles because of their deviating from German standards . . . might dislike Poles even more when they develop a European identity, because they generalize German standards to the European norm, which is then also binding on Poles."[5]

There are many ways to evaluate the strength of xenophobic attitudes across Europe. One general, if inexact, measure is electoral support for extreme right anti-immigrant parties. During the early 1990s, support in Germany for the Republikaner Partei and in France for the Front National hovered at about 10 percent. Yet opinion polls indicated that at least three times that proportion of respondents agreed with the anti-immigrant antiforeign thrust of these parties.[6]

In a seminal study, two academics used factor analysis to create a xenophobia index comparing the twelve EU member states of 1994. They found that respondents with stronger xenophobic tendencies were less supportive of the EU than those with tolerant attitudes towards foreigners. The fear of foreigners and the fear of the EU seemed to go hand in hand:

> The disposition to perceive foreigners and foreign institutions as threatening to one's culture appears to influence how Europeans respond to integration.

Those who identify themselves with a particular nation-state as the embodiment of their culture instinctively fend off foreigners as threats to the group. Consequently, those who fear foreigners will almost certainly feel an aversion to an organization that infringes upon their established cultural group, the nation-state.[7]

Lahav's empirical research on attitudes about immigration led to a related finding: "those who support European integration are more likely to prefer a common immigration policy for the EU, and to accept immigration levels and immigration rights, than those who oppose European integration."[8] When religion was included as an explanatory variable for attitudes towards European integration, she discovered that "Protestants from Northern and Central Europe may be slightly more resistant to [European] unification than other groups not only because of historical images of Christendom, an exclusive type of Europe, but because of perceived threats of an EU that includes traditional emigration nations with weaker economies." By contrast, "Catholics and Orthodox (often from these emigration nations) are somewhat more enthusiastic about the prospect of European integration, which could produce stronger economic powers and social standardization."[9]

There was cross-national variation in expressions of xenophobia (Table 5.1). The highest levels were found in Belgium, Greece, France, and Germany. While the belief that there were too many far-away locals in their midst could explain three of these countries' ranks, Greece constituted a

Table 5.1.   Expressions of Xenophobia in EU Members, 1994

| Country | Xenophobia Level (%) | | | |
	Low	Medium	High	N
Weighted Average	**33.3**	**32.4**	**34.3**	**12,799**
France	27.8	28.7	43.5	1,000
Belgium	16.9	29.5	53.5	1,003
Netherlands	37.9	33.7	28.4	1,005
Germany	27.6	33.0	39.4	2,134
Italy	30.1	37.5	32.4	1,067
Luxembourg	66.3	25.3	8.4	502
Denmark	36.7	31.9	31.4	1,000
Ireland	74.7	19.5	5.8	1,000
United Kingdom	40.5	34.3	25.2	1,183
Greece	16.3	36.3	47.4	1,002
Spain	55.8	28.9	15.3	1,000
Portugal	55.6	30.1	14.3	1,000

Source: Standard Eurobarometer 41.1 (June–July 1994). Note: Each row totals 100 percent. "Weighted average" is calculated from data weighting each country by its percentage of the total EU population.

special case. As the EU's poorest member at the time, having no contiguous border with any other EU state and just across the sea from Asia Minor, inhabited largely by Orthodox believers, the self-perception of isolation contributed to a wariness about foreigners. In addition, Greek respondents by nature may have been more outspoken and blunt in giving answers than the guarded, politically correct publics of Scandinavia, for example.

By contrast, Ireland—which was just beginning to experience immigration from other EU countries but had few far-away locals—was remarkable in the near absence of xenophobic attitudes. Paradoxically, the Irish Republic at this time was still a very Catholic society and had been lending support to their codenominationalists in the north in their struggle against Protestant Unionists.

In 2000, a Eurobarometer survey found that, once again, Greece (58 percent of respondents), Belgium (56 percent), and Germany (47 percent) led rankings on a xenophobia-related question—whether citizens felt that too many minority group members live in their country.[10] France was in a cluster with Britain, Holland, and Italy (between 41–44 percent). By far the country with the lowest percentage (17 percent) of respondents saying they did not feel there were too many minority group members in their midst was Finland. The reason for this is self-evident: Finns may have simply been describing a demographic fact of life—their country was ethnically homogeneous—rather than offering an opinion.

Levels of xenophobia are not related purely to intensity of fear or hatred of foreigners. As sociologist Anna Triandafyllidou contended, how individuals conceptualize the "us-versus-immigrant-other" relationship also affects xenophobic orientations. Drawing on her three Mediterranean case studies, she found that:

> Ethnic features predominate in Greek identity and nationhood is tied to common genealogical origins. Greekness is often seen as a transcendental essence that can be shared only by those born Greek. Contemporary Spanish nationalism, in contrast, is plural in character and politically decentralized. . . . Different national origins are accommodated as part and parcel of the Spanish state. Italian identity, finally, lies somewhere in the middle of the ethnic-civic continuum because, although originally based on common civic traditions and territory, it also displays some ethnic features such as the belief in a common national character.[11]

Each of these countries has had its national identity challenged from both without—by Europeanization—and within—the Macedonian, Basque, and Northern League questions respectively. The Greek response was to assume greater defensiveness, the Spanish to grant increased regional autonomy, and the Italian to embrace enthusiastic Europeanness in order to mitigate regional differences. The author was not surprised, therefore, that Greeks top the xenophobic list and Spaniards are at the other end: "The ethnic conception of Greek nationhood is confirmed by the high degree of intolerance towards immigrants. The openness of Spain is also reflected in the survey results, and the ambiguity of *Italianita* (Italianness) is expressed in Italians' attitudes towards immigrants: discriminatory tendencies are paradoxically combined with an attitude of acceptance."[12]

Let us jump forward to 2006. The annual report of Minority Rights Group International concluded that "Racism, discrimination and intolerance remained prevalent throughout the 48 states of Europe. Apart from overt racism and discrimination, ethnic and national minorities face socioeconomic exclusion and assimilation. Roma remain the most excluded and vulnerable group in Europe—closely followed by immigrants and some refugee groups—and face disadvantage in access to employment, education, housing and health care."[13] Even as the EU moves in the direction of greater institutional and discursive harmony, then, the reality on the ground is that it is also developing into an ethnic powder keg.

In the case of relations with immigrant groups, "ethnic" Europeans have seemingly painted themselves into a corner. As a critical American commentator put it, "Not one member of the EU has a birthrate among its native born to enable it to survive in its present form. Europe's welfare states are failing to produce the babies to replace the aging and shrinking population. Thus, virtually all the nations of Western Europe are undergoing invasions—from the Maghreb, Middle East, South Asia or sub-Saharan Africa."[14]

These same Europeans object to the arrival of others from afar. When asked if they agree that "immigrants contribute a lot to my country," only 40 percent of EU citizens said yes. The American author contended that new Europe was especially shaped by anti-immigrant views even though it had not played the role of receiving society to the extent that old Europe had. "Hostility to immigration is strongest in Eastern Europe. Not one in five Hungarians, Czechs, Estonians, Latvians or Slovakians thinks immigration is good for their country. They want to remain who they are, and their country to remain what it has been."[15]

DISCRIMINATORY PRACTICES IN NEW EUROPE

The total ethnic minority population in the EU increased significantly following enlargement in 2004. Excluding immigrant numbers, it rose from about 50 million to at least 80 million. The accession of Bulgaria and Romania in 2007 added over three million more, including close to a million Muslims. Bulgaria's population includes nearly 800,000 ethnic Turks and

400,000 Roma. Romania's minorities include 1.5 million Magyars and 500,000 Roma.

While eastern Europe has regularly been depicted as a hotbed of nationalism, racism, and discrimination against minorities, the incentive of joining the EU meant that the applicant states had to comply with established EU legal standards on minority rights. Conditionality of minority rights has grown in importance as the EU turned to a review of the records of potential candidate states from the Balkans, especially Serbia. The principal minority instrument of the forty-six-member Council of Europe is the 1995 Framework Convention for the Protection of National Minorities (FCNM), which enlargement states had to adopt. To be sure, several old Europe states had still not ratified the convention at the time of enlargement: Belgium, Greece, Iceland, and Luxembourg had signed but not ratified the Convention. France has not even signed since, following the letter of the 1923 Treaty of Lausanne, which only recognizes religious minorities, it continues to insist on promoting a unified homogeneous state. It is ironic, then, that on paper new Europe offers stronger minority rights protection than parts of old Europe.

Box 5.1. The Plight of the Pirese—Europe's Most Hated People
"An opinion poll taken in Hungary showed that Pirese refugees are more hated than any other group. Even those who admitted to disliking Arabs, Chinese and Romanians, said the Pirese were worse. The group who are statistically most likely to have the strongest feelings are elderly, far-left women from northern Hungary. It's widely believed the Pirese mix their beer with blood, have the evil eye and are hideously ugly. And of course they don't exist. They were made up by a research institute to test the level of xenophobia in Hungary. High apparently."

Source: "Europe Diary: How to Holiday," BBC News, July 28, 2006, http://news.bbc.co.uk/2/hi/europe/5217796.stm.

The question arises how energetically new Europe actually applies antidiscriminatory legislation. A revealing case is its approach to the Roma population scattered across the region. In 2006, the EU Parliament released a report on the situation of Roma women in the EU. It noted that Roma remain severely disadvantaged in access to housing, employment, education, and health services. They are frequently the targets of racism on the part of state officials. Moreover, "Romani women face extreme levels of discrimination including multiple or compound discrimination" that lead to shorter life expectancy than other EU females.[16] They often were denied basic health care, education, housing, and employment. In the Czech Republic and Slovakia some were possibly even victims of coercive sterilization—charges that were being investigated by the European Court of Human Rights. Romani women were frequently victims of trafficking as well.

Predictably, members of Roma groups were underrepresented at all levels of government. In 2006, two Roma women from Hungary served in the European Parliament, but none had been elected to the national parliament of an eastern EU state.

New Europe has pledged to rectify past discriminatory practices against the Roma. In 2003, the World Bank, the Open Society Institute promoted by Hungarian benefactor George Soros, and the Hungarian government initiated a program called The Decade of Roma Inclusion, which is to run from 2005 to 2015. Supported by the governments of Bulgaria, Croatia, the Czech Republic, Macedonia, Montenegro, Romania, Serbia, and Slovakia, the Decade's priority areas are improvements for Romani in education, employment, and health and housing, as well as policies promoting gender equality and nondiscrimination.

Western Europe's record on safeguarding minority rights is also spotty. In 2006, the EU Monitoring Commission (EUMC) published a pilot study based on data from twelve members—Austria, Belgium, France, Germany, Greece, Ireland, Italy, Luxembourg, the Netherlands, Portugal, Spain, and the UK. It found that a significant number of migrants in all twelve countries had subjectively experienced discriminatory practices in their everyday life. As one example, ethnic and national minorities experienced language difficulties in state schools, resulting in high dropout rates. The provincial government of Carinthia in Austria openly opposed providing Slovene-language education for its large Slovene population, viewing such a concession as a political victory for anti-German speakers. In France, religious minorities of all kinds failed to defeat the 2004 law restricting the wearing of any kinds of religious symbols in school.

Discrimination in the educational system against minorities is a serious concern, but establishing hurdles for minorities in obtaining citizenship may be even graver. According to the EUMC, minorities in some EU states—east and west—continue to face discrimination affecting their legal status. For one of Europe's leading specialists on citizenship issues, Rainer Bauböck, the lesson to be learned from recent "citizenship policies in the European Union is that these are increasingly contested in domestic politics and may become a source of conflict between member states. Spontaneous convergence towards liberal norms is no longer a plausible expectation."[17] Before presenting a case study of Germany, let us briefly consider the situation in three of the purportedly most Europeanized small eastern states.

In Slovenia—first in new Europe to join the euro zone and first to take over the EU Council presidency in 2008—large numbers of people from the other former Yugoslav republics were removed from the registry of permanent residents in 1992. Over a decade later, they had not had their status normalized. In Estonia—the "New Zealand" of the east—the number of persons without citizenship remained very high in 2006, according to the Council of Europe's Committee of Ministers. Neighboring Latvia, too, had adopted strict citizenship criteria in the 1990s: five years of permanent residence, renunciation of previous citizenship and a pledge of loyalty to Latvia, command of the Latvian language, knowledge of Latvian history and the constitution, and evidence of legal sources of income. Not surprisingly, in 2006 only 80 percent of Latvia's total population was citizens. Of noncitizens living in the country, two-thirds were Russians. In these more "Westernized" states, then, legal safeguards for minorities often took a backseat to majority rights.

RAGE AGAINST THE NEWCOMER

Even more than the subject of migrant workers, policy on asylum seekers has been a particularly contentious subject in many European countries. This is ironic given that asylum seekers express palpable fear of persecution and even death if they are sent home; migrants are up front that they have moved in pursuit of a higher standard of living.

EC policy on asylum and refugees only began to cohere in the mid 1980s after the Schengen regime had taken shape.[18] There was a "functional link between the opening of internal borders and the factual free movement of third-country nationals, including refugees and asylum seekers."[19] At first, the Schengen Agreement, signed in 1985, contributed to a more liberal—rather than restrictive—policy on asylum. At the low point in 1983, EU states had received a total of just 71,000 asylum applications. In 1992, Germany alone received 438,000 applications out of the EU total of 674,000. After that, the overall numbers began to drop and in 2005 the fifteen old EU states received 213,000 applications; the ten new members in their first year in the EU received just 25,000.[20] The next year the combined total for the EU was down to 180,000. Greece was one of the least popular destinations for asylum seekers since it had the lowest rate of asylum approvals in the EU, at about 0.05 percent in 2007 (representing several dozen people admitted). In the UK, new asylum applications fell by 73 percent between the peak year of 2002, when there were 103,080, and 2007, when there were just 27,900. EU totals increased slightly for 2007 because of a greater number of petitions filed by Iraqi war refugees. In the case of Sweden, from 2006 to 2007 Iraqi applicant numbers rose by 50 percent. This country, which took a liberal position on admitting displaced Iraqis shortly after the war began in 2003, led the EU with 36,000 Iraqi applications.[21]

The rising financial costs of, political backlash against, and security issues involved in accommodating asylum seekers forced a change of policy upon the EU. With a spate of racist attacks on hostels housing refugees and with the *Länder* pressing for greater jurisdiction over asylum matters, Germany took the lead in making changes.

In 1993, the law on asylum procedure was revised to include a "safe third state" provision. Entry into Germany from another EU state or other safe country (e.g., the United States) no longer ensured an individual's legal claim to asylum. In addition, "manifestly unfounded asylum applications" could be rejected at summary hearings held for airport arrivals rather than dragging through immigration courts. As a corollary, a humanitarian temporary residence status was established for indisputable war refugees and displaced persons.

The 1997 Amsterdam Treaty, we recall, confirmed the creation of a common EU pillar of freedom, security, and justice that had been advanced by the Maastricht agreement. One practical consequence was that refugee and asylum policy became treated as a matter of internal security. A burden-sharing approach to asylum seekers was therefore proposed. The key issue at the EU summit in Tampere in 1999 became harmonization of asylum and refugee policy. Member states still retained a veto on the harmonization checklist, but some human rights organizations believed the EU was on its way to creating "Fortress Europe" and a "European system of irresponsibility."

German foreign minister Joschka Fischer responded with a draft "Charter of Fundamental Freedoms of the European Union," which contained an explicit right of asylum while enabling the *securitization* of asylum and refugee policy. The EU draft constitution sought to incorporate a common policy on asylum, but by this time it was Germany, fearing an overly liberal policy that would affect it most, that pressed for and won a veto on the issue. "Front-line" states on the European side of the Mediterranean—Italy, Spain, and Malta—were also increasingly restive about a liberal asylum policy, since they were the first states that had to deal with potential applicants making the hazardous journey by sea from the African continent.

Lahav points to the growing influence of anti-asylum states within the EU. "Despite the incremental Europeanization of migration policy, protectionist states are tenacious; they have simply become better camouflaged." She believes that "The upshot of post-Amsterdam Europeanization has been a 'protective Union,' offering member states the opportunity to reinforce their restrictive and security-driven approach to migration control and in fact to gain new forms of power."[22]

With the Lisbon Treaty came grudging recognition by even "protective" states that some standardization of asylum policy in the EU was desirable.

Evidence of drastic differences in national policies had led to this view. For example, the European Council on Refugees and Exiles found that whereas Austria approved about 90 percent of asylum requests filed by Chechens, neighboring Slovakia rejected almost all Chechen asylum seekers.[23] The 2007 treaty adopted qualified majority voting—thereby removing the unanimity principle—for decisions involving asylum policy and control of EU external borders.

The dice have always been loaded against immigrant and asylum lobby groups. Let us consider one example. The EU established a Consultative Commission on Racism and Xenophobia that in 1998 issued its report "Action Plan Against Racism." Specific anti-racial discrimination provisions were to supplement the Maastricht Treaty. But the rub was that the action plan was not to apply to EU immigration and asylum policy.

Pro-immigrant lobby groups did not have the resources and access at the EU level to counter established interest groups like business and labor. As one study noted, "The EU is literally and metaphorically distant from many of the day-to-day concerns of migrants and their descendants in EU member states." The relevant lobbying level remains the nation-state or even subnational authorities. As a result "Pro-migrant NGOs have focused their activity on countering racism and xenophobia, seeking enactment of broader anti-discrimination legislation, expanding the rights of TCNs [third-country nationals] and ensuring that EU asylum policy accords with international legal standards."[24]

Throughout Europe—and elsewhere too—an anti-immigrant bias is sometimes justified in terms of the perceived higher crime rates that foreigners record. But it is not as if immigrants have different norms regarding the permissibility of killing or physical violence than, say, ethnic Germans. Thus "Cultural conflicts in terms of norm conflicts should not be regarded as accounting for large proportions of immigrants' crime because central criminal norms (theft, assault, rape, murder) do not differ along different cultures or nations to an extent that conflicting expectations could be produced."[25]

Setting aside questions of biased law enforcement and discrimination in the justice system, one plausible source of higher immigrant and minority crime rates may be that large proportions of the population are denied access to the rich material culture of the host society. Stability and integration, in this argument, are shaped less by shared values and collective morals and more by material gains. Accordingly, "people denied access to the material culture become susceptible to all types of social, religious or political movements stressing the importance of collective values"—and solidarity—of the movements.[26] Any recourse they make to violence will be justified in the name of defending ethnic, religious, or cultural identities. An example of this dynamic may be the riots by *les jeunes des banlieus*—Muslim Maghreb youth living in squalid conditions on the periphery of cities[27]—in France in 2005 and repeated in 2007, in each case triggered by the deaths of two Muslim youths blamed on careless police. Not least important is that lack of access to or participation in a wealthy country's affluent material culture has become the breeding ground for extremist groups, including Islamic fundamentalists.

Foreigner crime usually pales in significance when compared to the assaults of marginalized and disenfranchised "ethnic Europeans" on members of immigrant communities. The anti-immigrant violence of German youth in the 1990s—involving the random killing of foreigners, torching and bombing hostels for asylum seekers, and spreading anti-foreigner slogans and graffiti—furnishes a vivid example of host society crime. Much of it is enabled by widespread misoxenic attitudes among citizens, sometimes countenanced by law enforcement agencies and the political authorities.

CITIZENSHIP AND EXCLUSION IN GERMANY

How do citizenship laws affect attitudes of the majority and of far-away locals towards each other? Is it the case that making citizenship easy to obtain facilitates integration processes in a society? Or is there more involved in belonging to a society—the question we have raised here—than the fact of naturalization?

Much has been made of the differences in the French and German models of citizenship.[28] In France, "The republican values which are now most commonly associated with the revolutionary heritage include universalism, unitarism, secularism and assimilationism."[29] This signified that, first, the rights of man proclaimed in August 1789 apply to all humanity and, second, France's unitary corporate nature by definition has to be inclusionary.

Trapped in its own republican logic, to stem the tide of immigrants and, therefore, future French citizens, as early as 1974 France halted labor recruitment from non-EC countries. This was an example of France's color-blind yet race-oriented policy. Officially, no minority or race lives in the French Republic. But racism and discrimination are prevalent. While officially race-blind and discursively in favor of diversity, then, French politicians for several decades have played a game of *montré-caché de l'ethnicité* [ethnicity peekaboo]. "A symbolic rupture has undoubtedly occurred: in the name of the fight against racism, it is becoming legitimate for public authorities to take into account a criterion that not long ago was unspoken and unspeakable—the ethnic criterion."[30]

The politics of immigration and citizenship took a different course in Germany. It led not to the emergence of an electoral right, as in France, but to a more violent grassroots right. In part this was attributable to the more contested nature of German nationhood. It has been pulled in different directions by immigration and citizenship policies based on an unusual mix of old laws and contemporaneous improvisation, which are not always consistent.

Succeeding postwar generations of Germans have been taught to view their country's history and role in Europe critically. Forced to subject the past to an unsparing critique, young Germans have been socialized into a value system making skepticism a virtue and national pride a vice. The only German patriotism that was encouraged—and it was highly circumscribed—was what Jürgen Habermas calls *Verfassungspatriotismus*—loyalty to the 1949 constitution of the Federal Republic of Germany (FRG). This constricted and contingent nationalism supposedly offered grounds for optimism: "United Germans are not necessarily nationalist Germans. Big Germany is not necessarily mighty Germany."[31]

The constitution of the FRG, called the Basic Law, recognizes two categories of rights—general and reserved.[32] The first applies to all individuals living in the FRG and includes freedom of expression and conscience. The second is reserved for German citizens and includes freedom of association, peaceful assembly, and movement.[33]

Citizenship has been important, therefore, in determining not just voting privileges but also a wider package of rights taken for granted in most Western countries. Until 1999 when a new law was passed, German citizenship was based on the principle of *jus sanguinis*, or bloodlines. It reflected the myth of the unity of a German *Volk*, or people. Since the Basic Law did not delineate how citizenship was granted, rules were borrowed from the July 1913 imperial naturalization law. Its principle was that German citizenship was transmitted by descent from parent to child. Most other Western states also adopted *jus sanguinis*, in particular after the French Revolution, which viewed *jus soli*—place of birth as the determinant of nationality—as a feudal idea or as rooted in English common law.

German regulations on citizenship were of only scholastic interest so long as few foreigners migrated to the country. By the mid 1950s the economic miracle required an expanded labor pool and in 1955 the federal government signed its first employment contract with Italy to recruit workers to agricultural and construction jobs. The erection of the Berlin Wall in 1961 and the subsequent cutoff of East German labor led to additional employment contracts negotiated with Greece, Spain, Turkey, and, later, Portugal and Yugoslavia. By 1973, 12 percent (some 2.5 million) of the total German workforce was made up of guest workers. By 1980, Germany had granted resident alien status to an additional one million people. In 1991, foreigners comprised 8 percent of the workforce in a reunited Germany; only one-quarter of these were EC nationals.[34]

Reunification worsened the status of minorities because the federal government gave economic priority to developing eastern Germany. The dislike of foreigners was exacerbated by economic considerations. Xenophobia "reflects the desire on the part of the population of the affluent West European societies to protect their islands of prosperity against an outside world marked by poverty, environmental destruction, interethnic violence, and growing desperation."[35] As one of the most prosperous states in the world, Germany nevertheless decided to make it difficult for outsiders to share fully in its wealth.

Efforts to control the influx and presence of guest workers began when Kohl took office in 1982. This was around the time that opinion polls showed about half of German citizens harboring negative views on the presence of foreigners. Kohl formulated an emergency program that encouraged foreign residents—whose unemployment rate was up to 5 percent higher than of Germans—to return "home" if they had no jobs. They were offered a lump sum of approximately DM 10,000 (close to $6,000 at that time). But offering such a generous "separation package" to guest workers only attracted more foreigners, who calculated that they would be in a no-lose situation once in Germany.

Throughout the 1980s, many guest workers and their families decided to remain after their labor contracts expired. They accordingly applied to become permanent residents. With a rapidly expanding number of German-born, second- and even third-generation residents of foreign origin, a pressing issue became how to normalize the legal status of these resident aliens. For example, by 1990, 25 percent of all foreigners had been resident in Germany for over twenty years, and 60 percent for more than ten years. Two-thirds of Turks and three-quarters of Yugoslavs had lived in the country for more than ten years. At the end of 1998, 30 percent of the 7.3 million foreign nationals living in Germany had been there for twenty years and about a half for at least ten years. Only 3.4 percent of Germany's resident foreign population had acquired German citizenship in 1999, compared to 9.4 percent in the Netherlands.

Up until 1998, when the Social Democrats (SDU) under Gerhard Schröder took power, Chancellor Kohl's approach had been to treat naturalization as an exceptional process which might only occur under very strict conditions: a minimum of ten years of residence in the FRG (five years if married to a German citizen), mastery of German, residence in one's own dwelling, a demonstrated ability to support oneself and one's dependents financially, and, generally, "whether the applicant in his or her personal standing is a valuable addition to the population, but also, whether the naturalization of the applicant from a general political, economic, and cultural viewpoint is desirable."[36] Given such rigorous criteria, it was not surprising that even as it took in the largest number of foreigners Germany had one of Europe's lowest naturalization rates—about three percent of resident aliens per annum.[37] As a result, "two conflicting political conceptions of citizenship coexisted within the postwar consensus in the Federal Republic: the traditional ethno-cultural concept of the German nation characterized by a common history, language, culture, and descent; and a civil concept based on individual rights of citizens modeled after enlightened 'Western' traditions."[38]

The civic approach came into favor with the passage of the 1999 citizenship law. The two principal departures from *jus sanguinis* were: 1) children born in Germany to foreign nationals, with one parent who had been residing legally in the country for at least eight years and who had had a residence permit for at least three years, would acquire German citizenship by birth; 2) foreign nationals legally resident in Germany for eight years who professed loyalty to Germany's democratic order, possessed a residence permit, were able to support themselves without the help of welfare benefits, had renounced their previous citizenship, did not have a criminal record, and possessed an adequate command of the German language could obtain German citizenship. The stated purpose of the law was "guaranteeing and ensuring social and domestic peace in Germany."[39]

Germany's revised citizenship law still seemed very conservative. But compared to other EU states, was it really so? Let us consider two other cases. Neighboring Austria has stuck with a restrictive approach to the granting of citizenship based on *jus sanguinis*: a person obtains Austrian citizenship if a parent is Austrian. Being born in Austria is not sufficient to receive citizenship. Naturalization usually occurs after ten years of continuous residence in Austria plus demonstrating proficiency in German. The residency requirement may be reduced to four years for recognized refugees, citizens of another EU country, those born in Austria, or persons with "outstanding achievements in the fields of science, commerce, the arts, or sport." About 10 percent of the country's population consists of foreigners, of whom about 4 percent (a slightly higher rate than Germany) have been naturalized.

By contrast, up until the late 1990s the Irish Republic followed the principle of *jus soli*: anyone born in the Republic before January 1, 2005 was automatically an Irish citizen. A person also was entitled to Irish citizenship through descent, marriage to an Irish citizen, or naturalization—a five-year residency period (shorter than Germany's eight and Austria's ten) was the norm.

The large-scale arrival into the Republic of EU citizens and *excommunitari* seeking to take advantage of the country's economic boom forced a reconsideration of citizenship laws. In 2004, the government of Prime Minister Bertie Ahern called for a referendum on a constitutional reform bill with the stated objective of putting an end to "citizenship tourism." While Ahern emphasized that he supported a liberal approach to the right of asylum and immigration, the not-so-hidden agenda was what his minister for foreign affairs, Brian Cowen, had highlighted: the need to distinguish between "genuine migrants" and fraudulent ones.

By a large majority (79 to 21 percent), Irish voters said yes to the referendum question, which proposed doing away with automatic Irish citizenship—citizenship and nationality are the same thing in Irish law—for anyone born in Ireland. Accordingly, with several exceptions, the government eliminated *jus soli* for anyone born on the island (including the six counties in the north) in 2005 or later who was entitled to the citizenship of another country, was not entitled to Irish citizenship through descent, and had no parent living in Ireland in recent years.

An emotional issue persuading the electorate to support the change was the argument that women of foreign nationality had been traveling to particular EU countries to give birth so that their child would automatically acquire citizenship. The "Chen case" was before the European Court of Justice at the time and involved a Chinese woman who had gone to give birth in Northern Ireland on legal advice. Mrs. Chen then pursued a case in the courts to prevent her deportation on the grounds that her child had the right as an EU citizen—because of its Irish citizenship—to reside in a member state of the Union. Mrs. Chen won the case, but the referendum result meant that no one else would be able to partake of this right subsequently. In Dublin, a campaigner for a "yes" vote invoked the imagery of crowded maternity hospitals because of the influx of foreign women and some 200,000 people calling themselves refugees who were nevertheless living in new houses and flats. John Hume, a Catholic political leader in Northern Ireland and a Nobel Peace Prize recipient, took an even more ethnically grounded position: "certificates of Irishness" should be given to all those across the world who are of Irish origin.

Therefore, Germany's restrictive citizenship law is not so unusual. There is another core issue that we have been discussing in this book. Though undoubtedly important in validating a person's rights and identity, citizenship does not automatically guarantee that minorities will experience the feeling of belonging or not belonging to a society. As surveys discussed below suggest, Jews, asylum seekers, *Ossies* (East Germans), and non-EU citizens in Germany do not receive the same welcoming attitude as EU citizens from old Europe, like Italians.

The strict ethnic understanding of the German nation has persuaded some well-organized immigrant groups, like the Turks, to embrace a non-German identity around which a separate community living in Germany has been constructed. This community seeks recognition by the German state, including dual citizenship, as Turks—and as Turks in Germany.[40]

But the "Turks in Germany" identity became contested in a number of ways. By 2007, an "increasingly entrenched" parallel society to German society was developing among the almost 3 million German residents of Turkish descent. One sure sign of social integration is an increasing rate of intermarriage. Because the German rate was not increasing, the country's interior minister asked for a study of how the two groups "meet, mate, [and] marry." Young Turkish-Germans, it found, were uncomfortable with the "degenerate" values of Germans their age, and the majority still imported spouses from their homeland. Turkish-Germans continued to embrace the Muslim value of "sleeping on the same pillow until the end of your life," thereby cementing their parallel society.[41]

The 1999 citizenship law had excluded the possibility of dual citizenship or additional rights for foreign nationals. For example, under the "requirement to opt," children acquiring German citizenship by the fact of being born in Germany had to decide before their twenty-third birthday whether they wished to retain their German citizenship or opt for some other. In exceptional cases where renunciation of foreign citizenship was impossible, the law would not countenance the type of "negotiation" of recognition that some Turkish groups pressed for. "A German who holds multiple citizenship cannot use his other citizenship to assert additional rights or evade his obligations."[42] Thus, Schröder's citizenship reform was drafted so as to appease German sentiment at least as much as to normalize the status of foreign nationals.

The 2001 census provided comprehensive data on Germany's changing demographics. It found that 75 million of 82 million inhabitants of Germany were citizens of the FRG. Only 3 million of these (3.5 percent) had citizenship of another country. The remaining 7 million were officially foreigners who were legal residents, but about 1.5 million of these were born in Germany as children or grandchildren of immigrants.

Long-term resident foreigners and children born into the host society who are not citizens can be described as *denizens*. They can participate in the country's social and economic life and enjoy secondary political rights such as freedom of association and expression without having full legal status.[43] It goes without saying that while denizenship might be acceptable for a time to first-generation immigrants living in a host society, it cannot be a satisfactory resolution for both host society and its immigrants over the long term.

There is a simple structural reason, then, why xenophobia may be on the increase in both old and new Europe. "The EU has not only increased the interaction among European nation-states, but has also multiplied the points of contact between individuals of differing national and social backgrounds."[44]

ATTITUDES TOWARDS FOREIGNERS IN GERMANY

"Is Germany's xenophobia qualitatively different from everybody else's?" an American academic asked in the mid 1990s.[45] The answer he gave was a qualified yes. "The German attitude toward foreigners in their midst fuel doubts concerning whether the neo-Nazi movement, with its savage brutality, is but one of a considerable number of such movements throughout the world or whether it reflects a fundamentally distinctive German ethos." But the author regarded "German immigration policy as the litmus test of tolerance, the cornerstone of the country's dealings with foreigners in their midst. In Germany, that policy says that they see such people as irredeemably different from 'real' Germans."[46]

To be sure, over the years normative shifts have taken place in the country. "The attitude of Germans toward foreigners is characterized by considerable social distance, in particular in the eastern part of the country." But at a time when violence against foreigners was peaking in 1993, greater numbers of both German and foreigner respondents expressed the desire to lessen social distance by living together in shared neighborhoods. Accordingly, "support for integration reached its peak in 1993, at a time when xenophobia was highly likely to be viewed as a core problem."[47]

Support for immigration and integration weakened when the EU expanded into eastern Europe in 2004. German fears of losing control over their homeland were heightened. The perception spread that millions of citizens of new Europe wanted to work in the west, and surveys showed that the majority of prospective migrants identified Germany, with its strong economy and slack immigration laws, as their target country.

On the eve of EU labor market expansion, many Germans were bewildered by the paradox that so few foreign residents could become naturalized yet so many continued to come. The latter phenomenon was viewed partly as a product of the country's porous borders, its well-paid jobs, and its generous social services. In part, though, in-migration was perceived as often involving fraudulent foreigner entry into the country. Regulating the status of foreigners, many Germans felt, was a misdirected policy since attention should be focused on bogus immigrants. The stereotype of the disreputable foreigner living illegally in Germany exacerbated the feeling of *Auslanderfeindlichkeit*, or animosity towards foreigners, and provided additional structural conditions for the rise of the right.

Since 1990, ALLBUS, a German public opinion survey, has been asking respondents whether they believe the entry of certain groups of immigrants should be unrestricted, limited, or stopped completely. Between 1990 and 2000 more and more respondents shifted their views on asylum seekers towards restricted entry: among west German respondents the proportion over the ten years climbed from 50 percent to 73 percent. Surprisingly, the latter figure, for 2000, was higher than among the supposedly more xenophobic east Germans (69 percent).

Regarding people from other EU countries coming to work in Germany, there was also a marked shift towards restricted entry: from 54 percent in both parts of Germany to about 62 percent. Only 6 percent of respondents

in both parts in the year 2000 supported unrestricted entry of non-EU workers, representing a general hardening of attitudes towards this group. In addition, between 1980 and 2002 Germans increasingly felt that foreigners in
their midst should adapt their way of life more closely to the German one.
Thirty percent of those in the FRG thought this in 1980 compared to nearly
40 percent in both parts in 2002. The groups identified in 2006 as having
the least similar lifestyles to Germans were, by a wide margin, asylum seekers and Turks (Table 5.2).

It followed that marriage with a member of these groups was generally
frowned upon (Table 5.3). Respondents were just as adamant that asylum
seekers should not enjoy the same rights as Germans, though they were divided over whether Turks should have these rights (Table 5.4).

As evidence of increasing inclusionary orientations, in 1980 just about
the same number of west Germans (about one-quarter) completely disagreed with the view that foreigners in Germany should marry people of
their own nationality as completely agreed. By 2002, ten times more respondents in the west strongly disagreed with the call for endogamous marriages; in the east, though, the ratio was closer to three to one.[48]

Survey results from 2006 suggest that the average German is far more
hostile to groups coming from far away or which are Muslim than to culturally affiliated groups like Italians, east European German speakers, and
Jews. One noteworthy finding was that 48 percent of respondents expressed
indifference to having Jews as neighbors, reflecting a grudging acceptance of
the politically correct line. This indifference marked a contrast with evaluations of other possible neighbors, where opinion was more polarized. For
example, the prospect of an Italian neighbor was appealing: 22 percent were
very favorably disposed and just one percent very negative. At the other end
of the continuum, by a ratio of roughly three to one respondents did not
want an asylum seeker as neighbor.

**Table 5.2. How Significantly Do the Following Groups Living in Germany Differ in
Their Lifestyles from Germans (in %)?**

	Little or not at all	Somewhat or very much
Italians	42	6
German speakers from East Europe	13	24
Asylum seekers	4	59
Turks	4	45
Jews	52	11

Source: ALLBUS German General Social Survey, 2006, Tables V150–V154, 120–124. Little or not at all
scores included the first two (1, 2) on the seven-point scale. Somewhat or very much include the last two
(6, 7) on the seven-point scale.

Table 5.3.   How Pleasant or Unpleasant Would It Be for You If a Member of One of the Following Groups Married into Your Family?

	Very/quite pleasant	*Very/quite unpleasant*
Italians	32	7
German speakers from East Europe	17	20
Asylum seekers	9	43
Turks	12	40
Jews	19	16

Source: ALLBUS German General Social Survey, 2006, Tables V160–164, 128–131. Very/quite unpleasant included the first two (1, 2) on the seven-point scale. Quite/very pleasant scores included the last two (6, 7) on the seven-point scale.

The evidence we have reviewed largely supports a pessimistic assessment of the spread of transnational values in Germany. For several decades the combination of an anachronistic citizenship law and the influx of millions of guest workers facilitated the process of othering. Conceptualizing Germany differently than in exclusively ethnic terms remained a challenge for a long time. In order to revise this ethnically shaped modern historiography, some academics have called for writing a transnational history of Germany.

Three possible perspectives can shape this project. The first adopts a vantage point from the inside out, from the German nation to the world, a kind of "local transnationalism": "Germans over the past two centuries have had a particularly lively imagination of the world beyond the nation, ranging from their cosmopolitan knowledge and their proverbial embrace of the world to a sense of superiority and supremacy and on to utter panic."[49]

The second approach is an outside-in framework centered on actors and forces that circulate across boundaries. Their effects on national conditions, such as asylum seekers seeking security or capital in search of profits, can be

Table 5.4.   Members of the Following Groups Should Have the Same Rights in All Spheres as Germans

	Completely/ generally agree	Completely/ generally disagree
Italians	48	13
German speakers from East Europe	40	18
Asylum seekers	19	45
Turks	29	30
Jews	50	14

Source: ALLBUS German General Social Survey, 2006, Tables V165–169, 132–136. Completely or generally disagree included the first two (1, 2) on the seven-point scale. Generally or completely agree included the last two (6, 7) on the seven-point scale.

termed "global transnationalism." The third is located in between the two, a focus on the transformation of territoriality and transnationality—from the nation as longstanding anchor of identity and decision space towards the integration processes found in Europe over the past half century.

A German transnational history, then

> thinks of Germany and the Germans from the margins and peripheries. It opens up these social margins, borderlands, and enclaves to encompass the entire world. What has been emerging here is the exact opposite of a *Koenigsweg*: a genuinely subaltern history of Germany, which by its very nature must be transnational or, in any case, translocal history. It is, among other things, the history of the landless, the vagrants, the migrants, the pilgrims, the scholars, the expelled, and the expats.[50]

ATTITUDES TOWARDS FOREIGNERS IN POLAND

The data we have for Polish citizens' attitudes towards foreign groups are not comparable, but they still reveal much about xenophobic patterns in the country. A longitudinal analysis of survey results indicates important trends in the changing national likes and dislikes of Poles. In 1993, Italians, Americans, and French were bunched at the top of Poles' favorite nationalities. By 2006, however, six EU cohorts—Spaniards, Italians, Czechs, English (which Poles use interchangeably with British), Dutch, and Irish—ranked higher than Americans (Table 5.5). The sudden popularity of Spaniards and Irish is explained by the fact that these are two Catholic EU countries with which Poland has sometimes made common cause at EU meetings. They have also been welcoming to Polish workers looking for jobs in the west.

Poles' least-preferred nationalities changed only slightly over this same period. In 1993, Romanians were the least favorite: a -57 percent net difference between those saying they liked them and those saying they disliked them! When Roma were added to the survey the next year, they immediately overtook Romanians (-69 percent in 1994). Three largely Orthodox nations, Ukrainians (-53 percent), Serbs (-45 percent), and Russians (-39 percent) came next, and Belorussians did not fare well either (-28 percent). But they were still comfortably ahead of Germans (-53 percent) and Jews (-36 percent).

By a large margin (a -57 percent differential), Poles' least favorite "nation" in 2006 were the Arabs (Figure 5.1), who were first included in the survey in 2002. Roma came next (-44 percent) followed by their namesake, Romanians (-36 percent). Turks followed (-31 percent) with Jews, Russians, and Serbs Orthodox tied at -25 percent. As many Poles now said they liked their EU western neighbors as said they did not care for Germans (at 33 percent).[51]

Table 5.5. Polish Respondents' Attitudes Towards Other Nations

Nations	How would you describe your attitude towards other nations?				Mean
	A liking	Indifference	Dislike	Difficult to say	
		in percentage			
Spaniards	53	28	12	7	0.83
Italians	52	29	14	5	0.76
Czechs	52	30	14	4	0.70
English	50	31	15	4	0.76
Americans	49	32	16	3	0.70
Irish	49	28	15	8	0.72
French	48	31	16	5	0.62
Dutch	48	31	13	7	0.71
Greeks	47	29	17	8	0.58
Hungarians	45	32	18	6	0.53
Slovaks	44	33	18	5	0.44
Swedes	43	31	17	9	0.50
Danes	40	32	18	10	0.39
Belgians	39	34	19	8	0.38
Lithuanians	36	33	24	7	0.19
Austrians	36	34	23	7	0.19
Slovenes	35	34	22	9	0.24
Finns	35	32	21	12	0.27
Germans	33	31	33	3	−0.02
Japanese	30	31	30	9	−0.01
Latvians	29	33	28	10	0.00
Estonians	28	33	25	14	0.06
Bulgarians	24	34	34	8	−0.19
Ukrainians	24	29	42	5	−0.47
Belorussians	23	31	39	6	−0.34
Russians	22	28	47	3	−0.52
Jews	20	30	45	5	−0.64
Chinese	18	29	43	10	−0.58
Vietnamese	18	30	42	10	−0.56
Serbs	18	30	43	9	−0.54
Turks	17	27	48	8	−0.70
Romanians	16	26	52	6	−0.83
Roma (Gypsies)	14	24	58	4	−1.01
Arabs	9	19	66	6	−1.40

Source: Centrum Badania Opinii Społecznej, "Stosunek polaków do innych narodów" (Warsaw: CBOS, October 2006), BS/148/2006, www.cbos.pl.

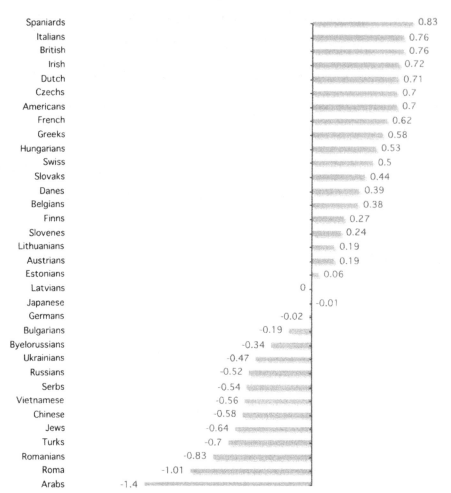

Fig 5.1. Polish Respondents' Attitudes Towards Other Nations. *Source:* **Centrum Badania Opinii Społecznej, "Stosunek Polaków do innych narodów" (Warsaw: CBOS, October 2006), BS/148/2006, www.cbos.pl.**

Special mention must be made of traditional Polish anti-Semitism. Its complex origins and evolution over centuries has raised questions as to why it remains a strong orientation even after the destruction of the Polish Jews during World War II.[52] Historian Jan Gross has written two books explaining the reasons for Poles' participation in the Holocaust and in pogroms in the immediate postwar period.[53] As a reviewer of his work summarized, "Rather than an inheritance passed down from the prewar anti-Semitic tradition, Gross finds that hatred of Jews in the postwar milieu was possible because of one simple factor: fear. The fear of what was to come with the encroaching communist regime, and the fear of Jews by Poles whose roles during the Nazi occupation were often dubious and sometimes worse. The surviving Jews witnessed their own destruction, and that was reason enough for Poles to fear them."[54] Needless to say, publication of Gross's *Fear* in Poland in 2007 stirred up long-simmering controversies.

Since Jews cannot be considered to be foreigners in eastern Europe, it is illogical to view anti-Semitism as a form of xenophobia. The history of the Jewish communities in Poland and Germany is embedded in that of ethnic Poles and Germans and, conversely, the history of these nations is embedded in that of Jews. A more accurate depiction is, then, of Jewish communities being perceived as far-away locals—even as "inner neighbors."[55] Since they may regard themselves as part of a worldwide Jewish diaspora, Jews have sometimes been treated as a non-national group, which can mean they are not eligible for protection by the state in which they live. This proved a moot issue in 1939 when the Nazi invasion of Poland immediately eliminated a Polish government. Poland's large Jewish community could justifiably claim that it had to defend itself with its own means, as there was no Polish state to do so. But there were no significant resources it could use to prevent the Holocaust from occurring.

We might have expected anti-Semitism in Poland to increase under the nationalistic, Catholic fundamentalist regime of the Kaczyńskis. Yet in terms of foreign policy, Poland's relations with Israel have never been better. As one writer asked, "Which European country is said to be one of the most favorably inclined toward Israel? Which has students organizing Israel Days at major universities? Whose president made the first visit by a head of state to Israel immediately after the war with Hezbollah? Amazingly, that country is Poland."[56]

Survey results point to a trend in Polish public opinion towards steadily more favorable ratings for EU nations. While Poles' greater affection for the western European nations is understandable—they promoted EU enlargement and directed EU funds towards the east—Poles are now even warming up to the peoples living in the new EU member states like the Czechs, Slovaks, and Baltic nations—all of whom once constituted Poland's quarrelsome neighborhood. The evidence we have strongly suggests that Poles suffer from Islamophobia—their strong dislikes of Arabs and Turks suggest such an interpretation. But to some extent Poles may be seen as "Orthodoxophobes" too, though it can be argued that dislike of Russians, in particular, has little to do with religious differences and everything to do with history and culture. Finally, even though dislike of Romanians, Roma, and Jews—the latter two groups, significantly, often perceived as homeless, nomadic nations—has been declining, Poles share the historic antipathy towards such perceived "bogeyman nations" with many of their fellow citizens in new Europe.

A different 2007 attitudinal survey sought to measure Poles' "social distance" from other nationalities and religious groups. Poles were asked the classic question: "Would you be opposed to your son or daughter marrying someone who was Jewish, or Russian, or Chinese?" One-third of Polish respondents said that they would oppose their child's marriage to someone who was Jewish or Chinese, and one-quarter said they would oppose their child's intermarriage with a Russian.

Poles voiced much stronger opposition, however, to interdenominational marriages. Respondents were somewhat more Islamophobic than anti-Semitic, with 55 percent expressing opposition to a son or daughter's marriage with a Muslim and 47 percent with a Jew. Poles relented somewhat if a possible son-in-law or daughter-in-law was Christian: Orthodoxophobic views were expressed by the 38 percent of respondents who would oppose a son or daughter marrying someone of this faith. Marrying a Protestant was less critically perceived (31 percent). Antipathy towards a possible atheist son- or daughter-in-law was at about the same level as for an Orthodox one (37 percent).

Same nationality and religion were two of the most important characteristics respondents looked for in a spouse—or friend, for that matter. Only the factor "way of comporting oneself in public"—let's call it "having good manners"—was seen as more important than religion or nationality in a potential spouse. Educational level, occupation, and political views were less influential.[57]

Poles admire the stereotypical image of the wealthy and civilized West. They want to be like Western nations and to belong in their midst. By contrast, Poles harbor a negative stereotype of the poorer, less developed East. Poles want to be distinguished from eastern nations and do not want to be included in their group. Unwittingly, by drawing a normative Iron Curtain between themselves and the nations to the east, Poles paint themselves into the east.

Above all, Poland does not wish to be identified with Russia. Its excellent vantage point on Russia makes it "at once the Western Slavic country that is geographically closest to Russia and—of the countries close by ethnic origin and geography—the most opposed to Russia."[58] Poland's imaginary of Russia has had consequences for the West, too. The West's image of Russia has been shaped by Poland as intermediary—more so in the case of some countries (like Britain) than others (like France).[59]

Many Polish citizens may suffer from many complexes ingrained in them by the nation's painful history. But elevating the Kaczyński twins to power seemed an act of folly and did not garner Poles much sympathy from the rest of Europe. So it is important to highlight how, at the first opportunity in late 2007 to undo the madness, the Polish electorate decisively voted the

Kaczyński-led government out of power. One of Poland's leading writers, Andrzej Stasiuk, paid them a grudging tribute:

> I'm going to miss them . . . . The Kaczynski brothers at the helm were theatrical beings. Each of their gestures, each word, each appearance had an element of drama. They could be as funny as a comedy, but never trite as a soap opera. Within their chubby bodies and beneath the masks of their childish faces seethed emotions that banned the dullness of modern politics to a shameful, hidden existence. The brothers gave a voice to the deepest human emotions. They were so authentically resentful, vengeful, reckless, full of complexes, malicious and petty, that it was painful to see. This is why the simple people loved them.[60]

EVEN IN SCANDINAVIA?

World-systems theory argues that global capitalism produces similar patterns of social development in whichever countries it touches. André Gunder-Frank, Immanuel Wallerstein, and to some extent Swedish academics like Gösta Esping-Andersen and Gunnar Myrdal have accepted this logic.

Sweden has always seemed to be different in Europe. It is one of the rare countries that has no national holiday to celebrate. It is among the highest-ranked states in the world in a number of key indicators of "progressiveness": quality of life, human development, postmaterialist values, empowerment of women, absence of corruption, and environmental regulation. The public's attitudes appear progressive. In a 2006 Eurobarometer survey, 79 percent of Swedes said that immigrants contribute a lot to their country. The EU average was 40 percent.[61]

Many Swedes see themselves as exceptional in Scandinavia: they are more concerned with ethical issues than the worldly Danes, the prosperous Norwegians, or the rustic Finns. Swedes regard themselves as different within the EU, which they associate with the "three C's—capitalism, conservatism, and Catholicism."[62] To that list some Swedes might add racism. Is that justified?

In focusing on outbreaks of xenophobia, the late Swedish-born Berkeley sociologist Allan Pred wrote "that the circumstances precipitated by global economic restructuring, by the everyday workings of interdependent capitalisms, have bred experiences throughout the highly industrialized world that readily lend themselves to being culturally and politically reworked into distinctive expressions of racism—*even in Sweden.*"[63]

Pred presents a powerful account of racisms *not only* in each and every state in Europe but also of why it occurs *even in Sweden.*[64] In 1985, the Swedish Social Democrats—the country's governing party more often than not—took a different approach than other European countries towards the increasing arrival of immigrants and refugees. Instead of seeing the choice as between a republican or multicultural policy, it adopted the "whole of Sweden strategy." It "was intended to stem the metropolitan concentration of migrants, and—in keeping with the Swedish Social Democratic notions of 'solidarity'—both to promote 'integration' and provide a 'sharing of the burden' among as many municipalities as possible."[65] Unlike in other states, immigrants had little say in where they would initially reside in Sweden.

As a result, the racial became the spatial and the spatial the racial: "The racialized become the segregated, and racial meanings become inscribed upon space. The discursively Otherized become the declared out of bounds, the physically Elsewherized and Isolated. The categorically excluded become the spatially enclosed. The socially marginalized become the geographically marginalized. The to-be-socially-avoided become out of reach, not easily socially knowable."[66]

In practice, even under the whole of Sweden policy, "The scapegoated become exiled to enclaves beyond the metropolitan core." Consequently, "The Physically Elsewherized and Isolated become further discursively Otherized."[67] The Stockholm suburb of Rinkeby is a case in point: in 1996 its population was 75 percent foreign-born, originating from more than one hundred countries. About 97 percent of children spoke a language other than Swedish at home. Nearly half of households received welfare payments. Rinkeby became the symbol for Sweden's failed integration policy.

The "problem" migrants were those from the Horn of Africa—Ethiopia and Somalia—fleeing wars and not easily blending into Swedish society as earlier groups of Hungarians, Czechs, and Chileans had. Nevertheless, they were not the only victims of Swedish racism, manifested in "labor-market discrimination, housing segregation, and social apartheid," not to mention that "racially inspired petty acts of intolerance and discrimination were everyday and innumerable."[68]

Supporting Pred's thesis, Bo Petersson describes how Swedish stereotypes of strangers are founded on constructions of sociocultural risk. Specifically, "notions of risk and threat co-construct an imagined 'normal' state of affairs that should be defended from perceived ills—whether it be a 'normal' or 'healthy' body at risk from disease or a 'healthy' and 'prosperous' nation endangered by outsiders or purportedly devious insiders."[69] Swedish newspapers in small towns were particularly instrumental in subdividing residents into Swedes and foreigners.

In a number of Western countries, pizzerias are viewed by the public with suspicion. The fact that they are often owned or managed by minorities adds to the distrust. Not surprisingly, then, in one Swedish town pizzerias owned by "foreigners" became identified as the abode of strangers where petty criminal activity was drawn. In one where stolen goods were found,

"The image of large footprints made in flour and tomato sauce on the pizzeria floor certainly invites amused smiles and sniggers about clumsy would-be perpetrators from a nearby reception centre for asylum-seekers."[70]

A newspaper account involving a rumor about a second pizzeria described a woman who had developed blisters around her mouth. She had supposedly contracted herpes after eating a pizza slice that had traces of sperm on it. Setting aside the newspaper's decision to feature the story, "the rumour itself seemed to testify to underlying sentiments of xenophobia in Älmhult"—a southern town that is home to the global IKEA furniture company.[71]

Petersson drew attention, then, to the

> connections between the stereotype-forming dynamics that depicted the immigrants as unreliable, deceitful, troublesome and generally unwanted, on the one hand, and the heightened experience of socio-cultural risks to the community of the majority, on the other. The most unruly members of the collective of asylum-seekers were taken to represent their entire general category. . . . Asylum-seekers were likened to misbehaving guests, at times even to parasites, and were generally portrayed as a wide-ranging burden to the community.[72]

In the Swedish *Folkhem*, then, as in the rest of Europe, it is debatable whether "unruly" and "misbehaving" foreigners belong. It may be possible to claim, then, that nowhere in the EU are immigrants made to feel at home, made to feel they fully belong. If a ranking of EU states in terms of their levels of xenophobia was compiled, Sweden would probably come in at the low end, with a relatively benign level of antipathy to foreigners when compared to other countries. Of the cases we considered in this chapter, the leading candidate for being described as fearful—even paranoiac—about foreigners and far-away locals was Poland, though it was the Poland that existed before its accession into the EU.[73]

NOTES

1. See Loek Halman, Ruud Luijkx, and Marga van Zundert, *Atlas of European Values*, European Values Studies 8 (Leiden, Netherlands: Brill, 2005).

2. European Commission against Racism and Intolerance, "Annual report on ECRI'S activities covering the period from 1 January to 31 December 2006," CRI(2007)21 (Strasbourg: ECRI, 2007), www.coe.int/t/e/human_rights/ecri/1-ECRI/1-Presentation_of_ECRI/4-Annual_Report_2006/Annual_Report_2006.asp.

3. Amélie Mummendey and Sven Waldzus, "National Differences and European Plurality: Discrimination or Tolerance between European Countries," in *Transnational Identities: Becoming European in the EU*, eds. Richard K. Herrmann, Marilynn B. Brewer, and Thomas Risse (Lanham, MD: Rowman & Littlefield, 2004), 68.

4. Sven Waldzus, Amélie Mummendey, and Michael Wenzel, "When 'Different' Means 'Worse:' In-group Prototypicality in Changing Intergroup Contexts," *Journal of Experimental Social Psychology* 41 (2005), 76–83.

5. Mummendey and Waldzus, "National Differences," 71.

6. Alec Hargreaves and Jeremy Leaman, "Racism in Contemporary Western Europe: An Overview," in *Racism, Ethnicity and Politics in Contemporary Europe*, eds. Hargreaves and Leaman (Brookfield, VT: Edward Elgar, 1995), 9–10.

7. Sara De Master and Michael K. Le Roy, "Xenophobia and the European Union," *Comparative Politics* 32, no. 4 (July 2000), 433–34.

8. Gallya Lahav, *Immigration and Politics in the New Europe: Reinventing Borders* (Cambridge: Cambridge University Press, 2004), 175.

9. Lahav, *Immigration and Politics in the New Europe*, 178.

10. Standard Eurobarometer 53 (2000).

11. Anna Triandafyllidou, *Immigrants and National Identity in Europe* (London: Routledge, 2001), 99.

12. Triandafyllidou, *Immigrants and National Identity in Europe*, 99.

13. Hugh Poulton, "Europe," in Minority Rights Group International, *State of the World's Minorities 2007* (London: MRG, 2007), 89–102.

14. Patrick Buchanan, "The EU at 50: Can It Survive Midlife Crisis?" *Investor's Business Daily*, April 2, 2007, www.ibdeditorials.com/IBDArticles.aspx?id=260406436848534&type=right.

15. Buchanan, "The EU at 50."

16. European Parliament, "Report on the Situation of Roma Women in the European Union," Report A6-0148/2006, April 27, 2006, www.soros.org/initiatives/women/news/landmark_20060602/EP_resolution.pdf.

17. Rainer Bauböck, "Who Are the Citizens of Europe?" *Eurozine*, December 23, 2006, www.eurozine.com/articles/2006-12-23-baubock-en.html.

18. See Robert Miles and Dietrich Thränhardt, eds., *Migration and European Integration: The Dynamics of Inclusion and Exclusion* (London: Pinter, 1995). Also Demetrios G. Papademetriou, *Coming Together or Pulling Apart? The European Union's Struggle with Immigration and Asylum* (Washington, DC: International Migration Policy Program, 1996).

19. Monika Bösche, "Trapped Inside the European Fortress? Germany and European Union Asylum and Refugee Policy," in *Germany's EU Policy on Asylum and Defence: De-Europeanization by Default?* ed. Gunther Hellmann (London: Palgrave, 2006), 42.

20. European Council on Refugees and Exiles, "Statistics," www.ecre.org/factfile/statistics.shtml.

21. "Iraqi Asylum Seeker Numbers Jump," BBC News, March 18, 2008, http://news.bbc.co.uk/2/hi/middle_east/7301985.stm.

22. Lahav, *Immigration and Politics in the New Europe*, 50–51.

23. "Europe Considers Single Asylum Policy," BBC News, June 6, 2007, http://news.bbc.co.uk/2/hi/europe/6726045.stm.

24. Andrew Geddes, *Immigration and European Integration: Towards Fortress Europe?* (Manchester: Manchester University Press, 2000), 143.

25. Hans-Jörg Albrecht, "Ethnic Minorities, Culture Conflicts and Crime," *Crime, Law and Social Change* 24, no. 1 (1995), 26.

26. Albrecht, "Ethnic Minorities," 31.

27. In the 1995 French film *La Haine* (Hatred), one of *les jeunes de banlieu* is portrayed as ethnically French.

28. Rogers Brubaker, *Citizenship and Nationhood in France and Germany* (Cambridge, MA: Harvard University Press, 1992).

29. Alec G. Hargreaves, *Immigration, 'Race' and Ethnicity in Contemporary France* (London: Routledge, 1995), 160.

30. Gwénaële Calvès, "Color-Blindness at a Crossroads in Contemporary France," in *Race in France: Interdisciplinary Perspectives on the Politics of Difference*, eds. Herrick Chapman and Laura L. Frader (New York: Berghahn Books, 2004), 224.

31. Niall Ferguson, "Uber the Hill: Why the New Germany's a Weakling," *New Republic* 204, no. 5 (February 4, 1991), 8.

32. Part of this account is based on Douglas B. Klusmeyer, "Aliens, Immigrants, and Citizens: The Politics of Inclusion in the Federal Republic of Germany," *Dædalus* 122 (Summer 1993), 81ff.

33. Articles 2–5 of the Basic Law, reprinted in Elmar Hucko, ed., *The Democratic Tradition: Four German Constitutions* (Oxford: Berg Publishers, 1989), 194–95.

34. See Ray Rist, *Guestworkers in Germany: the Prospects for Pluralism* (New York: Praeger, 1978). Also see Ulrich Herbert, *A History of Foreign Labor in Germany, 1880–1980* (Ann Arbor: University of Michigan Press, 1990).

35. Hans-Georg Betz, *Radical Right-Wing Populism in Western Europe* (Basingstoke, UK: Palgrave Macmillan, 1994), 103. See also Meredith Watts, *Xenophobia in United Germany: Generations, Modernization, and Ideology* (New York: St. Martin's Press, 1997).

36. Cited by Klusmeyer, "Aliens, Immigrants, and Citizens," 86.

37. Gerhard de Rham, "Naturalization: the Politics of Citizenship Acquisition," in *The Political Rights of Migrant Workers in Western Europe*, ed. Zig Henry Layton (Newbury Park, CA: Sage, 1990), 182.

38. Jeffrey Peck, Mitchell Ash, and Christiane Lemke, "Natives, Strangers, and Foreigners: Constituting Germans by Constructing Others," in *After Unity: Reconfiguring German Identities*, ed. Konrad H. Jarausch (Providence, RI: Berghahn Books, 1997), 78.

39. "Germany's New Citizenship Law 'A Foundation for Peace,'" REGIERUN-Gonline, www.bundesregierung.de/english/01/0103/04875/index.html.

40. Riva Castoryano, *La France, l'Allemagne et leurs immigrés: négocier l'identité* (Paris: A. Colin, 1997).

41. Christopher Caldwell, "Where Every Generation is First-Generation," *New York Times Magazine*, May 27, 2007.

42. "Germany's New Citizenship Law 'A Foundation for Peace.'"

43. Tomas Hammar, "State, Nation, and Dual Citizenship," in *Immigration and the Politics of Citizenship in Europe and North America*, ed. Rogers Brubaker (Lanham, MD: University Press of America, 1989), 81–96.

44. De Master and Le Roy, "Xenophobia and the European Union," 421.

45. Gilbert Geis, "Is Germany's Xenophobia Qualitatively Different from Everybody Else's?" *Crime, Law and Social Change* 24, no. 1 (1995), 65–75.

46. Geis, "Germany's Xenophobia," 66.

47. Ferdinand Böltken, "Social Distance and Physical Proximity: Day-to-Day Attitudes and Experiences of Foreigners and Germans Living in the Same Residential Areas," in *Germans or Foreigners? Attitudes Toward Ethnic Minorities in Post-Reunification*

Germany, eds. Richard Alba, Peter Schmidt, and Martina Wasmer (London: Palgrave, 2003), 252

48. ALLBUS German General Social Survey, *Cumulated ALLBUS 1980–2004*, V196–V199, V202, 172–175, 178.

49. Michael Geyer, "Where Germans Dwell: Transnationalism in Theory and Practice," *German Studies Association Newsletter* 31, no. 2 (Winter 2006), 29–37.

50. Michael Geyer, "Where Germans Dwell: Transnationalism in Theory and Practice," *German Studies Association Newsletter* 31, no. 2 (Winter 2006), 29–37.

51. Centrum Badania Opinii Spolecznej, "Stosunek polakow do innych naro-dów" (Warsaw: CBOS, October 2006), BS/148/2006, www.cbos.pl.

52. Raul Hilberg, *The Destruction of the European Jews* (New York: Holmes and Meier, 1985).

53. Jan T. Gross, *Neighbors: The Destruction of the Jewish Community in Jedwabne, Poland* (New York: Penguin, 2002); also Gross, *Fear: Anti-Semitism in Poland after Auschwitz* (New York: Random House, 2008).

54. Carolyn Slutsky, "Did Jan Gross Get it Right?" *The Jewish Week*, December 1, 2006.

55. Adam Krzeminski, "The View from the Vistula," *Sign and Sight*, March 8, 2007, http://print.signandsight.com/features/1242.html.

56. Tad Taube, "Poland and Israel Share More Than Just a Painful History: Modern Relations Flourish and So Do Investments," *San Jose Mercury News*, March 5, 2007.

57. Centrum Badania Opinii Spolecznej, "Przejawy dystansu spolecznego wobec innych narodów i religii" (Warsaw: CBOS, January 2007), BS/3/2007.

58. Jacques Le Goff, "Poland, Europe, and Russia," in *The Cultural Gradient: The Transmission of Ideas in Europe, 1789–1991*, eds. Catherine Evtuhov and Stephen Kotkin (Lanham, MD: Rowman & Littlefield, 2003), 278.

59. See Martin Malia, *Russia under Western Eyes: From the Bronze Horseman to the Lenin Mausoleum* (Cambridge, MA: Harvard University Press, 1999).

60. Andrzej Stasiuk quoted in *Die Welt*, November 27, 2007.

61. Standard Eurobarometer 66 (2006).

62. Annelin Andersen, "Is Swedish Identity About Being Different to Europe?" (paper presented at Center for German and European Studies, Georgetown University, February 3, 2007).

63. Allan Pred, *Even in Sweden: Racisms, Radicalized Spaces, and the Popular Geographical Imagination* (Berkeley, CA: University of California Press, 2000), xiii.

64. Pred, *Even in Sweden*, 3–6.

65. Pred, *Even in Sweden*, 37.

66. Pred, *Even in Sweden*, 98–99.

67. Pred, *Even in Sweden*, 125.

68. Pred, *Even in Sweden*, 270.

69. Bo Petersson, *Stories About Strangers: Swedish Media Constructions of Socio-Cultural Risk* (Lanham, MD: University Press of America, 2006), 15.

70. Petersson, *Stories About Strangers*, 114.

71. Petersson, *Stories About Strangers*, 108–9.

72. Petersson, *Stories About Strangers*, 78.

73. In a conversation, the author suggested to Jan Gross that he use *Paranoia* as the title of the Polish edition of his book *Fear*. But it was published as *Strach*—the direct rendering of the word fear into Polish.

6

Ethnic Hierarchies

MUSLIMS IN OLD EUROPE

Pluralism in Europe means more than just twenty-seven states working together in EU institutions whose leaders articulate shared norms. It also refers to Europe becoming the site of massive migration from the rest of the world. Europe is no longer merely "European" in terms of its traditional assumptions about peoples, cultures, and identities. The recognition of diversity as an absolute value in the EU's normative framework is consistent with—and provides further legitimation of—Europe's self-styled universalistic mission. There is a problem with this, however: "The EU is now caught in the contradictory situation of having to define a common European culture that is universal—but not so universal that it is global and thus not distinctively European—and at the same time does not negate national and regional cultures."[1]

Europe's social construction was never based on the premise of the existence of a specific European *Volk* or *ethnos*, that is, a community of descent and memory. As Bauman wrote, "Europe is not something you discover; Europe is a mission—something to be made, created, built."[2] It is a site of adventure. While Europe discovered various parts of the globe, no one— literally or, it is argued, metaphorically—has been able to discover Europe. Some historians would disagree with this perspective, to be sure. John Hobson among others took exception to this Eurocentrism and asserted that Europe was constructed with the discoveries of the rest of the world. It was therefore derivative.[3]

Even with large-scale in-migration, Europe's identity has not been constructed on the basis of ethnocentric prejudices about other peoples in a way that, for example, Canada's identity rests on not being American. Regardless of right-wing politicians' rhetoric to the contrary, whether in the past or today, Islam is not Europe's Other. Within the considerable body of evidence that can support this view is European public opinion. Survey results found that in the years that George W. Bush was president, the majority of European respondents considered the United States a greater threat to world peace than Islam.

If anything, Muslims are becoming Europe's largest group of far-away locals (Table 6.1). Before evaluating Islamophobia's reach in Europe, we need to put the phenomenon into context. According to Doudou Diène, a Senegalese diplomat who served as United Nations special rapporteur on contemporary forms of racism, racial discrimination, xenophobia, and related intolerance, the contemporary world has witnessed "an alarming resurgence" of defamation of religions, including anti-Semitism, Christianophobia, and, especially, Islamophobia. Diène singled out "the central involvement of politicians in national and international impact of manifestations and expressions of Islamophobia."[4] The question considered in this chapter is whether European political leaders are part of this current and, if so, whether they can count on the backing of much of their publics.

Table 6.1. Muslims in Europe 2005

	Total Population (in Millions)	Muslim Population	%
Albania	3.1	2.2 million	70.0
Austria	8.2	339,000	4.1
Belgium	10.3	400,000	4.0
Bosnia-Herzegovina	3.8	1.5 million	40.0
Bulgaria	7.7	1 million	12.0
Denmark	5.4	270,000	5.0
France	62.3	5–6 million	9.0
Germany	82.5	3 million	3.6
Italy	58.4	825,000	1.4
Macedonia	2.1	630,000	30.0
Netherlands	16.3	945,000	5.8
Serbia & Montenegro	10.8	405,000	5.0
Kosovo	2.7	1.8 million	90.0
Spain	43.1	1 million	2.3
Sweden	9.0	300,000	3.0
Switzerland	7.4	310,000	4.2
Turkey	68.7	68 million	99.0
United Kingdom	58.8	1.6 million	2.8

Source: "Muslims in Europe: Country Guide" BBC News, December 23 2005), http://news.bbc.co.uk/2/hi/europe/4385768.stm#uk.

It may be an understatement to observe that "in the postcolonial states of Western Europe, Islam is not always accepted without conflict as one religious mediation of national identity among others (just as, in the preceding generation, Jewish identity was excluded from the system of national mediations, at the cost of horrifying tragedies)."[5] But it is important to recognize that each European country has a distinct history in its relations with the Islamic world. Let us review cases from old Europe involving the relations between Muslim groups and the majority population. We do not consider Germany here as chapter 5 described the status of the sizeable Turkish minority in the country.

We also do not examine Muslim minorities in new Europe. The Czech Republic, Slovakia, and Poland have tiny Muslim minorities (about 5,000 each) while two parts of former Yugoslavia where Muslim populations constitute majorities—Bosnia-Herzegovina and Kosovo—are not in the EU. There has been limited Arab immigration, including Palestinian refugees, into eastern Europe, but it has not affected the demographic character of the countries in the way that western European ones have been impacted.

In this regard, Bulgaria is distinctive in new Europe. Of EU countries in the east it has the largest Muslim minority—about one million (two-thirds of them Turkish, the rest belonging to different ethnic groups), which represents over 12 percent of the total population. In the communist era, Turks were not treated as an ethnic minority but dismissed as "Turkified" Bulgarians. A crisis erupted in 1989 when the country shook off its communist system. Fearing the rise of Bulgarian nationalism, about 300,000 Turkish Bulgarians left the country for Turkey. But a predominantly Muslim party, the Movement for Rights and Freedom, became an influential actor in parliament after the 1990 elections. Partly for that reason, the 1991 constitution prohibited the formation of political parties on purely religious lines even though it also enshrined Christian Orthodoxy as the country's "traditional religion."

Nobel Laureate Elias Canetti described the cultural richness of a childhood spent in the Bulgarian city of Ruschük (today's Ruse): "People of the most varied backgrounds lived there; on any one day you could hear seven or eight languages. Aside from Bulgarians . . . there were Turks, who lived in their own neighborhood; next to it was the neighborhood of the Sephardim, the Spanish Jews . . . and there were Greeks, Albanians, Armenians, and Gypsies."[6]

Further up the Danube lies Vienna, which contains a large part of the explanation why Europe is what it is today and not some other civilization. It was in Vienna that the Islamic world's reach into central Europe reached its westernmost point. A critical battle here in the sixteenth century lost by the Turks marked the beginning of the decline of the Ottoman Empire. It was recognized as a turning point even at the time. The small Catholic church in Kahlenburg on the hills overlooking Vienna, where Jan Sobieski, king of Poland and commander of Europe's united Christian armies, prayed before going into the decisive battle, is therefore a centerpiece of Europe's history. Pope John Paul II recognized its historic character on his visit in 1983 to commemorate the three hundredth anniversary of the Christian victory.

Box 6.1. At the Gates of Vienna

"The Victory which the King of Poland has obtained over the Infidels, is so great and so complete that past Ages can scarce parallel the fame; and perhaps future Ages will never see any thing like it. All its Circumstances are as profitable to Christendom in general, and to the Empire in particular, as glorious to the Monarch."

Source: Polish Manuscripts, or The Secret History of the Reign of John Sobieski, The III of that Name, King of Poland, containing a particular account of the siege of Vienna, trans. François-Paulin Dalairac (London: Rhodes, Bennet, Bell, Leigh and Midwinter, 1700), 355.

The European country with the richest Islamic heritage is Spain. Its vibrant Islamic culture was the product of almost eight centuries of Moorish rule, which came to an end in 1492. Large-scale Muslim immigration into the country began in the 1970s. Many were Moroccans coming to work in the tourist industry. The March 2004 bombings on commuter trains around Madrid were largely the work of terrorists of Moroccan background, though 11-M (as the date is cited in Spanish) also involved unprecedented cooperation between Muslim and non-Muslim groups.

The Spanish state recognizes Catholicism as the country's official religion but affords Islam special privileges. These include the teaching of the Qur'an in schools and observation of Muslim religious holidays. Due to its geographical position, Spain has become a primary entry point for African migrants to Europe. In 2006, it was reported that close to 20,000 illegal immigrants had arrived from Africa to the Canary Islands alone. About one-third of all Africans are Muslim, so Spain's Islamic culture may be becoming less exclusively Moorish.

The country with the largest Muslim population in old Europe is France. About 70 percent originate in the north African states of Algeria, Morocco, and Tunisia. The rapid growth of the Islamic population has challenged the strict French practice of separating religion and public life. A ban on all religious symbols in public schools provoked a major national row when it was widely perceived as being a ban on the Islamic headscarf. The widespread and prolonged rioting among Muslim immigrant communities across France in 2005 was an angry response to the high unemployment rates and social marginalization in poor suburbs that young Muslims faced.

There are numerous paradoxes in the status of French Muslims.[7] Some fit into the category of *inexpulsables irregularisables*—immigrants who cannot be forcibly removed from France but also are not eligible for residency permits, for example, foreign parents of French-born children or asylum seekers whose appeals have been rejected. A few Muslims have become successful and even adored by all sections of French society, no one more than football star Zinédine Zidane, born in Marseille of Algerian descent. North African culture has become "cool" in France and leading exponents of *raï*, a form of Algerian pop—and rebel—music play to multiethnic audiences.

Some French Muslims even support the right-wing National Front because it says it supports wholesome family values. As one Arab regional councillor and National Front member in Paris inveighed, "When we're eating our dinner, watching TV at night and we see two homosexual men kissing, it upsets us. As Muslims, and as decent French citizens, it shocks us." The National Front leader's supposed civic nationalism also had appeal: "Why is there this fundamental injustice in France? Because we are called Fayid, Zubeida, Monir? We are French citizens, have masters degrees, and yet we only get jobs at fast food restaurants. Well, if Mr. Le Pen gets elected we will get proper jobs because he believes in putting French citizens—and that's what we are—first."[8]

But French Muslims have themselves been labeled as racists. After the fall 2005 riots that included attacks by young people belonging to ethnic minorities against *français-français* high-school students, several prominent intellectuals including Bernard Kouchner (former and future government minister), philosopher Alain Finkielkraut, and sociologist Pierre-André Taguieff spoke out against "anti-White racist attacks" (*ratonnades*). Finkielkraut's remarks provoked controversy by identifying rioters as Blacks, Arabs, and Muslims. Taguieff, a much-published pioneer on racisms in France, contextualized racist prejudices. Racism had evolved from an intellectual debate about races that initially wanted to explain inequality between "biological" groups as natural. The debate had now switched to how racism centers on cultures, has naturalized historical differences, and has been used to justify exclusion.[9] According to Taguieff, the Muslim minority is susceptible, therefore, to anti-White prejudices.

In Belgium, France's northern neighbor, Islam is one of seven recognized religions, allowing it to receive limited public funding. A majority of Belgium's Muslims are of Moroccan or Turkish origin while new arrivals from Albania have added to the overall number. Citizenship is generally available after seven years of residence but Belgians' above-EU-average Islamophobic attitudes exemplify how an officially proclaimed civic nationalism does not easily dislodge the ethnic kinds, which in this country are anchored in

Flemish (58 percent of the total population) and Walloon (French speakers; 32 percent) linguistic communities. So as to address this problem, in
2004 the government in Brussels launched the Intercultural Dialogue initiative aimed at increasing the sense of inclusion of minorities in the country. But it is the Flemish-Walloon standoff that has overshadowed other ethnic fault lines in the country.

In the 1950s, Muslims began to arrive in the Netherlands from its former colonies of Surinam and Indonesia. Other Muslim groups include
the Somali minority as well as Turks. In total, about 6 percent of the
Dutch population is Muslim. Polarization after the murders of ethno-
centrists Pim Fortuyn in 2002 and Theo van Gogh in 2004 produced an
Islamophobic backlash in Holland. In the case of van Gogh, the killer
was a Muslim of Moroccan background who issued an open letter calling for holy war against unbelievers. The Dutch tradition of religious tolerance was severely tested. The minister of finance added fuel to the fire
by proclaiming that there was indeed a clash of civilizations between Islam and the West and that if Muslim fundamentalists wanted war they
would get it. A number of mosques were burned in reprisal to the van
Gogh killing. Muslim immigration into the Netherlands began to de-
crease in succeeding years.

Denmark's Muslim population is relatively small and the pressure on foreigners to assimilate into Danish culture is great. Of the countries described
so far, it is the only one not to have a colonial history (unless the now
American Virgin Islands count). As with Germany, the first Muslims to arrive in Denmark were Turks and Yugoslavs (who would today be called
Bosnians). Refugees from the wars of the 1990s included Bosnians and Somalis.

It was not altogether surprising that in 2006 Denmark figured at the center of a maelstrom involving alleged Islamophobia. A provincial newspaper
published twelve controversial drawings including a likeness of the Prophet
Mohammed, triggering violent anti-Danish demonstrations, including attacks on its embassies and boycott of its products, in various countries with
significant Muslim populations.

The UN's special rapporteur on contemporary forms of racism, racial discrimination, xenophobia, and related intolerance became involved in the
conflict. Doudou Diène alleged that "the cartoons illustrated the increasing
emergence of the racist and xenophobic currents in everyday life." Diène
also referred to the enabling political context in Denmark, where an extremist political party had obtained 13 percent of the popular vote and
placed third in the 2005 elections, subsequently joining the governing
coalition. "The development of Islamophobia or any racism and racial discrimination always took place in the context of the emergence of strong

racist, extremist political parties and a corresponding absence of reaction against such racism by the country's political leaders."[10]

In 2006, Denmark's director of public prosecutions upheld the decision not to press criminal charges against those responsible for the cartoons. He contended that their publication was protected by legislation guaranteeing free speech. The cartoons were neither racist nor blasphemous, he claimed. But the Islamic Faith Community, a coalition of some twenty-seven radical Muslim organizations in Denmark, filed a complaint against the state of Denmark with the Office of the United Nations High Commission for Human Rights (OHCHR).

Italy's Muslim population is the fourth largest of any EU country, but it represents just 1.5 percent of the country's total population—a significantly lower proportion than other major EU states. The arrival of Islam in parts of today's Italy (especially Sicily, Sardinia, Calabria, and Puglia) dates to the seventh century and reached its high point in the middle of the ninth. In contrast to Spain, where the Christian *Reconquista* was completed in Grenada in 1492, the last Muslim strongholds in Italy fell earlier, in 1300. Also in contrast to Spain, Islam's legacy in Italy is usually seen in negative terms.[11]

Today, Muslim communities are spread across all of Italy. Slightly more than half of them reside in the industrial north, with a quarter living in the middle and the rest in the traditional south. Their origins are also diverse: in the 1970s most were Arabs and Berbers from North Africa. In the 1990s, the largest Muslim waves were of Tunisians and Albanians, from across the Mediterranean and Adriatic seas respectively.

As with Spain, Roman Catholicism is Italy's official religion. But unlike in the Iberian state, even though Islam is the next-largest faith in Italy it does not receive any state support. By contrast, other religions, such as Judaism and small Protestant denominations, have concluded agreements with the state making them eligible to receive a percentage of revenues from the national religion tax.

From 2001 to 2006, Silvio Berlusconi, founder of the center-right movement Forza Italia, served at the head of a coalition government. One of his coalition partners was the Northern League (*Lega Nord*), which regularly engaged in anti-Muslim discourse. The *Lega* even sponsored a bill to restrict the building of mosques. One of its leaders inveighed that mosques "aren't simple places of prayer" but sometimes serve as "centers of recruitment for terrorists and for propagation of hatred for the West."[12] As in other countries in old Europe, headscarves and burkas worn by Muslim women also became a lightning rod in Italy's politics. Whereas France banned the wearing of any kind of religious symbols, the corresponding Italian law forbids wearing clothing that obscures a person's identity. Some Muslim groups contest that the law discriminates against their religious practices.

MUSLIMS IN BRITAIN: CONTRADICTORY EXPERIENCES

As a much larger country with an unparalleled imperial history and a tradition of receiving foreigners, it is to be expected that Britain is at the heart of European-Islamic relations.[13] The number of supposed terrorist plots hatched by British Muslims to attack the country in recent years also speaks to the importance of the British case.

A watershed in British immigration history was the partition of British India in 1947 into separate Muslim and Hindu states. Following its creation, many citizens of Pakistan—and after its independence in 1971, of Bangladesh—opted to move to the metropole. By the time the 1968 Commonwealth Immigration Act was passed tightening former colonials' right to UK citizenship and residency, Britain had already received large numbers of Muslim South Asians. So-called family reunification programs (sometimes dubbed "daisy-chain" immigration), in which a member of one family can sponsor an ever-widening circle of relatives to immigrate to his or her new homeland, further increased immigration numbers to Britain. By 2005, half a million immigrants were arriving in the UK each year.

Periodic unrest in Muslim communities, especially in cities in the north of England with substantial Pakistani and Bangladeshi populations, revealed underlying ethnic tensions in parts of the country. The Cantle report on community cohesion, commissioned after race riots in a number of cities in the North of England in 2001, described a multiethnic Britain composed of separate communities without a meta-community to tie them together.[14] The conclusion of the report about the disturbances in Oldham, Burnley, and Bradford in 2001 was that people from different groups were not mixing and the towns displayed a "depth of polarization" around segregated communities living "a series of parallel lives."[15] Home Secretary David Blunkett went further to speak of a breach of norms in the British home caused by the arrival of so many foreigners.

One British academic tried to see the positive side of the events. Riots could have an instrumental value in bonding a community together. They could even prove more consequential than mutual perceptions of communities towards each other. "The spectacle of sanctimonious violence connects a dispersed and diffuse population as a community: one to be identified through the victimhood of its past and present, the collective vulnerability of its future, and the ethical and historical imperative to identify with and act as part of it."[16]

For Christian Joppke, a specialist on immigration, the 2001 riots marked a turning point in the Labour government's embrace of multiculturalism. Seeking to go "beyond multiculturalism," British policy appeared to Joppke to be evolving in a more civic and centrist orientation, requiring newcomers to bind to a particular society.[17]

It was conceivable, then, that both the ethnically English and British Muslims now rejected the UK's multicultural model in which immigrant communities were to enjoy considerable cultural autonomy and no assimilationist pressures would be applied on them. The first group could claim it was too accommodating, the second that it subtly imposed restrictions, conformity, and taboos.

Only months earlier, a special report on the future of multiethnic Britain, written by a commission of experts headed by academic and Lord Bhiku Parekh, had challenged long-held assumptions about multiculturalism.[18] The study was written in the spirit of the catchphrase "there ain't no black in the Union Jack."

The report provocatively suggested that the very term "British" had racial connotations and was inappropriate in describing the UK's multicultural society. Britishness had "systematic, largely unspoken, racial connotations. Whiteness nowhere features as an explicit condition of being British, but it is widely understood that Englishness, and therefore by extension Britishness is racially coded." Put into cliché form, whiteness and Britishness go together like roast beef and Yorkshire pudding.

Parekh rejected *Englishness* as an alternative term. "To be English, as the term is in practice used, is to be white. Britishness is not ideal, but at least it appears acceptable, particularly when suitably qualified—Black British, Indian British, British Muslim and so on."

But neither riots sparked by young people of South Asian origin nor a contentious commission report on Britain's multiethnic future chaired by a South Asian academic could possibly have had the impact on ethnic relations of the London subway bombings of July 2005. Carried out by several second-generation British citizens of Pakistani origin, the event proved to be the most serious challenge yet to the British policy of multiculturalism and exacerbated mutual suspicion between English and Muslim communities.

A few prominent British Muslims blamed the Blair government's policy on Iraq for giving ammunition to extremists. Nobel Prize–winning dramatist Harold Pinter joined in the fray with the charge that Tony Blair was "a hired Christian thug."[19] A small but significant minority of ordinary Muslims seemed to share such a view. In a July 2006 poll of UK Muslims, 13 percent of respondents believed that the suicide bombers "could be regarded as martyrs."[20]

A month later, the Secretary of State for Communities and Local Government established a Commission on Integration and Cohesion. The minister hinted at the weaknesses in Britain's multicultural system: "We have moved from a period of uniform consensus on the value of multiculturalism, to one where we can encourage that debate by questioning whether it is encouraging separateness."[21]

The final report of the Commission on Integration and Cohesion, published in June 2007, brought welcome good news.[22] It defined cohesion as "the process that must happen in all communities to ensure different groups of people get on well together." In turn, "integration is principally the process that ensures new residents and existing residents adapt to one another." The Commission reported that 79 percent of people agreed or strongly agreed that people of different backgrounds got on well in their local areas. While cohesion rates ranged from 38 percent to 90 percent, just 10 of 387 areas had a rate under 60 percent. Finally, 58 percent of people surveyed in a 2007 MORI-IPSOS poll agreed that immigrants make Britain more open to new ideas and cultures.

Britain was on the cusp of achieving "super-diversity": migrants come from all over the world—and not just places with historical ties to the UK. In the borough of Haringey (close to Heathrow airport), residents have over 120 different countries of origin. For the Commission, super-diversity also signified different immigration routes, legal statuses, demographic breakdowns, and settlement patterns in England.

The Commission report also employed the concept of transnationalism. It represents "a particular form of multiple identity developed as a result of globalization and its associated cheap transport and advances in communications, and meaning for the first time that migrants can easily maintain links with their place of origin." Transnationalism does not hinder integration, but helps it because "a transnational identity may give people the confidence in their own identity to engage with wider society. Transnationalism also allows people to express their attachment to their homeland in a way that does not clash with being part of the new society." Consequently, "those least integrated into a society often identify most strongly with their country of origin, but have fewest links to it."[23]

In a circuitous way, the Commission on Integration and Cohesion outlined the context in which the 2005 London bombings could take place. "When taken alongside super-diversity, transnationalism means that the UK is far more plugged in to events around the world and that cohesion in local areas can be affected by events in another country."[24]

The Commission pointed to some negative features of British society that could, hypothetically, rebound on the country. It cited the Equalities Review report, published in early 2007, that estimated that at the current rate of progress, children of Pakistani ethnicity would close the attainment gap in English and Maths only by the year 2017. The outlook was much worse for children of Black African ethnicity: the gap would be closed by 2053!

The Equalities Review report also listed other ethnic and gender inequalities. The employment rate among immigrant Somalis was just 12 percent, compared with 62 percent for all other new immigrants. And, on the basis of current trends, Pakistani and Bangladeshi women would continue to have the highest rates of economic inactivity for many years.[25] In an indirect way, the report made clear the underlying conditions for the recent rise of Islamic fundamentalism in Britain.

In its 2006 report on Islamophobia, the EU Monitoring Centre on Racism and Xenophobia analyzed statistics on racially motivated victimization in Britain—the EU country collecting the most comprehensive data on the issue. In a "racial" hierarchy made up of White, Black, Indian, and Pakistani/Bangladeshi, since 1993 the latter group had consistently suffered the most racially motivated threats and victimizations. This group in Britain is the closest proxy indicator to Muslim. Therefore, the urban myth of "Paki bashing" in Britain has empirical substance.[26]

British multiculturalism has come under attack. It has been challenged in many different ways and by various groups—not only by people who are ethnically English or who are radical British Muslims. The Office of National Statistics provides periodic data that feed the multiculturalism backlash. At the end of 2007, for example, it reported that Muhammad would soon replace Jack as the most common name given in Britain to boys. A principal reason for this, the office explained, was that the birth rate of women born in Pakistan but living in the UK was three times higher than that of British-born women. But Muslims are not the only group eroding Britishness.

Another group of migrants to Britain often uneasy with multiculturalism are Poles. In a matter of several years, they became a significant minority group in the British Isles and helped make practicing Catholics a larger group than practicing Protestants—thereby threatening to undermine Britain's dominant Anglicanism. Since 2004, over one-half million eastern Europeans—two-thirds of them Poles—have moved to Britain to find work.[27] The main reasons have been Britain's open-door policy towards 2004 accession states' workers plus the lag in competitiveness of new Europe's economies. Of the twelve new accession states, only Slovenia has managed to leapfrog older EU states (Greece and Portugal) in the 2006–2007 National European Competitiveness Index.[28]

Many Poles in Britain reported that their whiteness helped them find jobs. While one-third of Polish respondents agreed that London's multiculturalism is an asset, a similar proportion expressed covert racist views. According to one study, 90 percent of Polish respondents asserted that "Poles are not very tolerant" towards other ethnic minorities, Asians, and Blacks.[29] They found it difficult to understand "positive discrimination," which they equated with negative discrimination. "Unaccustomed to Britain's multiracial character, in turn they engaged in unpleasant behavior towards visible minorities, often encouraged by British nationalists and Nazi groups."[30] A few Polish groups even began to cooperate with a German-based racist organization called Combat 18, coded after Adolf Hitler's initials (the first and eighth letters of the alphabet).

In Britain today, being uncomfortable with and even disapproving of multiculturalism cuts across ethnic, racial, and religious categories. But antimulticulturalism and Islamophobia are two separate issues, one attacking a policy, the other a group of people. Let us survey public attitudes in Europe towards Muslims.

EUROPEAN PUBLIC OPINION ON MUSLIMS

Since the 2001 terrorist attacks in the United States and the subsequent U.S. invasion of Iraq, studying the West's relations with the Islamic world has grown exponentially in importance. A leading polling agency tracking worldwide attitudinal change has been the Pew Global Attitudes Project based in Washington. Let us start by looking at the survey results it collected in thirteen countries in 2006.

A central issue in this survey was how Westerners and Muslims viewed each other. In the four EU countries included in the survey, a slight drop from 2004 was noted in the general public's favorable ratings of Muslims.[31] Admittedly, Muslims invariably were given significantly lower ratings than Christians and Jews (Table 6.2).

By contrast, overwhelming majorities of Muslim respondents in France and Spain, and strong majorities in Britain and Germany too, had positive attitudes towards Christians (Figure 6.1). The normative divide is illustrated best by attitudes in Spain: whereas eight in ten Spanish Muslims viewed Christians favorably, only 29 percent of the general Spanish public (which included Muslim respondents) thought well of Muslims.

The general public (including a country's minority population) in the four EU samples believed relations between Westerners and Muslims were generally bad, ranging from 70 percent in Germany and 66 percent in France to a lower 61 percent in both Britain and Spain (paradoxically, both recent targets of jihadist terrorist attacks). When Muslim respondents alone were considered, British, French, and German Muslim respondents were slightly less negative about the state of Western-Muslim relations (hovering around 60 percent). Spanish Muslims were the only group in Europe believing relations were generally good (by a 49 to 23 percent margin).

Finally, differing majorities of the public in Germany (70 percent), Spain (58 percent), and Britain (54 percent) asserted that there is a conflict between being a devout Muslim and living in a modern society. The French general public strongly disagreed, with 74 percent seeing no conflict, about the same level as Muslim respondents in France and Spain. British Muslims were just about split down the middle on the question, again suggesting that the cultural schism in this country was not as sharp as elsewhere. Ar-

Table 6.2. Rating of Christians, Muslims, and Jews

	Rating in . . .	Christians %	Muslims %	Jews %
United States	2006	88	54	77
	2005	87	57	77
	2004	84	48	77
Russia	2006	90	59	59
	2005	92	55	63
	2004	93	53	65
Great Britain	2006	88	63	74
	2005	85	72	78
	2004	84	67	76
France	2006	87	65	86
	2005	84	64	82
	2004	84	64	81
Germany	2006	79	36	69
	2005	83	40	67
	2004	75	41	63
Spain	2006	79	29	45
	2005	80	46	58
Turkey	2006	16	88	15
	2005	21	83	18
	2004	31	88	27

Source: Pew Global Attitudes Project, "The Great Divide: How Westerners and Muslims View Each Other," June 22, 2006, www.pewglobal.org, accessed April 3, 2007. Rating is based on percentage of respondents having a very or somewhat favorable opinion.

guably, Britain did have above-average community cohesion, as the Commission on Integration and Cohesion had suggested.

By large margins blame for poor social relations was placed by respondents on the other community. The greatest polarization was in Germany: twice as many Germans blamed Muslims for the bad relations as did not, while nearly eight times as many German Muslims blamed Germans. The only exception to this rule were British respondents who, by a narrow margin, blamed themselves more for the bad relations than they did Muslims living in their country. In this important respect, Britain was significantly less Islamophobic than the three other large countries of old Europe.

ANTI-AMERICANISM AS MARKER OF EUROPEAN IDENTITY

Europe has been shifting eastwards. Given that the geographic center of Europe is near the city of Grodno in Belarus—whose government was far

Muslims

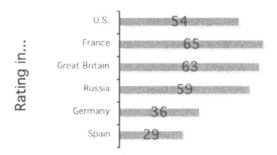

Rating in...
U.S.	54
France	65
Great Britain	63
Russia	59
Germany	36
Spain	29

Christians

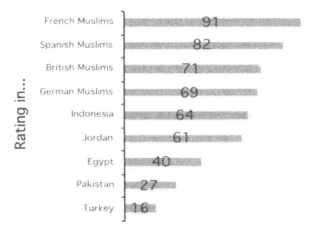

Rating in...
French Muslims	91
Spanish Muslims	82
British Muslims	71
German Muslims	69
Indonesia	64
Jordan	61
Egypt	40
Pakistan	27
Turkey	16

Fig 6.1. How Christians and Muslims View Each Other. *Source:* **Pew Global Attitudes Project, "The Great Divide: How Westerners and Muslims View Each Other," June 22, 2006, www.pewglobal.org.**

removed from European norms—there remains space for further eastern expansion if former Soviet republics take the necessary steps. Through the European Neighborhood Policy, the EU is also looking southwards.

Some believe that the eastern and southern direction of the EU has undermined its Atlanticist character—its historic partnership with the United States on the other side of the ocean. The rise of widespread anti-Americanism among European elites and publics is an additional factor that has weakened Atlanticism.

It is giving excessive attention to the George W. Bush presidency to suggest that anti-Americanism, and even a kind of anti-Atlanticism (we must remember there is Canada—a country that tries very hard to be like Europe—on the other side of the ocean), were largely products of his administration. Very few observers would question that Bush was responsible for increasing anti-Americanism. But it was already there when he took office. In the case of Europe, the development of a Europeanness galvanized by anti-Americanism has a long, subtle, noteworthy history.

In the early 1950s, Hannah Arendt—known for her devastating criticism of totalitarian systems—criticized a "Europeanism" being built on populist notions of exclusion and *réssentiment*. In 1954, she argued in a lecture that "If it is true that each nationalism . . . begins with a real or fabricated common enemy, then the current image of America in Europe may well become the beginning of a new pan-European nationalism." Europe had "a tendency to consider the establishment of a European government an act of emancipation from America."[32] Arendt supported the construction of a federated Europe lacking an anti-American cement because "America has been both the dream and the nightmare of Europe."[33]

One of the most outspoken anti-American European intellectuals at the turn of the new century was former French foreign minister Hubert Védrine. He attacked the United States as *un hyperpuissance*—a term that caught on as a description of America's unprecedented power—and urged Europe to unify politically in order to check it. The catalog of America's faults included: "ultraliberal market economy, rejection of the state, nonrepublican individualism, unthinking strengthening of the universal and 'indispensable' role of the U.S.A., common law, *anglophonie*, Protestant rather than Catholic concepts."[34] He made these statements *before* the onset of the Bush administration.

French anti-Americanism is widely regarded as exceptionally pointed. In the 2005 French referendum on the EU constitution, both supporters and opponents used anti-American arguments. President Chirac argued that only a strong Europe could balance the United States. Skeptics claimed the EU constitution was itself quasi-American, permeated by Anglo-American liberalism.

President Bush's invasion of Iraq proved to be a watershed in EU-American relations. Antiwar demonstrations were held throughout Europe on February 15, 2003. One French minister's hyperbole even included the assertion that "On Saturday, February 15, 2003, a nation was born on the streets. This nation is the European nation."[35]

German philosopher Jürgen Habermas and his French counterpart Jacques Derrida published an essay underscoring the separate paths that Europe and the United States had embarked on with the war in Iraq.[36] Appearing in Germany's *Frankfurter Allgemeine Zeitung* and France's *La Liberation*, the article appealed for a unified European response—without embracing a Eurocentrism—to balance out the hegemonic unilateralism of the United States. This required the creation of a European identity shaped by a shared political fate which, the two philosophers stressed, the Franco-German avant-garde core would articulate.

Habermas and Derrida identified Europe's legacy to the entire Western world: "Insofar as Christianity and capitalism, natural science and technology, Roman law and the Code Napoléon, the bourgeois-urban form of life, democracy and human rights, the secularization of state and society have spread across other continents, these legacies no longer constitute a *proprium*." Instead, the EU's uniqueness is to "have confirmed Europeans in their belief that the domestication of state power demands a *mutual* limitation of sovereignty, on the global as well as the nation-state level."[37] For the two philosophers, the EU was nothing less than the rejection of the Westphalian order that had consolidated the modern system of nation-states.

The article initiated a debate among some of Europe's best-known thinkers about how to construct a European identity. In contextualizing America's war in Iraq, Italian novelist Umberto Eco observed that "Europeans have a lot in common—joy and sorrow, pride and shame, traditions to defend and remorse still to process."[38] Citing the motto that "Europe is where there is no death penalty," Spanish philosopher Fernando Savater emphasized Europe's indispensable role in a renewed civilizing project. For his part, Italian philosopher Gianni Vattimo added: "That which Rumsfeld and Bush call Europe is characterized by values that we do not perceive as our own; and therefore, by contrast, it evokes in us the awareness of what Europe 'truly' is."[39]

Significantly, no intellectuals from new Europe, the Nordic countries, or Britain were invited to take part in this conversation. A journalist from central Europe was incensed about the exclusionary nature of the debate:

> The deliberate non-invitation of Poles, Hungarians or Czechs to the great debate about the European spirit might have been meant as a pedagogical measure; however, it follows an old tradition. The message is unequivocal: Europe's spiritual driving forces are we, the Germans, French, Italians, Spanish, and Anglo-Saxons. All the others must first show that they deserve to belong among this group. Whether they deserve it or not, the East-Central Europeans will come. In fact, they are already here, *intra muros*.[40]

Western European elites and publics share a negative image of Americans, though with some subtle differences between them. Culture-driven anti-Americanism has deep roots in western Europe, historian Andrei Markovits claimed. Thus, Heinrich Heine hated America: in the German poet's words, "there are no princes or nobles there; all men are equal—equal dolts."[41] Bertolt Brecht came to believe that "The mistakes of the Russians are the mistakes of friends; the mistakes of the Americans are the mistakes of enemies."[42] Markovits summarizes Charles Dickens's views of Americans as "conceited, ill-mannered, repulsive, sanctimonious, immoral, boastful, uncultivated, tasteless, moralizing, insulting, insulted, abusive of liberty, materialistic, religious and blasphemous at one and the same time."[43]

Box 6.2. Against America as Alterity

"Exploiting an unfavorable view of Americans in order to define Europe in opposition to something negative—just as the Athenians defined themselves in opposition to the Persians or the Europeans in relation to the Arabs, Tartars or Turks—is a strategy which destroys the chances of Europe emerging on the international scene as a useful partner."

Source: Bronisław Geremek, "Thinking about Europe as a Community" (speech delivered at the conference Quelles valeurs pour quelle Europe? organized by the République des Idées, Paris, June 19, 2003), http://myeurope.eun.org/ww/en/pub/myeurope/home/activities/citizenship/geremek.htm.

Markovits believed that Europe's identity has become dependent on a shared anti-Americanism. This view is also embraced by Russell Berman: "anti-Americanism serves as a peculiar social psychology, based on the collectivistic identity formation that provides an antireformist ideology for European unification. European anti-Americanism is the primary cultural and ideological substance for the otherwise only bureaucratic process of European unification."[44]

Contemporary eastern Europe did not figure in Markovits' study. Findings there might well have been the opposite of those in the west. As we have noted in our study, much of new Europe—at least initially—was favorably disposed both towards the United States—seen as the force behind its liberation from Soviet rule—and the Bush administration—viewed as a likeable maverick.

A series of public opinion surveys measured changing attitudes towards the United States throughout the world. The Pew Charitable Trust issued a report in 2007 that made clear how anti-Americanism had become a global phenomenon since the U.S. invasion of Iraq. It was strongest in the Muslim world ranging from Turkey (where only 12 percent of respondents had a favorable view of the United States in 2006), across the Middle East (the corresponding figure for Jordan was 15 percent) through Pakistan (27 percent) and down to Indonesia (30 percent).

But the United States's NATO partners and EU core states also witnessed a dramatic decline in support for the United States. In Germany it toppled from 78 percent in 1999 to 37 percent in 2006; in France from 62 percent to 39 percent; and in Spain from 50 percent to just 23 percent. British pro-Americanism also fell, from 83 percent in 1999 to a still high 56 percent in 2006.[45]

Anti-Americanism has become an intensely held opinion that targets not only the U.S. government but also the American people.[46] In 2003, 53 percent of respondents to an EU poll regarded the United States as a threat to world peace—about the same percentage as for Iran and North Korea. Of western European publics surveyed, Spaniards led the way with 56 percent believing that the U.S. presence in Iraq constituted a great danger to world peace. But Spaniards also had the least favorable opinion of Americans themselves: in 2006, only 37 percent had a very or somewhat favorable opinion. This compared to two-thirds of British, French, and German publics. Generally, a small minority (around 20 percent) of European respondents believed that the United States took the interests of countries like theirs into account when making policy.

In a 2007 BBC World Service poll of 28,000 people across twenty-seven countries, the United States ranked just behind Iran and Israel as countries viewed as having a mainly negative influence in the world. Overall, 51 percent of respondents evaluated U.S. influence negatively and only 30 percent positively. When we focus on opinion in the EU, negative perceptions are even greater, especially in Greece (78 percent), Germany (74 percent), and France (69 percent). But even Poland's usually positive view of the United States was tempered: its positive rating dropped twenty-four points in one year, from 62 percent in 2006 to 38 percent in 2007.[47] We might say that Polish attitudes towards America seem to be undergoing Europeanization.

Conversely, the 2007 global survey found that the EU was generally seen as a force for good. Overall, 53 percent of all respondents had a positive view and just 19 percent a negative one. Of EU member states, France's ratings were nearly as good as the EU's. The EU and France followed closely behind top-ranked Canada and Japan as forces seen as exerting positive influence in the world.

Among EU member states, the EU received the highest rating in Portugal (79 percent), but there were large favorable majorities in Italy (76 percent), Germany (73 percent), Poland (70 percent), France (68 percent), and Greece (63 percent). The most Eurosceptic countries were Britain (59 percent positive) and Hungary (50 percent positive, though only 11 percent gave negative views). The existence of a continental divide in North America is supported by contrasting levels of positive support for the EU in Canada (70 percent) compared to the United States (53 percent).

One particular source of anti-American views has been the perception of America's extreme religiosity. The Pew Trust poll found that in 2005 about 60 percent of French and Dutch respondents found Americans to be too religious; pluralities in Britain and Germany concurred with this view. Yet 58 percent of Americans thought of their society as not being religious enough and only 21 percent as too religious. That perception was very similar to Poles' belief that America wasn't religious enough (56 percent, compared to a scant 6 percent who thought it was too religious)—an indication of lingering Polish exceptionalism in the EU. Significantly, by majorities as large as or larger than in Poland, all Muslim countries surveyed regarded America as not religious enough, but for very different reasons.

When respondents in various countries were asked whether they thought emigrants to the United States have a better life than at home, most supported this assertion. In Europe, it ranged from a margin of 43 percent in Russia and 35 percent in Britain to 12 percent in France and -2 percent in Germany. Generally, the United States has maintained its status as, in the term used by J. G. A. Pocock, a closed "American geopolitical utopia."[48] The United States as a specific place to live was rated much higher than when presented as an abstract entity. Positive attitudes about the United States as a place to live were largely unrelated to favorable attitudes to the United States generally.

TYPOLOGIES OF ANTI-AMERICANISM

A major comparative study of anti-Americanism and its impact on world politics was published by international relations scholars Peter Katzenstein and Robert Keohane.[49] They identified different varieties of this orientation. A "liberal anti-Americanism" is associated with the advanced democratic societies of the West. Arguing that liberal anti-Americans—many British intellectuals can be counted in this number—do not detonate bombs against Americans, the authors explained that "The more the United States is seen as a self-interested power parading under the banners of democracy and human rights, rather than a true proponent of those values, the less willing other liberals may be to defend it with words or deeds."[50]

A second type of anti-Americanism is commonly found in Europe. "Social anti-Americanism" is "marked by a more encompassing support for a variety of social programs than are politically feasible or socially acceptable in the United States."[51] Both social and Christian democratic welfare states in Scandinavia and on the European continent are cradles of social anti-Americanism. Everything about "American conditions"—from the hegemony of the market to the death penalty, gun laws, and foreign-policy unilateralism—shape the value divide between the United States and Europe. A comparison of France and the United States found, for example, that evaluations made on the basis of civic solidarity were stronger in the European country, evaluations made on the basis of market performance stronger in the United States.[52]

Two other kinds of anti-Americanism—"sovereign-nationalist" and "radical"—are less salient to the European context. The first involves the effort by a state threatened by American influence to maintain control over its destiny. During the Cold War, for example, there was a current in Europe that expressed fear that the two superpowers—the United States and the Soviet Union—would gang up on Europe or at least restrict its influence in world politics.[53] "Radical anti-Americanism" is a version of Occidentalism that regards the United States, the self-proclaimed leader of the West, as constituting the principal source of evil in the world. This was the official position of the Soviet bloc and some radical regimes today, in particular, those labeled as rogue states by the United States.

"Legacy anti-Americanism," in its turn, is a resentment of past wrongs committed by the United States. This form could subsume Mexican hostility towards the colossus to the north. It could also describe antipathy towards the United States in nations which were invaded by it, such as Puerto Rico, Nicaragua, and the Philippines.

Drawing a continuum of the constancy of anti-American attitudes, Katzenstein and Keohane identified three points on the scale. On one end was unbiased opinion in which citizens are open to new information which may change their views. On the other end are predispositions, or bias, where no amount of new information is likely to change views about the United States. In between is distrust, based on negative evaluations of American conditions.

The authors' optimistic conclusion is that "with the exception of the Arab Middle East, bias is not yet deeply embedded in global public opinion."[54] Anti-Americanism is highly contingent, they believe, on time and place. They would strongly disagree that we have entered the "anti-American century."[55]

Katzenstein and Keohane went further to make the contentious claim that in old Europe such transient anti-Americanism has not had any real consequences for support for the struggle against terrorism, NATO cooperation, diplomatic agreements, or trade relations.[56] The "coalition of the leaving"—countries which had initially supported the U.S. invasion of Iraq but which later decided to withdraw their forces from there—would disprove their thesis.

The president of the Pew Research Center, Andrew Kohut, summarized the values gap between the United States and Europe this way:

> it is true that Americans are different. We are more individualistic and we feel a stronger sense of personal empowerment than people in most countries. We are more likely to resist government efforts to restrict personal freedom. Consistent with our history as an immigrant nation, we have more positive attitudes about immigration than do citizens in much of the developed world.

And our religiosity sets us apart—the U.S. is by far the most religious rich country in the world.[57]

The notion of the United States as Europe's Other enabling Europe to construct its own otherwise murky identity has appeal to some writers. But as we have seen, the social construction of a European identity involves normative, demographic, territorial, and institutional dimensions and by now extends well beyond the atavistic attitudes towards America identified in some recent efforts to debunk anti-Americanism.

Anti-Americanism is not usually classified as a xenophobia because dislike of America, it is argued, is a more encompassing issue than dislike of Americans visiting or living in Europe. It is sometimes argued that anti-Americanism largely constitutes a radical ideology having little in common with a xenophobic thrust. This interpretation stands in need of modification. During the Vietnam War years—and again during the Bush administration—Americans themselves were identified by some radical groups as "ugly Americans"—following British novelist Graham Greene's terminology. It is presumptuous to hold that European anti-Americanism is never *ad hominem* and has nothing to do with perceptions of individual Americans—their behavior, culture, manner of speaking, eating habits, and looks (Markovits cites their perceived obesity). That method of evaluating a group has, after all, helped consolidate and spread another antipathy—Islamophobia.

NOTES

1. Gerard Delanty and Chris Rumford, *Rethinking Europe: Social Theory and the Implications of Europeanization* (London: Routledge, 2005), 60.

2. Zygmunt Bauman, *Europe: An Unfinished Adventure* (New York: Polity Press, 2004), 22.

3. John Hobson, *The Eastern Origins of Western Civilization* (Cambridge: Cambridge University Press, 2004).

4. Sarah el Sigany, "Islamophobia and Racism Discussed at the UN Human Rights Council," *Daily News: Egypt*, September 21, 2006, www.dailystaregypt.com/article.aspx?ArticleID=3066.

5. Étienne Balibar, *We, the People of Europe? Reflections on Transnational Citizenship* (Princeton, NJ: Princeton University Press, 2004), 29.

6. Quoted in Stephen Lewis, "Islam in Bulgaria," *Saudi Aramco World* 45, no. 3 (May/June 1994), www.saudiaramcoworld.com/issue/199403/islam.in.bulgaria.htm.

7. See Jonathan Laurence and Justin Vaisse, *Integrating Islam: Political and Religious Challenges in Contemporary France* (Washington, DC: Brookings Institution, 2006).

8. "Le Pen Urges Halt to Immigration," BBC News, April 16, 2007.

9. See Pierre-André Taguieff, *Force of Prejudice: On Racism and its Doubles* (Minneapolis: University of Minnesota Press, 2001).

10. "Racism and Racial Discrimination on Rise around the World, UN Expert Warns," UN News Centre, March 7, 2006, www.un.org/apps/news/story.asp?News ID=17718&Cr=racis&Cr1.

11. See Robert D. Putnam, Robert Leonardi, and Raffaella Y. Nanetti, *Making Democracy Work: Civic Traditions in Modern Italy* (Princeton, NJ: Princeton University Press, 1994).

12. Sophie Arie, "Italian MPs Plan Control of New Mosques," *Guardian Unlimited*, March 25, 2004, www.guardian.co.uk/italy/story/0,12576,1177464,00.html.

13. In the spirit of Bhiku Parekh's notion that use of the word Britain may have an imperial ring to anyone non-English subsumed under it, and also so as not to presume that the experience of England is the same as that of Scots and Welsh and northern Irish, unless otherwise made clear I do not have in mind anyone other than the English when referring to interethnic relations with British Muslims.

14. British Home Office, *Community Cohesion: A Report of the Independent Review Team Chaired by Ted Cantle* (London: HMSO, 2001), 9.

15. British Home Office, *Community Cohesion*, 9. See also "Key Points of the Cantle Report," *Guardian Unlimited*, December 11, 2001, www.guardian.co.uk/racism/Story/0,2763,617138,00.html.

16. Shane Brighton, "British Muslims, Multiculturalism and UK Foreign Policy: 'Integration' and 'Cohesion' in and beyond the State," *International Affairs* 83, no. 1 (January 2007), 15.

17. Christian Joppke, "The Retreat of Multiculturalism in the Liberal State: Theory and Policy," *British Journal of Sociology* 55, no. 2 (2004), 253.

18. Commission on the Future of Multi-Ethnic Britain, sponsored by the Runnymede Trust, *The Parekh Report*, October 11, 2000. See also his *Rethinking Multiculturalism: Cultural Diversity and Political Theory* (Cambridge, MA: Harvard University Press, 2002).

19. "Pinter Takes Final Bow," *Guardian Unlimited*, February 28, 2005, http://books.guardian.co.uk/news/articles/0,6109,1427404,00.html.

20. "Populus Poll of British Muslims," *UK Polling Report*, July 4, 2006, http://ukpollingreport.co.uk/blog/archives/262.

21. Ruth Kelly, speech at the launch of the Commission on Integration and Cohesion (August 24, 2006), www.communities.gov.uk/index.asp?id=1502280.

22. Commission on Integration and Cohesion, "Our Shared Future," June 14, 2007, www.integrationandcohesion.org.uk/Our_final_report.aspx.

23. Commission on Integration and Cohesion, "Our Shared Future," section 2.50, p. 28.

24. Commission on Integration and Cohesion, "Our Shared Future," section 2.50, p. 28.

25. Equalities Review, "Fairness and Freedom: The Final Report," February 28, 2007, www.theequalitiesreview.org.uk/publications.aspx.

26. European Union Monitoring Centre on Racism and Xenophobia, *Muslims in the European Union: Discrimination and Islamophobia* (Vienna: EUMC, 2006), tables 12–13, 88–89.

27. Andrew Taylor, "Poles Dominate in Migration of Workers," *Financial Times*, November 21, 2006.

28. "New EU States 'Poor Competitors,'" BBC News, November 24 2006, http://news.bbc.co.uk/2/hi/business/6179630.stm. Based on a University of Sheffield and George Washington University study.

29. Richard Ford, "Jobs Easier to Find As We're White, Poles Claim," *The Times*, May 18, 2006, 7. Based on a report by The Centre for Research on Nationalism, Ethnicity, and Multiculturalism, University of Surrey.

30. Krystyna Bleszynska (Warsaw University), quoted in "Polish Race Hate Groups Spark Concern," BBC News, November 29, 2006.

31. Pew Global Attitudes Project, "The Great Divide: How Westerners and Muslims View Each Other," June 22, 2006, www.pewglobal.org, accessed April 3, 2007.

32. Hannah Arendt, *Essays in Understanding 1930–1954* (New York: Harcourt, Brace & Company, 1994), 416–17.

33. Arendt, *Essays in Understanding*, 410.

34. Hubert Védrine, *Les cartes de la France à l'heure de la mondialisation* (Paris: Fayard, 2000).

35. Former finance minister Dominique Strauss-Kahn, quoted in Andrei S. Markovits, *Uncouth Nation: Why Europe Dislikes America* (Princeton, NJ: Princeton University Press, 2007), 202.

36. For an English-language version, see Jürgen Habermas and Jacques Derrida, "February 15, Or, What Binds Europeans Together: Plea for a Common Foreign Policy, Beginning in Core Europe," in *Old Europe, New Europe, Core Europe: Transatlantic Relations After The Iraq War*, eds. Daniel C. Levy, John C. Torpey, and Max Pensky (London: Verso, 2005), chapter 1. Essays by other prominent intellectuals are included in this volume.

37. Habermas and Derrida, "February 15," 8, 12.

38. Umberto Eco, "An Uncertain Europe between Rebirth and Decline," in *Old Europe, New Europe, Core Europe*, 17.

39. Fernando Savater, "Europe, Both Needed and In Need," 43; Gianni Vattimo, "The European Union Faces the Major Points of its Development," 31. Both in *Old Europe, New Europe, Core Europe*.

40. Adam Krzeminski, "First Kant, Now Habermas: A Polish Perspective on 'Core Europe,'" in *Old Europe, New Europe, Core Europe*, 151.

41. Quoted in Markovits, *Uncouth Nation*, 57.

42. Markovits, *Uncouth Nation*, 69.

43. Markovits, *Uncouth Nation*, 72.

44. Russell A. Berman, *Anti-Americanism in Europe: A Cultural Problem* (Stanford, CA: Hoover Institution Press, 2004), 80.

45. Andrew Kohut, "America's Image in the World: Findings from the Pew Global Attitudes Project" (speech to the U.S. House Committee on Foreign Affairs; Subcommittee on International Organizations, Human Rights, and Oversight, March 14, 2007).

46. David Farber, *What They Think of Us: International Perceptions of the United States since 9/11* (Princeton, NJ: Princeton University Press, 2007).

47. BBC World Service Poll, "Israel and Iran Share Most Negative Ratings in Global Poll," February 2007, newsvote.bbc.co.uk.

48. J. G. A. Pocock, "Civic Humanism and its Role in Anglo-American Thought," in Pocock, *Politics, Language and Time: Essays on Political Thought and History* (Chicago: University of Chicago Press, 1989), 100.

49. Peter Katzenstein and Robert Keohane, eds., *Anti-Americanisms in World Politics* (Ithaca, NY: Cornell University Press, 2007).

50. Peter Katzenstein and Robert Keohane, "Varieties of Anti-Americanism: A Framework for Analysis," in *Anti-Americanisms in World Politics*, 30.

51. Katzenstein and Keohane, "Varieties of Anti-Americanism," 31.

52. Michèle Lamont and Laurent Thévenot, "Introduction: Toward a Renewed Comparative Cultural Sociology," in *Rethinking Comparative Cultural Sociology: Repertoires of Evaluation in France and the United States*, eds. Lamont and Thévenot (Cambridge: Cambridge University Press, 2000), 2.

53. Pierangelo Isernia, "Anti-Americanism in Europe during the Cold War," in *Anti-Americanisms in World Politics*, 57–92.

54. Keohane and Katzenstein, "The Political Consequences of Anti-Americanism," in *Anti-Americanisms in World Politics*, 276.

55. Ivan Krastev and Alan McPherson, eds., *The Anti-American Century* (Budapest: Central European University Press, 2007).

56. Keohane and Katzenstein, "The Political Consequences of Anti-Americanism," 273–305.

57. Kohut, "America's Image in the World."

7

Narrations of Home across Borders

CULTURAL PRODUCTION IN AN ENLARGED EUROPE

The novel is an imagined arena of contested realms. Its essential task is the representation of an ordinary experience and a circumstantial reality. But it also doubles as an agent of cultural change by intervening in discourses of identity and in opposing hegemonic narratives. For example, it often interrogates political thinking about intercultural encounters.[1]

The previous chapters have examined the different interweaving threads that go into the making of a common European home: the historical struggles for integration, the institutional solutions proposed, the platitudes and attitudes of governing elites and concerned citizens, the public's national antipathies and biases, the power of ethnic stereotypes and auto-types. Some of the clearest insights into and truths about weaving a common home are lent, paradoxically, by writers of fiction. They bring into relief a country's—and at times even a continent's—partialities, phobias, and premises through the fictional characters they create. Employing different literary devices, novelists relate the reality around them and deconstruct what its values seem to be.

Let us recall the two epistemological approaches to the study of culture today. The first, positing the presence of a metaculture, seeks organic unity and coherence in its subject. This top-down approach may play an important ideological role in multiethnic societies, prescribing a unifying culture and sense of a common political home in conditions of ethnic, religious, and cultural diversity. Many EU leaders see their jobs as presenting synthesizing metanarratives about transnationalism. They highlight the shared

European essentialism supposedly found across all member states. Meta-narratives generally possess more of a prescriptive than ontological character.

The second approach is the recognition that cultures are invariably de-centered, fragmented, and polyvocal. The focus is on the particularistic rather than the holistic. Because there are many contending voices, under-standings of the political home and the sense of belonging to it are con-tested by different groups, never more than when a majority culture asserts its hegemonic claim on an identity. Polyvocality can be best appreciated in the narratives spun by a nation's cultural producers and re-producers. They adopt a bottom-up approach and articulate nationalized and sometimes ethnicized views of Europe. While some voice support for the Europe-building project, others are pessimistic that national phobias can ever be transcended.

This chapter considers voices from old and new Europe that address the question of whether Europe's diversity can ever give way to effective unity. The writers whose work we examine are concerned with interrogating their national and European identities. They also share a concern for under-standing how belonging is constructed in their societies.

At the outset we need to recognize that many contemporary European writers—and especially those in the east—reject the notion of cultural bor-ders. Introducing the notion of the existence of a central Europe—an idea less politically divisive and therefore less contested—is an assertion that Eu-ropean nations cannot be neatly compartmentalized into west and east. No one has championed the view of a distinctive central Europe more than Mi-lan Kundera, a writer from Prague who left for Paris after the Soviet inva-sion of Czechoslovakia in 1968. Let us review his arguments for positing a central European home.

To begin with, Kundera believed in the possibility of a transnational Eu-ropean culture precisely because of its fragmented makeup: "cultural diver-sity is the great European value." He added: "I formulated my own ideal of Europe thus: *maximum diversity in minimum space.*"[2] Oddly, many other parts of the globe would insist on the same ideal, and we can debate whether the African continent or the Asian subcontinent are not markedly more diverse than Europe.

The Czech writer conceptualized Europe's progress towards transnation-alism as a foot race: "the history of each European art (painting, the novel, music, and so on) seems like a relay race in which the various nations pass the baton from one to the next." He described how the success of the Eng-lish novel of the eighteenth century was followed in turn by that of the French, Russian, and Scandinavian novels of the nineteenth.[3]

Kundera always advocated central Europe's uniqueness because he be-lieved that it is the principal site of Europe's synthesizing forces. By contrast, he was dismissive of categories like old and new Europe. Central Europe cannot be reduced to *Mitteleuropa*, which Kundera ridiculed as a perspective from Vienna and the Habsburg days. Central Europe is essentially polycentric: "while there is a *linguistic* unity among the Slavic nations, there is no Slavic *culture*, no Slavic *world*." Polish, Czech, Slovene, Croat, and Hungarian history "is entirely Western: Gothic, Renaissance, Baroque; close contact with the Germanic world; the struggle of Catholicism against the Reformation. Never anything to do with Russia, which was far off, another world. Only the Poles lived in direct relation with Russia—a relation much like a death struggle."[4]

Central Europe's vitality has rested in its music, not in the great novel. But it shares with France a literary tradition condemning kitsch. Emerging in mid-nineteenth-century Munich, "Kitsch long ago became a very precise concept in Central Europe, where it represents *the supreme aesthetic evil*." But in France, too, there is no greater scorn than for the *vulgaire*, for *vulgarité*.[5]

In turn, provincialism is easy to condemn but hard to overcome. Kundera asked: "How to define 'provincialism?' As the inability (or the refusal) to see one's own culture in *the large context*." The provincialism of the large nation is seeing its own literature as sufficiently rich as to not be interested in others. Small nations have a reverse logic for being provincial: "they hold world culture in high esteem but feel it to be something alien, a sky above their heads, distant, inaccessible, an ideal reality with little connection to their national literature."[6] Nevertheless, cultural forces can be powerful and contagious and can negotiate political boundaries, even those that were drawn in the communist era.

Kundera's explanation for the rise of political dissent in the Soviet bloc is not one most political scientists or historians would have formulated: "the Prague Spring began eight years before 1968, with the Ionesco plays that were staged at the little Theatre on the Balustrade."[7] It is not surprising, therefore, that he follows Goethe in proclaiming that "we are entering the era of *Weltliteratur*."[8]

Hungarian writer Péter Nádas adopted a more sanguine view about the speed with which cultural change occurs: "it does not take just ten years— it takes well over two hundred to change a nation's most singular characteristics."[9] He employed the metaphor of being on the road, on a train, "in transition between 'East' and 'West' in a geographic and cultural sense."[10] His mapping exercise—one of several drawn by novelists examined in this chapter—assumes textual rather than political borders. At the same time, there is recognition that instead of overcoming this divide, the process of Europeanization can lead to the subalternization of non-Western cultures.[11] Under this scenario, new Europe would become old Europe's colonies.

One of the most cynical depictions of central Europe offered in recent years was by William Vollmann, an American novelist who wrote many lengthy books on many different countries and periods of world history.

His misnamed novel, *Europe Central*, is a fictionalized study of the German-Russian front in World War II. Personages like the poet Anna Akhmatova, the anti-Bolshevik general Andrei Vlasov, and the composer Dmitri Shostakovich—none of whom thought of themselves as central Europeans—make appearances.

In one of the few references to central Europe, Vollmann colorfully observed that "Europe Central's not a nest of countries at all, but a blank zone of black icons and gold-rimmed clocks whose accidental, endlessly contested territorial divisions (essentially old walls from Roman times) can be overwritten as we like, Gauleiters and commissars blanching them down to grey dotted lines of permeability convenient to police troops."[12] The stereotype of the divided region's pathologies, phobias, hatreds, and violence is reproduced.

From its vulnerability and weakness, Vollmann imputed guilt to central Europe. He inquired, ironically: "What once impelled millions of manned and unmanned bullets into motion? You say *Germany*. They say *Russia*. It certainly couldn't have been Europe herself, much less Europe Central, who's always such a good docile girl. I repeat: Europe's a mild heifer, a plump virgin, an R-maiden or P-girl ripe for loving, an angel, a submissive prize. Europe is Lisca Malbran. Europe's never burned a witch or laid hands on a Jew!" He added that "Europe's watchful since she's already been raped so many times. . . . Europe feels all, bears all."[13] Put differently, rape victims bear responsibility for their victimhood and central Europe has gotten what it deserved.

Most of today's writers from the other Europe—the new one that has emerged from a totalitarian past—would strongly disagree with the American novelist's negative stereotyping of the region. Some of these writers might also grudgingly agree with Andrew Wachtel's assertion that after the Promethean struggle against communism in which the literary intelligentsia played a vanguard role, "Lucky is the people whose literature need no longer be universally relevant."[14] Let us consider the work of one of the most eloquent and persuasive voices from new Europe—a Romanian who repudiated the premise that the continent could still be divided into two cultural parts and instead insisted on the universalist character of new writing from new Europe.

THE EUROPEAN EXPANSES OF MIRCEA CĂRTĂRESCU

"My writing is my only motherland. I could be Portuguese or Estonian or Swiss. I could be a woman or a Hellene or a Barbarian."[15] This statement furnishes an example of the new transnationalism rising up in the Balkans—a region all too often associated with ancient hatreds and ethnic cleansings. Writer Mircea Cărtărescu is a leading representative of Romania's so-called Eighties Generation. He has argued that the nation as a geographical and political organism is a burdensome legacy. It had been aggressively policed by the former communist regime, by other regimes before it, and today it serves as a handy tool for compartmentalization by elites whose interests are served by it.

For Cărtărescu, it was time to contextualize the national self as part of a vaster geography—cultural and psychological tracks that run parallel to EU and NATO integration. In order "to step across the borders into an ampler ensemble, one must first break the mold of inherited national self-representation—and thus break with certain prescriptions of collective identity."[16]

The novelist emphasizes that the Iron Curtain defined not only geopolitics but also mindset. The curtain was removed but "even now, Europe is not united and this will not change in the foreseeable future, not even when all the nation-states in the would-be 'East' have become officially integrated into that equally fantastic notion of the 'West.'" Cărtărescu draws on Samuel Huntington's clash of civilizations thesis. Huntington "saw Europe as split along the borders between opposing Christian beliefs, Protestant, Catholic, and Orthodox" and consequently he only partly understood the reason for disunity.[17]

The Romanian writer contends that Europe's division is engrained in the mindset of western Europeans. The equations they make are: "Western, Central and Eastern Europe. Civilization, neurosis and chaos. Affluence, culture and chaos. Rationality, subconscious awareness and chaos."[18]

Writers from the east have been told: "Remain in your designated ghetto and write away on your typically southeastern European stories. Write about your *Securitate* and that dictator of yours, Ceaușescu, and his People's Palace. Put in something about the feral dogs, the street kids and the Gypsies. Proudly demonstrate what a brave dissident you were during the communist era. We will deal with happiness and agony and ecstasy."[19]

At least with respect to Gypsies, Cărtărescu has done just that. But he has put the blame on Romanians themselves for relegating the Roma to poverty and delinquency by enslaving them. "Over the course of centuries the Roma could be bought and sold, families were torn apart, children separated from their mothers, women from their menfolk, young women were regularly raped by their owners, and the so-called 'crow-scum' was the target of widespread contempt and discrimination. . . . Tied to localities and kept like animals, the gypsies in the Romanian principalities multiplied faster than anywhere else in Europe. So we created the gypsy problem ourselves. This is our historical responsibility."[20]

This admission still did not justify old European stereotyping of Romania as a site of darkness. If proof were needed of Cărtărescu's invective against stereotyping, the 2007 International Film Festival in Cannes furnished it. The festival's Palme d'Or was awarded to a Romanian film, *4 Months, 3 Weeks and 2 Days*—described as "an unsparing yet humane look at life during the dictatorship of Nicolae Ceauşescu."[21] And the main award given by a sidebar to the main competition went to *California Dreamin'*—a film by a young Romanian director killed in a car crash, which was set in Romania during the Kosovo War of 1999. One movie critic from the region inveighed: "This is exactly what people in the West expect to see as a picture of the Balkans and Eastern Europe, a stereotype."[22]

Unlike Nádas, Cărtărescu does not acknowledge even textual borders. The brain "is a ridged and deeply grooved organ, but nowhere has it stone walls or iron curtains. It knows no borders."[23] He adamantly rejects post–Cold War balkanization and fragmentation and opts instead for a view of Europe as relational rather than unitary.

Box 7.1. Europe Has the Shape of a Brain
"I do not believe we, Easterners, have been lobotomized by propaganda and you, Westerners, no less, by commercials. I do not believe you are more hard-working than me because you are Protestant, as much as I do not believe I am closer to God than you because I am an Orthodox Christian. No matter how painful, unjust, and reckless history may be, I think we should not help it cook up differences between one human being and another where there are no differences at all or blow these distinctions out of proportion where they do exist. No, the 'Easterner,' as long as the person is educated, tolerant, open-minded, is nothing unlike the Westerner (as long as this one is also educated, tolerant, and so on), regardless of what they have experienced in the past. No wall keeps them apart 'inherently.'"

Source: Mircea Cărtărescu, *Pururi tînăr, înfăflurat in pixeli*, 201–2. Translated by Christian Moraru, "Beyond the Nation: Mircea Cărtărescu's Europeanism and Cosmopolitanism," *World Literature Today* (July–August 2006), 43.

As a postcommunist cosmopolitan, he, too, claims to embody a part of Europeanness and even of Whitman-like multitudes. "My generation was born free, and its language was the Occident's own from day one. This very language . . . is our most precious common treasure, yours, my dear Western reader, and mine. The similarities between us, not what makes us different—that is what I find important . . . . Once we have agreed on these similarities, we will have plenty of time to tease out the differences."[24]

Christian Moraru, a specialist on Romanian postmodernism and Cărtărescu, was drawn to the following conclusion: "In the postcommunist era, the ongoing hegemony of the nationalist model and East European ethnic strife, in particular, have consolidated in the West a set of assumptions about what the East European writer should be like. Based on them, according to Cărtărescu, a new division is about to replace previous walls and curtains and threatens to muffle his voice, put new constraints on what he can be, and prevent others from seeing who he truly is."[25]

Cărtărescu is concerned that a new othering of eastern Europe that is convenient for the west is taking place. The region is "seen as completely determined by past and present history, hence spatially and culturally outside 'true,' forward-moving Europe." Artists here are expected "to convey their 'uniqueness' from a position of radical alterity, in idiomatic rhetorics of sectarian resentment, necessarily 'bearing witness' to communist-era unspeakable pain, and so forth."[26] In short, for a writer from the region to gain recognition in the west, she or he must refer to the barbarian characteristics—xenophobia, pogroms, senseless killing, and wars—that set this world apart.[27]

Moraru reviews the ascribed status of writers from the region: "Milan Kundera, Milorad Pavić, Péter Esterházy, Danilo Kiš, Ismail Kadare, Joseph Brodsky, and the like are supposed to 'speak for' and come, as Philip Roth notes, from this 'other Europe.' Following as they are in the footsteps of Kafka and Nabokov, Bulgakov and Pasternak, they nevertheless continue to be quarantined—with the possible exception of Kundera—on Europe's troubled fringes."[28] In highlighting Cărtărescu's pioneering cosmopolitan project, Moraru skewered the west's depiction of "Eastern Europe and East Europeans as one big freak show; former communist countries' literature as a cultural safari in Europe's irrevocable other."

Cărtărescu rejects "the fetish of this other, projected from the outside—and its quasi-Orientalist colonizing by images and constructions that do little justice to what this other means." There can be no cosmopolitan reconstruction of Europe "if East European identity in general and Romanian identity in particular continue to be measured by the yardstick of touristlike expectations. In effect, the reinscription of difference, of different national bodies and identities into the nation's body politic, and, ultimately, the nation's genuinely European 'integration' itself require a critique of this neosegregationist mindset."[29]

Andrei Codrescu, a Romanian poet living in the United States for several decades, implicitly recognizes the existence of borders, but *within* new Europe. Writers from central—as opposed to eastern—Europe found it relatively easy to find translators of their works into English. Czech and Polish politics gave a sense of urgency to disseminating works by Kundera, for example. By contrast, "The suspicion of Romania as a land of beastly antisemites and talented but shady writers was not helped by the addition in the last two decades of superagile but crazy gymnasts, vampires, orphans, child prostitutes, and wild dogs. Having missed a historical opportunity during the Cold War, Romanian writers found themselves associated with a multitude of old and new sins." In his introduction to Cărtărescu's *Nostalgia*, Codrescu appeals: "Perhaps now is the time for the last Europeans to put in their two cents, hard earned, I might add, through communist censorship, Western neglect, and postcommunist disinterest."[30]

So we have to realize that what applies to writers also applies to entire cultures. Moraru avers that

> Inside its borders, Europe must take in its Eastern hinterlands and thus expunge the cultural 'ghettos' of unexamined 'clichés' that East European writers are supposed to corroborate. Likewise, it must open itself up to others outside it and thus give itself 'absolutely necessary new blood.' Insofar as East/West 'mentality' barriers are still in place, Cărtărescu disavows Europe's 'geopolitical, cultural, or religious' division. His dream is a 'diverse,' not a 'schizophrenic' Europe, cut up in zones that do not communicate and itself a zone cut off from the rest of the world.[31]

Nostalgia is the only novel by Cărtărescu to be published in English—supporting Codrescu's position that there is no real market for the Romanian novel. It is a kaleidoscopic narrative charting his partly real, partly imagined personal history under communist rule.[32] To a degree, he enacts the role of communist bloc victim which, as he subsequently recognized, was exactly what the west demanded of him. Summarizing the shift of perspectives in his later writings to European cosmopolitan, Moraru emphasized Cărtărescu's distaste with "an old-style, Cold War sort of cartography," and "clichés and presumptions that skew Western representations of Eastern Europe." Moraru was bewildered why, "By and large, we have cast aside this questionable approach of broad brushstrokes and hard-and-fast binaries in other, formerly colonial zones; here, however, things appear to be changing at a slower pace. While a few Central and East European writers have been making inroads, we still perceive them as a fairly undifferentiated bunch—once more a 'bloc'—and lump them together as Europe's (our) 'others,' 'out there,' hopelessly hemmed in by squabbles, styles, and frames of reference of clannish relevance."[33]

In *Nostalgia*, Cărtărescu drew attention to the fact that the world's problems are not reducible to the problem of borders, othering, and hierarchies. As he has a student warn in his Borgesian work, "We're headed toward catastrophe, sir! The arms race, sir! Growing hatred, sir! Suspicion, paranoia! The apocalypse is nearly here, my friend!"[34] The main threats to the world transcend the nation-state. This warning lends support, therefore, to the political process promoted by the Lisbon Treaty that aims at boosting a common EU security policy, even if Cărtărescu did not say so himself.

HOME FOR MAKINE: FROM THE
ATLANTIC TO BEYOND THE URALS

Ever since his first novel, *Dreams of My Russian Summers* (the French title is *Le testament francais*) was published in 1995, critics have debated whether Andreï Makine is really a French or a Russian writer. Born and educated in Siberia, he arrived in Paris in 1987 seeking asylum before the breakup of the Soviet Union. Still in his twenties, he had few material possessions and no support network to launch a career in France.

He did have knowledge of the French language, however, which was to serve him well. As a child in Siberia, French had been Makine's "grandma-ternal tongue."[35] Proficiency in this foreign language "made a dreamer of him."[36] As a reviewer of his first novel put it, "Dreams of France are an old Russian tradition."[37] Makine is a French and Russian romantic at the same time.

The *sans papiers* immigrant is a much-discussed figure in contemporary French society. His best shot at remaining in France is to destroy any personal documents, which might identify him as a citizen of another country to which he could be deported. The French, with a tradition of rus-sophilism, were not about to send Makine back to Soviet Russia, in particular because he had brought with him an extraordinary talent for writing prose—and in French. The most repeated story told about this master storyteller is that he had quickly to compose a Russian-language draft of his first novel *after* he had submitted the original French-language manuscript to a publisher. Only the existence of a Russian-language draft could establish the authenticity of his voice.

Makine's debut on the Parisian literary scene was spectacular. He achieved the unprecedented honor of winning two of France's top literary awards (Prix Goncourt and Prix Médicis) in the same year, 1995. Back in Russia, however, the literary establishment, slow to shed its rigid hierarchical mentality even after the disappearance of the Soviet Writers' Union, refused to recognize Makine as a Russian novelist in exile. "He writes about us but does not speak to us"[38] was the most grudging acknowledgement he could expect in his native country. Tatyana Tolstoya, herself a Russian writer living in the United States, contended that he was "Russian, but he is not a Russian writer." She labeled him "a philological halfbreed, a cultural hybrid, a linguistic chimera, a literary basilisk."[39]

All of his novels and a collection of essays have dealt with Russian and French identities.[40] In *Dreams of My Russian Summers*, for example, the narrator and his sister leave the USSR each summer for the mythical land of "France-Atlantis." This country is a romantic construction of the mind of the narrator's grandmother. The novel is that rare love story about grandmother and grandson, an ode to the Russian *babushka*.

Charlotte's birth in France, her adolescence in that country, and the memento from her first lover—a brown pebble, souvenir from the battle of Verdun—make her an untypical Russian *babushka*. Among her earliest memories of France of the Belle Epoque was of Proust playing tennis—it is impossible to imagine a more profound Frenchness than this image. While in Russia in 1921 to find her mother, Charlotte becomes trapped by revolution and war.

Even though she lives in a town on the edge of the steppe, each night Charlotte takes a journey to the Paris of long ago, telling tales that the children then russify: "The president of the Republic was bound to have something Stalinesque about him in the portrait sketched by our imagination. Neuilly was peopled with kolkhozniks. And the slow emergence of Paris from the waters evoked a very Russian emotion—that of fleeting relief after one more historic cataclysm."[41]

We gain further insight into Makine's interrogation of hybrid identity in the novel *Once Upon the River Love*.[42] Its bittersweet nostalgia results from the story having a more remote Russian setting and a more pervasive Western theme. In it the symbol of a pendulum is employed to describe the pull of two worlds.

One of the three Siberian boys who are the novel's protagonists recalls how "The pendulum kept the measure of passing time . . . . Ever since our childhood, however, the pendulum seemed to have stuck. It was as if its immense weight had become entangled in the innumerable lines of barbed-wire fencing stretched across its path."[43] The Soviet Union's imminent collapse is also depicted by this metaphor: "It was swinging more and more freely, and now its movement back and forth across the immense empire was becoming threatening."[44] The primary significance Makine ascribed to the pendulum was as a marker of a cultural divide, a clash of civilizations.

The Western world is brought home to the boys living in the Siberian village through the movies. It is again French culture that opens up the world to parochial eyes. A film starring Jean-Paul Belmondo captivates the villagers. The character played by Belmondo has his way with women: "We saw a strength that took pride in itself with no thought for the result; the gleam of muscles that were not concerned to break productivity records. . . . From now on we had a name for this marvelous 'in itself:' Western World."[45] The political power of the West, exerted by way of an action movie, evokes awe. "Belmondo settled in, established his headquarters at the Red October, just halfway between the squat building of the local militia and KGB and the Communard factory, where they manufactured the barbed wire that went to all the camps in that region of Siberia."[46]

Makine is a prolific writer. *L'amour humain* (Human love), published in 2006, was his tenth novel in about as many years.[47] We observe changes in the author's concern with identities. The fusion of French and Russian romanticism gives way to a fundamentally cynical, even intolerant, view of racial relations; race features more in the book than nationality. It may be that Makine's values have changed in step with those of French society—the mass market that has lapped up his work.

For the first time the main setting is not Russia or France but Africa. The principal character, Elias, is an idealistic Angolan freedom fighter engaged in the bitter struggle to drive the Portuguese colonialists out. He is an *assimilado*, "which signifies, he learns pretty quickly, that he, a black hardly different from an ape, could one day gain entrance into the world of the whites."[48]

The narrator is a decades-long friend of Elias who recounts the twists and turns in Elias' life. But he lashes out along the way against the smug bourgeois globalized societies of the post–Cold War era.

Makine's evocations of the sexual act have often been overwrought. But he reaches a new level of insensibility in depicting Western forms of exploitation today. A French woman attends a literary conference in Africa and ends up in bed with a trophy African male—a naïve native artist. Engaging in lovemaking does not deter her from simultaneously talking on the phone with her husband back in France. Makine's narrator overhears the goings-on in the next bedroom and debates whether to march in on the couple and moralize to the woman: "In this world there is a child who is six years old, this Delphinette, your daughter, who you will kiss, Madame, with those same lips that are sucking this erect black member."[49]

The West's liberal rhetoric irritates Makine. A 1960s *gauchiste* turned TV pundit warns in the novel that "if the French don't get back to work it will be the developing countries that will teach them liberalism."[50] The West's fetishization of globalization is a pathology that unleashes "the energy of thousands of men who crash into each other, plot with each other, who sell unfathomable riches, stow billions away in secret accounts, flatter their rivals and devour their partners, drag their countries into long years of war, starve entire regions, pay hordes of penpushers to eulogize their policies."[51]

The novel is an indictment of Western culture. It depicts an American eating a sixteen-ounce steak and associates this with U.S. foreign policy: "America uses all of its power to protect the right of this man to eat such a quantity of meat."[52] While Makine's novels usually say little about the United States, they consistently hint it is an uncouth nation.

No Makine novel is complete without a denunciation of Soviet society. This time, the author exposes the deep-seated racism of that system. On spotting the Angolan on a street in Moscow where he has come for political training, a Russian hooligan remarks to friends: "I told you, fuck, they forgot to lock the cages at the zoo."[53] Elias is beaten up by "Men for whom he was nothing but a monkey . . . such hatred in a country that was promising a world without hate."[54]

Racism figured in an earlier work and also implicated Russian attitudes. But arguably it also reflected an ardent Russian francophile's disillusion with contemporary multiethnic France. In *A Hero's Daughter*, first published in English in 2003, Makine describes a fictional Soviet reporter sent to Paris to interview people living near the Place de Stalingrad. His assignment was to ask what they knew about the decisive World War II battle in that city that gave the Parisian square its name. In the end, the journalist could not conduct any interviews because "nobody but Blacks and Arabs" lived in the area. Any recorded interviews would make the Soviet audience "think that we filmed this in Africa, not Paris."[55]

While the more xenophobic, racist texture of *l'Amour humaine* distinguishes it from the transnational desideratum of earlier novels, in common with them is the theme of love, as its simple title suggests. Makine narrates a touching, doomed love between Elias the *assimilado*, maligned while visiting the Soviet Union, and Anna, a Russian moving up in society who is his only source of comfort on that first visit. Love is symbolized in the orchid blooming in the snow outside a remote Siberian village where Elias and Anna briefly find happiness.

Makine is driven to the nonpolitical, nonethnicized conclusion that a person's life begins when "history, having exhausted its atrocities and promises, leaves us bare under the sky, to experience only the look of the one he loves."[56] The debate about Frenchness or Russianness has been left behind. In its place is this: "The sovereign truth of life—the certainty that the passing of a man who has loved does not mean the disappearance of the love that he carried within himself."

In 2006, Makine published a short collection of essays whose title can be translated as *This France that We Forget to Love*.[57] Over the space of ten novels, the author was engaged in tortured grappling about French and, to a steadily lessening degree, Russian national identity. The quotation on the jacket of *This France* reaffirms his concern with the subject but surprises with his admonition: "I wouldn't have written this book if I didn't believe deeply in France's vitality, its future, and the capacity of the French to say 'enough!'"[58] But, we can ask, enough of what?

France's greatest contribution to civilization, Makine affirmed, lies in its intellectual life. He twisted the question Stalin is said to have asked about the Vatican and writes: "'Voltaire? Proust? Camus? How many divisions do they have?'"[59] Immaterial divisions, Makine replies, but with a fighting spirit that matches all the world's military-industrial complexes.

Makine admires France for all the habitual reasons—the arts, the way of life, the gastronomy, fashion, chivalry, the affection for verbs. He cites from a letter written by Pushkin: "I want to speak to you in the language of Europe."[60] *Français, naturellement*. There is the French wine master who endearingly observes, "This is an intelligent wine. It wants us to talk about it."[61] Makine adores France because it is where the preference for the cerebral over the physiological, the artistic over the material, holds sway.

It is no surprise, then, that he decries the reduction of French to just one of the many vernacular languages of Europe. But it is the shackles of political correctness that above all he cannot tolerate. He describes the disconnect between official multicultural propaganda celebrating *black-blanc-beur* [black-white-Arab] and the private attitudes of the French. The same doublespeak and collective schizophrenia exist here as in the former Soviet Union, he observes. France is becoming unloved because of the existence of taboo subjects, the absence of real public debate on issues of identity, the erosion of free speech, the censorship by "professional anti-racists."[62]

Box 7.2. Multiple Problems
"There have been decades of lies about France as multicultural paradise—multiracial, multi-denominational, multi-what? Multi-everything. Too many lies and now the sovereign reality explodes in front of our eyes."

Source: Andreï Makine, *Cette France qu'on oublie d'aimer* (Paris: Flammarion, 2006), 97.

Part of this reality is France's *proxénétisme* or what this book has termed xenophilia—the affection for all things foreign—which has forced the state to negotiate with leaders of street gangs engaged in violent disturbances, to tolerate drug traffickers, to recognize the wealth accumulated by car thieves, to excuse the behavior of *les jeunes des banlieues*. For Makine, the lyrics of one rap song (presumably sung by an Arab) sum up the rallying cry of angry immigrant youth and senselessness of the xenophilic approach: "I'll fuck France until she loves me."[63]

The responsibility for this degradation of France's stature lies less with immigrant groups and more with *français-français* (this hyphenated term is actually now used to refer to ethnic French). "France is hated because the French have allowed it to be emptied of its substance, permitted it to be transformed into a simple populated territory, a little corner of a globalized Eurasia."[64]

The response to Makine can be, of course, to point to the French national soccer team that all French love. *Black-blanc-beur* has made France into a winning side—everyone boasts—notwithstanding the injustice of the ethnically pure Italian side winning the 2006 World Cup.

The fate of the *français-français* National Rugby XV—one which Makine would presumably embrace—might also suggest that homogeneity leads to failure. The team with which France won the 2007 Six Nations Championship contained no player in the forty-man squad with an Arabic name. But at the 2007 Rugby World Cup, hosted by France, the French XV finished in fourth place—a poor result considering how few rugby-playing nations there are. Yet the composition of that side was more in keeping with Makine's ethnic imaginary as well as the Frenchness that National Front leader Jean-Marie Le Pen espoused.

But it was not just Le Pen anymore who expressed anti-foreigner sentiments. In the runoff to the 2007 presidential elections, both candidates appealed to the French-French vote. Winner Nicolas Sarkozy proudly pointed to his record as interior minister when he was responsible for expelling tens of thousands of illegal immigrants from France. In 2005, he had attacked the "scum" living in ethnic Arab and Muslim neighborhoods who took part in three weeks of violent protests about living conditions. His electoral promise was to establish a ministry of immigration and national identity that would oversee the propagation of French secular values among all immigrants.

Socialist candidate Ségolène Royal also emphasized the need to return to traditional French identity. Instead of direct broadsides against France's minorities—oops, officially France does not have any—she called on all residents to memorize the words to *La Marseillaise* and to publicly display the French flag on Bastille Day.

Makine's narratives on the topics of the West, national and transnational identity, xenophobia, and racism have reflected more general trends found in one particular country of old Europe. The romanticized notion of intercultural understanding and advancement, which permeated his most famous novel, has been replaced with a soured depiction of France's troubled multiethnic society. It is a sign of the times, a reflection of Europe's Zeitgeist.

IDENTITY LOSS IN EUROPE: DUBRAVKA UGREŠIĆ

Dubravka Ugrešić, born and educated in Croatia when it was a part of socialist Yugoslavia, became labeled a public enemy in Croatia when the Balkan wars broke out in the 1990s. As individual republics separated from the Yugoslav federation, she had taken an unpopular position against nationalism and war; she even advocated neutrality in the Croatian-Serb conflict. These views were unpopular with her compatriots because Croatia was successfully parlaying nationalism and war to win its independence.

Ugrešić was branded a traitor and a witch. To understand the reasons for such invective, it is enough to read what Croatian nationalist writer Slobodan Novak was writing after the 1995 expulsion of Serbs from the country. "Croatia is cleansing itself of Yugo-unitarist and Great-Serb rubbish which had been spread all over it for a whole century."[65] Repulsed by the misoxenic discourse of Croatian cultural and political elites, Ugrešić had already departed for Amsterdam two years earlier. There, when she returned to writing, she faced criticism that she was exploiting her exile for literary gain.

In *The Ministry of Pain*, her most reflective novel about the migration experience, Ugrešić described the conscious effort she made to mete out the pain of war in small doses. Tanja, her alter ego, teaches languages in Amsterdam. Her students, who include refugees from Yugoslavia, learn how memory and language can help them cope and heal. They had "changed their names, given and sur; they bought cheap passports when they could. What had till recently meant everything to them—their faith, their nationality—was suddenly worthless currency. Survival took over."[66] In a collection of essays, *The Culture of Lies*, Ugrešić expanded on this theme: "The citizens of former Yugoslavia suddenly found themselves in the situation of having two biographies and one life."[67]

After the homeland disappears, identity is the next to go. Tanja catches herself fumbling for an identity in Amsterdam: "I overuse the personal pronoun *ik*. For the time being *ik* doesn't commit me to anything."[68]

Ugrešić's life seemed to her to be that of a modern-day Gypsy. Told by a little girl selling roses in an Antwerp restaurant that "I'm Yugoslav, a Gypsy," Ugrešić unearths the irony: "The Yugoslav Gypsies who have scattered all over Europe are the only remaining Yugoslavs today, it seems, and the leftover ex-Yugoslavs have in the meantime become homeless, exiles, refugees, countryless, excommunicated, new nomads, in a word—Gypsies."[69]

Living in Holland does not stem identity loss: "Flat, wet, nondescript as it is, Holland has one unique feature: it's a country of forgetting, a country without pain. People turn into amphibians here. Of their own accord. They turn the color of sand; they blend in and die out. Like fucking amphibians. That's all they care about: dying out. The Dutch lowlands are one big blotter: it sucks up everything—memories, pain, *all that crap*."[70]

What, then, is the identity that Ugrešić struggles to affirm? She rejects the notion of exile. "'Exile is a neurosis, an art of paranoia. . . . That's why we always have to be sure that we have an adaptor with us. So that we don't burn ourselves.'"[71]

She rules out other labels. "I myself am neither an émigré nor a refugee nor an asylum-seeker. I am a writer who at one point decided not to live in her own country anymore because her country was no longer hers."[72]

The "national" identity Ugrešić claims—in fact it really had always been a supranational one—had officially become nonexistent. "I felt Yugoslav, and that's how I described myself in my identity documents: a citizen of Yugoslavia, mixed, anational, unspecified, nationally indifferent."[73] She realizes, however, that she has lost control over her identity: "I am not and do not wish to be different. My difference and my identity are doggedly determined by others. Those *at home* and these *outside.*"[74]

To cling to the identity of a country that has imploded needs explication. How can pan-Yugoslavism be justified when it disintegrated so quickly? Ugrešić turns to realpolitik for the answer. "Yugoslavia was *a prison of nations,* they say." Accordingly, "Having established that Yugoslavia was a big lie, the Great Manipulators and their well-equipped teams (composed of writers, journalists, sociologists, psychiatrists, philosophers, political scientists, and . . . generals!) began the process of dismantling the *big lie.* At first it was easy, they accused the communist regime of every evil (of manipulating the people!)."[75] They replaced ideological formulae of brotherhood and unity with democracy and Europeanization.

Decommunization was a prelude to engineering the collapse of Yugoslavia.[76] "The Great Manipulators, *transformers,* dismantled the old system and built a new one out of the *same* pieces! And then they stopped to rest from their work and suddenly noticed that the country was still whole." So they went further. "And they set about dismantling the country . . . . the Great Manipulators and their teams offered the most effective formula, a new Utopia; the nation. But in order to awaken the dormant national consciousness, it was necessary quickly to establish differences: in what way were we different, that is, better, than them."[77]

Here was the process that led to the Balkan wars of the 1990s. "The *struggle for national identity* becomes acceptable in the newly established value system. It gives political legitimacy to war criminality, madness, hatred, collective and individual pathological behavior, pleasure in killing, profiteering, territorial ambitions, as well as to patriotism and the right to self-defense. So that the irony should be complete, the same notion has been used by both the stronger, who were conquering, and the weaker, who were defending themselves."[78]

Yet the author asks: "What is the point of newborn states, which, as their poetically disposed rulers like to say, *must be born in blood?*"[79] Moreover, their struggle for authenticity often leads these new states to adopt xenophobic practices: "The yes-sayers [to sincerity and authenticity] have chosen to live as authentically 'themselves,' with their authentically 'own kind,' having first cleansed the country of inauthentic elements: others, minorities, non-like thinkers and traitors."[80]

In one of her earlier books published in English, *The Museum of Unconditional Surrender,* Ugrešić described the type of xenophobia that would single out a Bulgarian girl for ridicule in a neighboring country: "the other little girls would often tease me, calling after me Bulgar (Bulgie! Bulgie!) with the same intonation that they would tease Gypsies (Gypsy! Gypsy!) when they went down our street. The words were pronounced in the same way and meant the same thing: someone else, someone who wasn't the same as them."[81]

National xenophobias are a subject that leads Ugrešić to theorize about what is western and what is eastern Europe. Coming from southeastern Europe, she early on learned to recognize its characteristics. "Before I was quite seven I would learn, like a blind person, the Braille of Eastern Europe . . . . I would recognize its east and its west, its north and its south."[82]

Box 7.3. Passport Control
"The EU people in the parallel queue enter quickly. I notice that none of them looks in our direction. There is not a single glance expressing sympathy, curiosity or, if nothing else, contempt. They have no time, the queue is moving too quickly. But we, others, have plenty of time to observe them. We are different, our skin is often dark, our eyes dart suspiciously about or stare dully straight ahead, our movements are sluggish and subdued. No one chats or laughs in our queue, we are quiet, there is something surreptitious about us. The tension of our bodies testifies that we have only one thought in our heads: just to get across this frontier."

Source: Dubravka Ugrešić, *The Culture of Lies* (University Park: Pennsylvania State University Press, 1998), 237.

The fall of the wall resulted in a culture shock to those living in old Europe, who now discovered how insubstantial their differences with the easterners were. Ugrešić reflects: "all at once, instead of feeling sorry for the 'Easterners' (for whom things are always worse), I felt sorry for the 'Westerners,' seeing how flimsy were the foundations of their self-assurance: toilet paper, passport, hard currency." Westerners had discovered the east's "queues, the empty shops, the grey people, ugly everyday life. All at once, it seemed to me that the 'Westerners' needed that border, that symbolic roll of toilet paper as large and firm as the Great Wall of China . . . because it showed, if nothing else, that they belonged to a softer, more fragrant and cleaner world."[83]

An anxiety took hold among westerners that resembled the fear of waiting for the barbarians: "And our Westerner feels a kind of discomfort (*What if Eastern Europe moves here, to me?*), loss (*Where are the frontiers? Is the whole world going to be the same?*), slight contempt (*Oh, couldn't they think of anything better to do than resemble us?*), self-pity (*When I took them jeans, they liked me!*)."[84]

For their part, easterners invariably exercised a defensive, roundabout logic when affirming European identity: "All in all, the *Easterner* did not doubt that he was a European, but his language gave him away. He never said 'We Europeans' but always 'Europe and us.' The *Easterner* lived in the mousetrap of that traumatic paradox, without being aware of either the mousetrap or the trauma or the paradox."[85]

The psychology of the cultural border plays on subtleties: "If an East European says that he wants to 'go to Europe' and insists that he is its inhabitant with equal rights, on the whole he is thinking of himself in 'Western Europe' and not of the European in himself."[86]

Borders, therefore, play a critical role in constructing identity even as they may appear to be disappearing: "the new European self-identity reemerged, in an almost textbook fashion, as a *derivative of the boundary*."[87]

Like Kundera and Cărtărescu, Ugrešić is concerned with the identity and role of the writer in old and new Europe. Writers need to be given a national label, she complains. They are like participants in the Eurovision Song Contest. It is "the hottest point of mental unification of Europe" where viewers learn about new countries, hear each national culture rendered in a kitschy way, and even discuss the nonparticipant: "The Serbs will never sing in Europe, not in a million years!"[88]

As with performers in the Eurovision Song Contest—Ireland was represented in 2008 by a puppet turkey—writers, too, are associated with a particular state and given an identity tag that is to function as a shorthand interpretation of the text. Ugrešić writes that applying its ideology of multiculturalism, "the cultural bureaucracy of the EU perpetuates its well-tried formula—*Me Tarzan, you Jane*—that is, the formula of recognizing different cultural identities."[89]

The author expresses her resentment at the appeal that this formula has. "Behind every writer stands his homeland. Invitations to literary gatherings with the names of the participants resemble lists of competitors in the Olympics: there is always the name of a country in parentheses. Only once did I see the word *transnational* in parentheses after the name of a writer and I immediately envied him."[90] Ugrešić makes her own position clear: "I refuse to be a writer of 'my nation.'"[91]

Or of "my new Europe," she could have added. The author worries about western expectations of art in the east that lead, for example, to award-winning Romanian films about dictatorship and war. Citing a counterexample—an "eastern European" novel, *Porcupine*, written by an English author, Julian Barnes[92]—Ugrešić inquires: "as we seek for the 'Easternness of East European culture, will we be unconsciously dealing in assumptions from an East European mindset constructed by 'Westerners,' or the cultural reality which was, after all, built up by 'Easterners' in the course of their socialist years?"[93]

The west's double standards are apparent: "East European writers do not live in the West, unless they have to. An American writer in Berlin, a German writer in Ireland, a Dutch writer in Portugal—all of them live the life which is expected from people of their profession. A Romanian writer living in Paris, without a clear political reason, is *suspect.*"[94]

In other words, the west demands an identity of the easterner. Living in exile "it is easy to perform anti-nationalism, but difficult to remain a-national. Even Western Europe will not tolerate the nationally indifferent: the proud West European ideology of multiculturalism wants declared ethnic cultural identities in order to generously grant them the freedom of self-realization."[95]

Bundling Yugoslavs and other peoples of the Balkans into the category of eastern Europe—or of new Europe as Rumsfeld did—demonstrated the arbitrary approach of the west's identity construction. "And then those 'Westerners,' always ready to invent marketable political labels, had suddenly discovered *Eastern Europe* and shoved him there with the Romanians and Bulgarians. The Romanians!"[96]

Box 7.4. The Peoples of Eastern Europe
"Precisely because they did not fight out their freedom for themselves, their values, which in large part had served a strategy of national and individual survival, overnight became useless, if they did not look like shameful collaboration. For precisely this reason a not inconsiderable portion of this society really did experience the dropping of freedom into their lap as a collapse. And when their arms were stretched out for support towards the democracies of western Europe, all they got was a brisk handshake and an encouraging clap on the shoulder. Western Europe couldn't make up its mind what to do with its eastern neighbors, while looked at from the other side, this was taken to be a sign of arrogance, which sent the poor relations into a sulk. The winning of freedom came not so much with a release of the spirit of regeneration as, far more, that of the bad past, of *ressentiment*, in the form of a national frenzy at the reopening of age-old national wounds that degenerated to murder and genocide or, elsewhere, into a more restrained nationalism in a democratic mask."

Source: Imre Kertész, "Europe's Oppressive Legacy" (keynote speech at the conference on Perspective Europe, Academy of Arts in Berlin, June 1, 2007), http://www.signandsight.com/features/1382.html.

Does Ugrešić, then, observe any evidence of the appearance of a transnationalism transcending borders in Europe? She does, and it comes in both negative and positive forms.

She narrates a scene set in Lisbon. "In his *gastarbeiter's* German, the taxi driver outlined his notion of life as work and order. And were it not for those million 'niggers' from Angola, who, incidentally, bred 'like rabbits,' were it not for Gypsies, Romanians, Russians, Poles and Yugoslavs, that East European scum which had learned nothing from communism except to avoid work, steal, get involved in petty crime and gorge themselves for nothing on Portuguese bread, life in Portugal would be quite satisfactory."[97]

Alongside transnational xenophobia is the division of labor in Europe that produces bizarre results. "The Pakistani standing in the place where the [Berlin] wall stood a short time ago selling cheap souvenirs [Russian fur hats with a red star, sickles, and hammers] of a vanished epoch is perhaps the most precise and condensed metaphor of the times in which we are living."[98]

Finally, there is the ideal of a cosmopolitan identity of the future. Referring to the children of Tomás and Tereza, characters in Kundera's *The Unbearable Lightness of Being*, Tanja, the protagonist of *The Ministry of Pain*, says enviously: "They will have multiple identities: they will be cosmopolitan, global, multicultural, nationalistic, ethnic, and diasporic all in one. They will wear any number of hats and be flexible in the extreme, ever ready to define and refine themselves, construct and deconstruct themselves."[99]

PLAYS ABOUT EMIGRÉS IN NEW AND OLD EUROPE

A particularly effective literary genre in depicting relations between far-away locals and people in a host society is the theater. The sense of belonging and the process of othering—both of which are emotional and psychological structures—can be captured in a concrete and palpable way on stage whereas written narrations may make them intangible.

An eastern European classic addressing this topic is Polish playwright Sławomir Mrożek's *The Emigrants*. Directed by Andrzej Wajda, the legendary film director, it premiered in a Warsaw theater in 1976 at a time when many Poles were, for the first time under communism, able to leave the country to work—usually illegally—in Western countries, then return with savings that made them rich back home.

The play features two characters: an intellectual and a peasant-worker from an unnamed far-away nation living together in a decrepit rented flat in a foreign country. The dialogue captures the hopes and fears of two men from very different social classes, brought together by their sense of belonging to a common home, by their living in a country alien to both of them, by their shared fear of an external power, and by their common realization that their personal identities were in flux. At the same time, their class differences cannot be transcended and keep them at a distance from each other. The educated emigrant mocks the crude tastes of his rural companion, for example, the sense of belonging he derives at the bus terminal: "And there everything is just right for you. First of all, the entrance is free. Secondly, there you are no longer a stranger. There are no strangers at a station, precisely because it has been made for strangers. At such a station your foreign ways are completely at home. In fact, at an international bus terminal, it's the locals who look like foreigners."[100]

More recently, the theme of emigration was resurrected by Polish theater director Krzysztof Warlikowski. His production of Israeli writer Hanokh Levin's *Kroum*, staged during the 2005 summer theater season in Avignon, was widely acclaimed.[101] The story concerns a man returning to his home country after a long trip abroad. Dressed in a cowboy hat and pulling a suitcase on wheels behind him, he arrives in his house in a dank quarter of Tel Aviv—a district that could be anywhere in Europe, or elsewhere.

Kroum is reunited with his mother, but he has an admission to make. "Mama, I haven't succeeded. I haven't found fortune or happiness abroad. I haven't progressed an inch, I didn't haven't fun, didn't marry, didn't even get engaged. I didn't meet a soul. I didn't buy anything and didn't bring anything back. There's only dirty laundry and toiletries in my suitcase."

Born in Tel Aviv, the playwright Levin is a descendent of a well-known line of Hassidic rabbis from Poland. His satirical writings have often had Israel as a target, including how it was transformed following its victorious 1967 Six-Day War. *Kroum* confronts the loss of meaning and identity in a globalized world where individuals roam about striving for social advancement. Home is where they are fixed in a social hierarchy, with few prospects of upward mobility.

Thematically similar to *Kroum* is Ariane Mnouchkine's "pageant of the uprooted"—*Le Dernier Caravansérail (Odyssées)*.[102] The title is meant to be ironic: *caravansérail* comes from a Persian word meaning palace or the spacious place where caravans put up to rest. Mnouchkine's odyssey is a testimonial to the new existential nomads who wander the world looking for landfall which they can call home.

The six-hour saga is told in two parts and in sixty-two scenes. Set in detention camps in France, Australia, New Zealand, and Indonesia, the story is interpreted by thirty-six actors on stage. For Mnouchkine, a French avantgarde stage director who improvised the piece from narratives collected from refugees between 1999 and 2002, these thirty-six actors represent the twelve million people trapped in the ghost life of detention centers and legal limbo around the world. "I hope the audience will follow our wanderings as we followed yours," Mnouchkine implores in the *Übertitel* that opens part two. Wandering and unknowing are the experiences of the asylum seekers, and they are the tropes of this sprawling production. Through the caprice of history, émigrés find themselves with no rights, no voice, no place.

The first scene in *Le Dernier Caravansérail* is of refugees trying to cross a raging river between Kyrgyzstan and Kazakhstan. They are hoisted over the torrent in a wicker basket whose rope and pulley are operated by a smuggler. The wind roars and the refugees' shouts are muffled. The actors rappel horizontally across the stage. They slip, they struggle. A woman hesitates, then plunges into the current before she is hauled back up into the bobbing basket. One man is not so lucky: he is swept away. While upstage the audience sees him disappear in a swell, downstage we witness a drama being acted out about payment to a human smuggler.

The image of water symbolizes the danger, bravery, desperation, and grueling physical and emotional costs of exodus. When, finally, the asylum seekers are safely on the other side, they trade insults with the smuggler: "Kyrgyz bastards! You race of dogs!" And the reply: "Kazakh bastard . . . ! Stop moving across my country."

Theater in both new and old Europe describes the aspirations and desperation of populations moving across the world's borders. For all the talk about globalization, the plays we have described underscore the individual's own small struggle to be part of the process.

Other themes have attracted the attention of European playwights. One persisting topic is of national self-loathing. Czech-born British playwright Tom Stoppard set his trilogy, *The Coast of Utopia*, in Russia of the 1830s. Featuring an imaginary debate among the great characters of the time, the play anticipates the questions that still haunt European identity today. Peter Chaadaev, the philosopher, asks about Russia: "How did we come to be the Caliban of Europe?"[103] Vissarion Belinsky, the literary critic, summarizes a manuscript he has been reading: "it's all about how backward Russia is compared with Europe . . . the *rest* of Europe, sorry."[104] The great anarchist Michael Bakunin expresses his frustration about rebellion in tsarist-governed Congress Poland: "Poland is simply impossible."[105] Stoppard gives us a clear and concise summing up of the longstanding antipathies in the east of Europe. However home is constructed—Kundera and Cărtărescu's insistent transnational one, Makine and Ugrešić's tenuous hybrid one, or playwrights' agonizing hierarchical one—there is always an inner tension involving who belongs to it. Whether from the perspective of Eurocrats, Eurocitizens, or European writers, constructing home is the process of negotiating competing hostilities.

NOTES

1. I have borrowed these ideas from Muhammad Siddiq, *Arab Culture and the Novel: Genre, Identity and Agency in Egyptian Fiction* (London: Routledge, 2007).

2. Milan Kundera, "Die Weltliteratur," *New Yorker* (January 8, 2007), 28.

3. Kundera, "Die Weltliteratur," 28.

4. Kundera, "Die Weltliteratur," 32.

5. Kundera, "Die Weltliteratur," 34.

6. Kundera, "Die Weltliteratur," 30.

7. Kundera, "Die Weltliteratur," 31.

8. Kundera, "Die Weltliteratur," 29.

9. Péter Nádas, "Training Practices of Freedom" (2001, in Hungarian) quoted in Attila Melegh, *On the East-West Slope: Globalization, Nationalism, Racism and Discourses on Central and Eastern Europe* (Budapest: Central European University Press, 2006), 11.

10. Melegh, *On the East-West Slope*, 15.

11. Melegh, *On the East-West Slope*, 30.

12. William T. Vollmann, *Europe Central* (London: Penguin Books, 2005), 4.

13. Vollmann, *Europe Central*, 9.

14. Andrew Baruch Wachtel, *Remaining Relevant after Communism: The Role of the Writer in Eastern Europe.* (Chicago: University of Chicago Press, 2006), 219.

15. Mircea Cărtărescu, "Europe Has the Shape of My Brain," in *Writing Europe: What is European about the Literatures of Europe?* eds. Ursula Keller and Ilma Rakusa (Budapest: Central European University Press, 2004), 64.

16. Christian Moraru, "Beyond the Nation: Mircea Cărtărescu's Europeanism and Cosmopolitanism," *World Literature Today*, July–August 2006, 41.

17. Cărtărescu, "Europe Has the Shape of My Brain," 62.

18. Cărtărescu, "Europe Has the Shape of My Brain," 63.

19. Cărtărescu, "Europe Has the Shape of My Brain," 63.

20. Cărtărescu, quoted in *Neue Zürcher Zeitung*, November 29, 2007.

21. Manohla Dargis and A. O. Scott, "Romania Rules at Cannes Film Festival," *International Herald Tribune*, May 27, 2007.

22. One comment made to the Internet Movie Database, June 17, 2007, www.imdb.com/title/tt0449573/.

23. Cărtărescu, "Europe Has the Shape of My Brain," 66.

24. Moraru, "Beyond the Nation," 43.

25. Moraru, "Beyond the Nation," 42.

26. Moraru, "Beyond the Nation," 42.

27. The barbarian motif is never explicitly employed by old Europe about new. But the sense of immanent threat and siege resembles the atmosphere depicted in J.M. Coetzee, *Waiting for the Barbarians* (New York: Vintage, 2004), first published in 1980.

28. Moraru, "Beyond the Nation," 43.

29. Moraru, "Beyond the Nation," 43.

30. Andrei Codrescu, introduction to Mircea Cărtărescu, *Nostalgia* (New York: New Directions, 2005), xi.

31. Moraru, "Beyond the Nation," 44.

32. Mircea Cărtărescu, *Nostalgia* (New York: New Directions, 2005).

33. Moraru, "Beyond the Nation," 42–43.

34. Cărtărescu, *Nostalgia*, 261–62.

35. Quoted in Natasha Fairweather, "A 'Frenchman's' Tale from the Russian Steppe," *St. Petersburg Times*, June 2–8, 1997.

36. Fairweather, "A 'Frenchman's' Tale from the Russian Steppe."

37. Tatyana Tolstoya, "Love Story," *New York Review of Books*, November 30, 1997.

38. Fairweather, "A 'Frenchman's' Tale from the Russian Steppe."

39. Tatyana Tolstoya, "Russkii chelovek na randevu," *Znamia* no. 6 (1998).

40. For a review of his first five novels, see Ray Taras, "À la recherche du pays perdu: Andreï Makine's Russia," *East European Quarterly* 34, no. 1 (March 2000), 51–79.

41. Andreï Makine, *Dreams of My Russian Summers* (New York: Touchstone, 1998).

42. Andreï Makine, *Once Upon the River Love* (New York: Arcade Publishing, 1998). First published in French as *Au temps du fleuve amour* (Paris: Le Felin, 1994). Its publication predated *Le testament français*. There is a pun on the word *amour* because it is pronounced the same way as one of Siberia's four great rivers, the Amur.

43. Makine, *Once Upon the River Love*, 12.

44. Makine, *Once Upon the River Love*, 207.

45. Makine, *Once Upon the River Love*, 98.

46. Makine, *Once Upon the River Love*, 127.

47. Andreï Makine, *L'amour humain* (Paris: Éditions du Seuil, 2006).

48. Makine, *L'amour humain*, 60.

49. Makine, *L'amour humain*, 29.

50. Makine, *L'amour humain*, 217.

51. Makine, *L'amour humain*, 227.

52. Makine, *L'amour humain*, 119.

53. Makine, *L'amour humain*, 133.

54. Makine, *L'amour humain*, 140.

55. Andreï Makine, *La fille d'un heros de l'Union sovietique* (Paris: Folio, 1996), 75. It was first published in French in 1990. The English version is *A Hero's Daughter* (New York: Sceptre Books, 2005).

56. Makine, *L'amour humain*, 236.

57. Andreï Makine, *Cette France qu'on oublie d'aimer* (Paris: Flammarion, 2006).

58. Makine, *Cette France qu'on oublie d'aimer*, back cover.

59. Makine, *Cette France qu'on oublie d'aimer*, 31.

60. Makine, *Cette France qu'on oublie d'aimer*, 60.

61. Makine, *Cette France qu'on oublie d'aimer*, 44.

62. Makine, *Cette France qu'on oublie d'aimer*.

63. Makine, *Cette France qu'on oublie d'aimer*, 98.

64. Makine, *Cette France qu'on oublie d'aimer*, 99.

65. Quoted in Dubravka Ugrešić, *The Culture of Lies* (University Park: Pennsylvania State University Press, 1998), 64.
66. Dubravka Ugrešić, *The Ministry of Pain* (New York: Harper Perennial, 2007), 16.
67. Ugrešić, *The Culture of Lies*, 227.
68. Ugrešić, *The Ministry of Pain*, 247.
69. Ugrešić, *The Culture of Lies*, 7.
70. Ugrešić, *The Ministry of Pain*, 207.
71. Dubravka Ugrešić, *The Museum of Unconditional Surrender* (London: Phoenix, 1998), 119.
72. Dubravka Ugrešić, *Thank You for Not Reading: Essays on Literary Trivia* (Normal, IL: Dalkey Archive Press, 2003), 130.
73. Ugrešić, *The Culture of Lies*, 269.
74. Ugrešić, *The Culture of Lies*, 237.
75. Ugrešić, *The Culture of Lies*, 108, 39.
76. For a similar view taking an international relations approach to the collapse of Yugoslavia, see Ray Taras and Rajat Ganguly, *Understanding Ethnic Conflict: The International Dimension* (New York: Longman, 2008), 247–60.
77. Ugrešić, *The Culture of Lies*, 39–40.
78. Ugrešić, *The Culture of Lies*, 193.
79. Ugrešić, *Thank You for Not Reading*, 99.
80. Ugrešić, *Thank You for Not Reading*, 68.
81. Ugrešić, *The Museum of Unconditional Surrender*, 134–35.
82. Ugrešić, *The Museum of Unconditional Surrender*, 135.
83. Ugrešić, *The Culture of Lies*, 173–74.
84. Ugrešić, *The Culture of Lies*, 241.
85. Ugrešić, *The Culture of Lies*, 242.
86. Ugrešić, *The Culture of Lies*, 171.
87. Bauman, *Life in Fragments*, 244. Quoted in Ugrešić, *The Culture of Lies*, 244.
88. Dubravka Ugrešić, "European Literature as a Eurovision Song Contest," in *Writing Europe: What is European about the Literatures of Europe?* eds. Ursula Keller and Ilma Rakusa (Budapest: Central European University Press, 2004), 327.
89. Ugrešić, "European Literature as a Eurovision Song Contest," 332.
90. Ugrešić, *Thank You for Not Reading*, 140.
91. Ugrešić, *The Culture of Lies*, 272.
92. Julian Barnes, *The Porcupine* (New York: Alfred Knopf, 1992).
93. Ugrešić, *The Culture of Lies*, 158
94. Ugrešić, *Thank You for Not Reading*, 135.
95. Ugrešić, *Thank You for Not Reading*, 137.
96. Ugrešić, *The Culture of Lies*, 35.
97. Ugrešić, *The Museum of Unconditional Surrender*, 162.
98. Ugrešić, *The Culture of Lies*, 158
99. Ugrešić, *The Ministry of Pain*, 135. Milan Kundera, *The Unbearable Lightness of Being* (New York: Harper Perennial, 1999).
100. Sławomir Mrożek, *The Emigrants* (London: Samuel French In., 1984), 11.

101. Fabienne Darge, "Kroum," *Le Monde*, July 23, 2005.

102. From a review by John Lahr, "The New Nomads," *New Yorker*, January 8, 2005. The Théâtre du Soleil's production ran at the Lincoln Center Festival until August 2005.

103. Tom Stoppard, *The Coast of Utopia: Part I Voyage* (New York: Grove Press, 2002), 82.

104. Stoppard, *The Coast of Utopia: Part I*, 30.

105. Stoppard, *The Coast of Utopia: Part I*, 13.

8

Narrating Europe's Phobias

HOW THE EAST WAS TO BE CIVILIZED

Are xenophobia and racism perched on an east-west slope, with eastern Europe on the top with its many smoldering antipathies and phobias, and the west lower down with its civic, inclusive, cosmopolitan approach to interethnic relations? Some authors in the east are defensive about it and if they acknowledge that such a slope exists, they say it exists in the minds of western leaders and publics.

The author who proposed the slope idea highlighted how it was based on xenophobic attitudes, not differing levels of economic development. Accordingly, "racism is linked to different positionings on the East-West slope." Specifically, racism is a sign of being non-European and 'Eastern,' which are traits that must be left behind in order to enter the 'West.'"[1]

To put eastern Europe's racism behind it, EU conditionality put the Amsterdam Treaty's minority rights framework on the agenda for the region.[2] The east's xenophobias were to be combated—under western eyes. So the French began to champion the rights of the Roma of eastern Europe, in this way interchanging racist roles: as surely as the Czechs looked down on the Gypsies, the French would look down on the Czechs. An unintended consequence of old Europe's patronizing approach was an eastern backlash that engendered more frequent ethnic-based conflicts. The "power arrangements of the 'Eastern enlargement', or 'Westernization,' . . . per se leads to the rise of 'Eastern' racism."[3]

In *Imagining the Balkans*, historian Maria Todorova contended that the region plays an indispensable role as foil for western Europe. "As in the case

of the Orient, the Balkans have served as a repository of negative characteristics against which a positive and self-congratulatory image of the 'European' and the 'West' has been constructed."⁴ Differences between old Europe and the Balkans do not involve just contrasting norms of tolerance
and inclusion; eastern Europeans are portrayed as the lower classes, "a virtual parallel between the East End of London and the East End of Europe."⁵

When Bulgaria and Romania formally joined the EU in 2007, the BBC
provided the basic background about the two Balkan states' cultures to its
listeners and readers.⁶ In Bulgarian marketplaces, cafes, and bars, the BBC
reported, *chalga* music will be blaring out of stereos. "This vibrant, heady
mixture of traditional Balkan folk music with Roma (gypsy), Turkish and
Arab influences is highly popular. But it is sometimes frowned upon for its
scantily-clad female singers and appeal to 'low class people.'" The best
known exponent of *chalga* was flamboyant, cross-dressing male vocalist
Azis, who represented Bulgaria at the 2006 Eurovision Song Contest.

The BBC tried to be just as illuminating and discerning about Romania's
pop culture. Its musical phenomenon was Cleopatra Stratan—age three:
"this diminutive talent dominated the charts recently with her song Ghita
and has already recorded an album. The daughter of singer Pavel Stratan is
said to have been discovered when she performed at his recording sessions."

The most popular Romanian TV show was "Surprize, Surprize." According to the BBC, "Its tearful reunions are interspersed with regular appearances by *bebelusele*—female dancing girls [sic]—which are a common feature on numerous Romanian TV programs." The country's most popular
comedy show was *Cronica Carcotasilor* ("The Fault Finder's Chronicle"),
which lampooned political leaders and celebrities. "This program also has
a coterie of female dancers who perform between sketches."

The news from Britain was not so upbeat for potential job seekers from
Bulgaria and Romania. One report summed up their situation. "When the
two countries joined the European Union in January, Britain capped the
number of low-skilled workers it would admit to 20,000, despite offering
an open door to migrants from new EU states such as Poland three years
ago."⁷ If over 600,000 eastern Europeans had come to Britain following the
2004 EU enlargement, only 40,000 Bulgarians and Romanians were expected to arrive in 2007.

To be sure, one report suggested that it was not anti-Balkan discrimination but a skill set not fitted to the British labor market that may have kept
the numbers low: "Rather than the plumbers and builders many expected,
the top profession listed by Romanians is 'circus artiste.' Most Bulgarians
claim to have worked as chefs or carers while musician, researcher and ho-
tel worker also make the cut."⁸

Has Britain interchanged racist roles with the Bulgarians and Romanians? Are the stereotypes popularized of these nations in the UK a mirror image of Balkan stereotypes of their Roma populations? Can we really talk about a descending xenophobic slope from east to west, or does it simply exist in the western popular imagination?

Introspection into orientalism—the generally negative features of the east that give it definition—should not be carried out exclusively from a Western vantage point. Accordingly, the first two writers we examine in this chapter come from Turkey and Albania, though they have settled in Germany and France. In their novels, they reveal the oriental phobias and demons that have not been destroyed.

PARANOIA IN ISMAIL KADARE'S BALKANS

For a long time, Albanian writer Ismail Kadare was largely unknown in the English-speaking world. The author of many gripping novels set in Albania and other Balkan nations, Kadare found that getting his books into English involved a circuitous path: first out of Albanian into French, then out of French into English. Was there really no one capable or willing to translate his books into English directly out of the Albanian? Kadare must have savored those times. It added to the exotism of his works, and of the esoteric Balkan cultures he evoked.

Under Albania's Stalinist-governed system, Kadare was never a dissident and he never claimed to be one subsequently, when he moved to Paris in 1990 as the communist world disintegrated. Few of his books could be read as veiled critiques of the hardline Albanian leadership. If anything, he may have enjoyed a privileged relationship with the country's longtime strongman, Enver Hoxha, in particular as they came from the same small village.

Despite the lack of dissident credentials that would have catapulted him high in Western literary circles, what established Kadare's reputation was the extraordinary quality of his writing and storytelling. Literary critics who followed his career began to think of him as a potential Nobel Prize winner. In 2005, he was awarded the next best thing: the Mann Booker International Prize for the full body of his work. He was commended by the three-person jury as "a universal writer in a tradition of storytelling that goes back to Homer."[9]

Running through many of his novels is the theme of a small nation besieged by outside forces. The paranoia that results and the conflicts that are entered into are facts not to be underestimated. The part played by the Slavs and the Turks as the country's historic Other is deftly analyzed in his works. Kadare understands Albanian identity as primordial, rooted in history,

ethnicity, and culture. There can hardly be an identity in Europe less like a
transnational European identity than Albania's traditional one, founded on
long-established oaths, codes, blood feuds, and ancient rituals impervious
to modern times.

Arguably the most nationalistic of his novels is *The File on H.*, first published in Albania in 1981 in the last years of Hoxha's paranoiac dictatorship.[10] In it, Kadare seemed to amplify the anti-Slav, anti-Serb campaign
that permeated Hoxha's rabid national communism. While dismissing nationalism's "absurd and morbid passions," the author embraces Albania's
national interests, especially in opposition to the Slavs who had invaded
the Balkan peninsula—towards the end of the sixth century! Islam had not
yet started on its conquest of Italy and Spain because it did not yet exist.

> It seemed the Slav tide would never stop; unlike the Roman invasion, the con-
> quest was achieved without armies, flags, or treaties. It must have been an un-
> ending straggle of women and children moving forward to the muddled
> sounds of yelling and squalling, a cohort obeying no orders, leaving no mile-
> stones or monuments, more like a natural disaster than a military invasion. . . .
> All of a sudden they were in the midst of a Slavic sea: a gray, unending, anony-
> mous Eurasian mass that could easily destroy all the treasures of a land where
> art had flourished more than anywhere else on earth.[11]

Many of Kadare's books highlight how ancient a culture Albania is, having roots in the Illyrian civilization of classical antiquity. The barbarian Slav
invasions threatened Albanian culture. An important identity marker became, then, the Albanian contribution to Homeric verse. Kadare outlines
the context. "For more than a thousand years, Albanians and Slavs had been
in ceaseless conflict in this area. They had quarreled over everything—over
land, over boundaries, over pastures and watering holes—and it would have
been entirely unsurprising had they also disputed the ownership of local
rainbows." But the dispute did not end there. "[T]hey also squabbled over
the ancient epics, which existed, just to make things completely intractable,
in both languages, Albanian and Serbo-Croatian. Each of the two peoples
asserted that it had created the epic, leaving the other nation the choice of
being considered either a thief or a mere imitator."[12]

The File on H.—for Homer—follows the work of two foreign scholars
studying the Greek bard who are inserted into this conflict. "Slav chauvin-
ists" attack the scholars because "Any mention of the Illyrian origins of the
Albanians, in particular, arouses in them barbaric and murderous jeal-
ousy."[13] Set in the most inaccessible backward parts of Europe of the 1980s,
the story seems surreal until we realize that Kadare's purpose is indeed to
capture the historic and irrational paranoias and hatreds of the region. The
novel describes how an Albanian newspaper article simplistically concluded that Serb-Albanian hostility was so intractable "no dialogue was

possible between two peoples whose names derived, on the one hand, from the word for 'snake' and, on the other, from the word meaning 'eagle.'"[14]

Kadare's obsessions are those of an ethnographer. He believes in the power of a local self-regulating culture to perpetuate itself and maintain its hold on all aspects of public and private life. In the Albania before 1990, he had the perfect laboratory.

Doruntine is a simple tale of medieval folklore, set around the twelfth century and therefore good material for an anthropological study. It also again juxtaposes Albania with the Slavic world. A small Albanian town's police officer, Stres, is asked to investigate the veracity of a ghost story. Constantine, one of nine brothers who had died three years earlier, had apparently risen from the dead to bring his sister, Doruntine, back home from a foreign land. Or at least that was how it had seemed: neither Doruntine herself nor anyone else could be sure that the mysterious horseman who brought her home was really her brother.

The marriage to the foreigner had been opposed by Doruntine's mother and the eight other brothers. By contrast, "Constantine believed that far-off marriages, hitherto the privilege of kings and princesses, should become common practice for all. The distance between the families of bride and groom was in fact a token of dignity and strength of character."[15] Constantine appears to be a precocious Albanian transnationalist.

But there may have been more to Constantine's acceptance of the marriage with the foreigner. Perhaps he was in love himself with his sister and preferred she be married to a foreigner so that he would not be constantly reminded of her if she had stayed close to home. If Constantine was driven by an incestuous love of his sister, was the horseback ride home their honeymoon? Or was encouraging her to go far away a premonition Constantine had that many deaths were about to visit the family and he wanted to save her life?

About her three years in Bohemia, Doruntine herself lamented: "I lived in the most awful solitude."[16] But was that reason enough for her to want to return home? "What young woman would want to return to a house that was more ruin than home and on which, it was said, the seal of death had been fixed?"[17] Perhaps "She returned to close the circle of death, that's all."[18]

Stres is unable to come up with any evidence to contradict the story that Doruntine was brought home by a mysterious horseman who may well have been her brother. But the police officer faces pressure from all around to discredit the ghost story. The local Catholic official tells him that he will face dire consequences if he does not make short work of the idea that a man was resurrected; Constantine had no right to ape Jesus Christ and be resurrected from the dead.

Kadare launches into a description of the power struggle in the Balkans between different religions. "The struggle between Catholicism and Orthodoxy

since time immemorial had greatly weakened religion in the Albanian principalities" and Constantine's resurrection could trigger a civil war.[19] Was
Constantine's return from the grave, therefore, generated by "the intrigues
and rivalry of the world's two major religions?"

The news had even reached Constantinople and the emperor. Its significance had multiplied.

> It was not a simple case of a ghostly apparition, nor even one of those typical
> calumnies that the Church had always punished with the stake and always
> would. No, this was far more serious, something that, may God protect us, was
> shaking the Orthodox religion to its foundations. It concerned the coming of
> a new messiah . . . for if one believed that someone today had succeeded in do-
> ing what Jesus had done in His time, then it was but one small step to admit-
> ting—may God preserve us!—that this someone else may be His rival.[20]

Albania was in a bind. It would have to devise new ways of defending itself from "'external' laws and institutions, structures eternal and universal,"
as were found in Constantinople. Frustrated by how elusive truth is, Stres
decides that local culture must triumph over the threat of religious persecution. He therefore proclaims the power of the *Bessa*—a type of social contract among Albanians cemented through kept promises and uncompro-
mising honesty. The authority of the *Bessa*, Kadare tells us, transcends any
form of religious authority.[21]

Another novel set in medieval times is *The Three-Arched Bridge*. Published
in Albania in 1978, it too is a paean to Albanian culture as it faces external
threat, this time from the Turks. In 1377, the country of Arberia, or
Shqipëria—"a community of eagles"—as it had recently become known,
got a new neighbor. The Ottoman Empire had replaced the Greeks on the
country's eastern frontier. This spoiled the historic symmetry of the area, for
the Arberian population, along with the ancient Greeks, were the oldest
people in the Balkans. The Ottomans were parvenus as surely as the Slavs
were. "The Slavs, who have recently become so embittered, as often happens with newcomers, arrived from the steppes of the east no more than
three or four centuries ago."[22]

The new imperial neighbor inspired awe in the Albanians. The narrator
reflects: "Since the Ottoman state became our neighbor, I do not look at the
moon as before, especially when it is a crescent. No empire has so far chosen a more masterful symbol for its flag. When Byzantium chose the eagle,
this was indeed superior to the Roman wolf, but now the new empire has
chosen an emblem that rises far higher in the skies than any bird."[23]

Turkish expansion had followed Slav and Byzantine encroachment into
the Balkans. The region's population scrambled to preserve its autonomy
and identity as its borders were penetrated: "The famous 'Arbanon Line' of
seven fortresses from Shkodër to Lezhë, which defended Byzantium from

the Slavs, was crumbling. Byzantium itself had lost its vigor. The Balkan nobles—Albanians, Croats, Greeks, Serbs, Romanians, Macedonians, and Slovenes—sent their couriers sometimes to Venice and sometimes to Turkey, and sometimes in both directions simultaneously, to choose the lesser of the two dangers."[24]

The Turks had coined the term Balkans to describe the region they were conquering. Not all of the local population resisted the pressure of assimilation. Ottoman emissaries had been "buying up the great western highway that had once been called the Via Egnatia and was now called the Road of the Balkans, after the name the Turks have recently given to the entire peninsula, which comes from the word *mountain*. More than by the desire of the Ottomans to cover under one name the countries and peoples of the peninsula, as if subsequently to devour them more easily, I was amazed by our readiness to accept the new name."[25]

Box 8.1. Turks are Appearing Everywhere
"Sometimes they turn up as political or commercial envoys, sometimes as trade missions, sometimes as wandering groups of musicians, adherents of religious sects, military units, or solitary eccentrics. . . . There is something deceitful in their smiles and courtesy. It is no accident that their silken garments, turbans, breeches, and robes have no straight lines, corners, hems, or seams. Their whole costume is insubstantial, and cut so that it changes its shape continually. . . . But after all, how can straightforwardness be expected from a people who hide their very origins: their women?"

Source: Ismail Kadare, *The Three-Arched Bridge* (New York: Arcade, 1997), 46.

The main character in *The Three-Arched Bridge* is an Albanian monk who chronicles the construction of a bridge spanning a river whose name in Turkish means wicked waters. What starts out as a project that looks like ordinary capitalist competition—a bridge company hoping to steal the ferryman's business—turns out to be something much more. A state-of-the-art, intricately designed structure meant to put the "Boats and Rafts" company out of business ends with medieval conquest and death.

What are the intentions of the bridge builders and who is behind them? Is the bridge meant to breach? Or to confine? Is it supposed to bring cultures together? If so, no such links are forged in the story. Is it designed to facilitate Turkish expansion? The monk refers to the Turkish Great Royal Commination, whose rules of war require that a curse—in this case it may be the bridge—be placed on the target first—which is Europe.[26]

No one is sure, but the deceptions and self-deceptions, and with them the quarrels, multiply as the bridge is under construction. It becomes itself the target of sabotage, but the man carrying it out becomes immured within one of the arches. Is this a sacrifice or merely an ordinary crime? In the end, delirium, superstition, and madness become pervasive. The bridge may be the sign of progress, but the wicked waters it spans seem to have won out after all.

A skirmish takes place on the bridge. One Turk is killed and the Albanian narrator explains the makings of orientalism: "We had seen their Asiatic costume. We had heard their music. Now we were seeing their blood . . . the only thing they had in common with us."[27] Soon after, "I saw Ottoman hordes flattening the world and creating in its place the land of Islam. I saw the fires and the ash and the scorched remains of men and their chronicles."[28]

The monk's mind is overwhelmed by stories about the Ottoman hordes. He hears of how the Emperor of Byzantium ordered the eyes of an entire Bulgarian army put out, then sent the blinded soldiers stumbling home.[29] The Turks' language, their music ("hashish dissolved in the air in the form of song"), their garments ("among such diaphanous folds it is hard to tell whether a hand is holding a knife or a flower"), all seem sinister and deeply threatening. "Bad news continues to come from the east, as Byzantium crumbles and carts loaded with barrels of pitch move down the western highway. 'As soon as tar begins to move fast along the highways, you know that blood will flow after it.'"[30]

The Three-Arched Bridge conveys a gloomy symbolism when compared to Bosnian Nobel laureate Ivo Andric's *Bridge on the Drina*.[31] Kadare's metaphor of the bridge is different from the image of bridges found on euro coinage. It does not lead to the "happy end" that the massive span across the Öresund, opened in 2002 to link Copenhagen with Malmö in Sweden, seeks to achieve. Instead, for the Albanian author bridges—like transnationalism—pose a threat to an ancient culture.

Bridges are a means to impose rules from outsiders on an old culture. Kadare may be advising us that a culture is best off when faithful to its own unique rules. These rules are most evocatively summarized in *Broken April*.[32] Set on the high plateau of northern Albania, blood feuds are a way of life and are strictly governed by the *Kanun*, a comprehensive set of guidelines to regulate everything in life. Revenge killings are common, but the institution of the *Bessa* (or oath) may provide a temporary or spatial refuge from being killed. On the high plateau, there is a steward of the blood who collects death taxes. It is in his interest to ensure that blood feuds continue.

Stereotyping and heterotyping characterize *General of the Dead Army*, a story about an Italian general who, twenty years after the end of World War II, travels to Albania to recover the remains of his soldiers. His army had been defeated and disgraced in the war and the general resents the Albanian victors: they are paranoid, beastly, truculent, "these Albanians . . . You would never believe that in battle they would turn into wild beasts."[33] The Italian priest who accompanies him adds: "Almost as soon as they are born someone puts a gun into their cradle, so that it shall become an integral part of their existence."

Kadare uses the bigoted comments of the priest and the general to highlight the stereotyping and xenophobia that survive war. But then the Italians come upon the cruelties carried out by their own compatriot, the venerated Colonel Z. The general becomes defensive about the Italian colonel's horrific actions: "I want to explain that all our officers don't shut themselves up in their tents with little girls of fourteen, neglecting their duties, and getting themselves killed for a woman."[34] But the Italian seems to make no such allowances for Albanians.

The author has written a number of books dealing explicitly with the politics that have affected his country. *The Concert*, for example, is a satirical examination of Hoxha's international relations as Albania steers from alliance with the USSR to alliance with Maoist China to, finally, being left to its own devices.[35]

In the Borges-like *The Palace of Dreams*, published in Albania in 1981 but immediately banned, a vast bureaucracy keeps track of the dreams of a police state's subjects. It represents a nightmare of totalitarianism in which government attempts to control the subconscious.

Set inside the labyrinthine Tabir Sarrail, the dreams of citizens living in a Balkan empire are collected, sorted, and interpreted. Why? "For in the nocturnal realm of sleep are to be found both the light and the darkness of humanity, its honey and its poison, its greatness and its vulnerability. All that is murky and harmful, or that will become so in a few years or centuries, makes its first appearance in men's dreams."[36]

The custodians of dreams are in search of the crucial Master-Dreams, those which may affect the security of the Empire and of the Sovereign. A Master-Dream, "with its significant omens, is sometimes more useful to the Sovereign than a whole army of soldiers or all his diplomats put together."[37]

One such dream had suggested that "all modern states, including the Ottoman Empire, were merely old, bloodthirsty institutions buried by time, only to return to earth as specters."[38] The Tabir's archives revealed that on the eve of the battle of Kosovo in 1389, around seven hundred dreams had anticipated the pivotal event.

This novel also describes the conflicts between clans in this imperial society. The protagonist, Mark-Alem, who is employed in the Palace of Dreams, is a member of the Quprili family. Its name means a three-arched bridge! It symbolizes the access that the clan provides between the worlds of dream and of reality.

The Sovereign, however, grows increasingly suspicious of the Quprilis. A Master-Dream is brought to his attention: "The Quprilis (the bridge), through their epic (the musical instrument), were engaged in some action against the State (the angry bull)."[39] Mark-Alem realizes that he has become a pawn in a dynastic struggle.

From this examination of his writings it becomes clear that Kadare is fixated on hierarchies, whether within a society—nobles, religious authorities, police chiefs, and commanders of blood feuds—or among nations. Albanians, as the descendants of Illyrians, are at the top of his list, if only because of faithfulness to ancient customs: "The very saying, 'I've nourished a snake in my bosom,' proved that the custom had once been quite widespread in Albania."[40] Turks but also Slavs are at the bottom.

In one novel, he even describes the literary hierarchy of a Moscow residence hall for writers. On the first floor lived first-year students who still had committed few literary sins. On the second were conformist dramatists, those who whitewashed everyday life. On the third were schematics, sycophants, and Slavophiles. The fourth housed women, liberals, those discontented with the socialist system. On the fifth were the slanderers and informers. And on the highest floor, with a view over Moscow, were "the denationalized—those who abandoned their languages and wrote in Russian."[41]

We conclude our analysis of Kadare's eastern world with his essay about Kosovo—for centuries an Albanian enclave in Serbia—published in 2000.[42] It serves as a reference point for the more general study of empires, conquests, identities, and phobias.

Kadare believes that in the distant past the Balkans could accommodate an extraordinary mix of peoples and cultures. "There were times when the peninsula seemed truly large, with enough space for everyone: for different languages and faiths, for a dozen peoples, states, kingdoms, and principalities—even for three empires."[43] But on the plains of Kosovo in 1389 "Torrents of Christian and Turkish blood mingled more forcefully than they would have in a thousand years of intermarriage."[44] Kadare has Sultan Murad I, victor at Kosovo, lament that the Balkans have attacked each other for the seven hundred years since the battle. "During my worst hours I am seized by the suspicion that maybe my blood [on the fields] is the origin of all this horror."[45]

The author acknowledges the internecine history of the Balkan peoples. It went well beyond the battle on the plains of Kosovo: "the princes in the big tent laughed at the songs, for the princes had come together to fight the Turks while the minstrels were still singing songs against one another, the Serbs cursing the Albanians and the Albanians the Serbs. And all the while, across the plain, the Turks were gathering to destroy them both the following day!"[46]

Eleven peoples made up the Balkan peninsula. The very name carried a stigma: "they would have to carry this new name, fossilized and ponderous, on their backs like a curse as they stumbled like a tortoise in its shell."[47] Europe was not much different but not fatally cursed: "Twenty-odd empires, a hundred different peoples. Some jammed against each other, others far apart. Which was Europe's true mass—constricted or distended?"[48]

But Kadare makes no apologies for the ethnic blood feuds that have punctuated Balkan history. Local cultures and their codes of conduct may have enabled much spilling of blood. But Kadare's assessment of one such code—the *Kanun*—is ambiguous. And it represents a source of fascination for him because it continues to this day to mark out the special identity that someone from the region possesses.

At the turn of the twenty-first century, even as the EU was codifying its liberal normative regime, Albania was returning to its ancient code of laws.[49] According to Kadare, the code would have died a natural death had it not been banned by the communist regime, which made it more appealing. Efforts were undertaken by various political institutions to eliminate it, without much success.[50] In *Spring Flowers, Spring Frost*, a more recent novel, one of his characters bawls: "'Vendettas are back! The terrible law of the *Kanun* has been restored!'"[51]

This led to an ironic twist. A boy sentenced to death for carrying out a revenge murder made a bizarre request: "that in this case the state would assume the role of the opposing clan's executioner. He was perfectly aware that in ordinary circumstances such a request would be considered insane. But in current conditions, with so many Albanian issues going to Brussels and Strasbourg and suchlike, and also more especially because the National Ferment Party was demanding that the ancient *Kanun* be incorporated into the revised penal code, everything was possible."[52]

Kadare seems to take a perverse pride in the notoriety and backwardness of the *Kanun* and the way it is a thorn in the side of the EU and Council of Europe. He relates a scene in which a foreign delegation—two Germans and a Dutchman—from the Council of Europe are taken to the northern Albanian plateau to learn about the ancient code. A revenge killing was about a single shot, a speaker proclaimed to applause from the local crowd. "'The *Kanun* does not allow the use of knives, axes, fire, or stone. Nor does it condone drowning, strangling, whipping, or the use of explosives.'" But there were restrictions even about the one shot. "'The Kalashnikov rifle, like everything that comes from the Slav, undermines the *Kanun*'" and is its "'number-one enemy.'"[53]

The phobias of the Balkans are as original as they can be deadly.

ÖZDAMAR'S LINGUISTIC HOMES EAST AND WEST

Emine Sevgi Özdamar was among the first wave of Turkish immigrants who made their way to Germany. Born in eastern Turkey, she was only nineteen when she arrived in the Federal Republic in 1965 to work in a factory. After two years, she returned home to take up theater, but after the Turkish military coup of 1971 she returned once again to Germany.

Özdamar became fluent in German, giving her the opportunity to be a writer as well as an actress in her adopted home. Her first novel published in English was *Mother Tongue*. Her work "aimed to capture an elaborate, multicolored snapshot of Turkish culture and migration experience" and to express "her longing for forgotten words and sounds of Turkish and Koranic Arabic."[54] Her identity is located both in the home country and the receiving society, both in the remnants of a mother tongue (Turkish) and a foreign tongue (German) that has become her native tongue. Not surprisingly, "'For Germans, I'm a Turk, for Arabs German.'"[55]

The author describes herself as a storyteller who narrates in German, "the language of my day-to-day experiences" and "the language of some five million *Gastarbeiters*."[56] In *Mother Tongue*, the narrator is told to explain what she is doing in her adopted country: "'What are you doing in Germany?' asked the girl. I said: 'I'm a word collector.'"[57] She lists all the Turkish and Arabic words that she has collected. In the afterword Özdamar writes: "We have no choice but to rebuild the tongue which we have lost with the tongue that we have found."[58]

One of the reasons for constructing a working language is practical. "The Turks spoke in their language with German words mixed in, words for which they had no others in Turkish: employment office, tax office, income-tax card, vocational school."[59]

Although xenophobia is not palpable in her novels, ethnic stereotypes abound. Mutual constructions of the Other are on the surface respectful but in reality absurd. A donkey and farmer are heading for "Alemania." The donkey says: "'Didn't you hear? It rains pearls in Germany.'"[60] A Turkish woman traveling to Germany tells her companions: "'I have seen their women. They iron and iron their hair. They sew up their bosoms every day or flop, let them hang down. Allah gave each of them an arse, but they only jiggle with it, zirr—zirr—zirr.'"[61] A Turkish man with his flock of sheep stands at the "Door to Germany" and warns a Turkish woman standing beside him: "'Woman, if you don't want to take the man's smelly cock in your mouth, then you should have cut off your legs and stayed at home.'"[62]

Apart from Turkish self-loathing and stereotyping, Özdamar draws a pastiche of the xenophilic German who prides himself in his knowledge about Turkish culture. But even the self-congratulating advocate of multiculturalism finds a way to be cutting while trying to be nice. The author elaborates: "along came a German, a lover of Turks" who talked incessantly about his friend who was Turkish. The German and his wife once stayed at the Turk's house. What did his wife and the Turk do? "They fucked and they fucked." Later the German tells some Turks he meets on the street: "In your country, you wash your arse with water after you have a crap, isn't that true? You see,

I know that . . . I also always wash mine here."[63] The absurdity of rote multicultural discourse is made evident.

Similar tropes are presented in Özdamar's *Life is a Caravanserai*, published in English in 2000. The novel describes a girl growing up in a rough social milieu in Turkey in the 1950s and 1960s before deciding to emigrate to Germany. There was a hurdle to leap in order to qualify for emigration to Germany: "In order to go to Germany you had to have medical tests, give urine samples, give blood samples, show your teeth." The narrator happily reported she had received her visa: "I had good urine. My path was clear."[64]

Prospective immigrants were given a "Handbook for Workers Going to Work Abroad." There was some plain but prescient advice for women: "In Europe you don't wear headscarves. If Turkish women wear headscarves, Europe will not love them."[65]

The images of Germany were favorable. Turkish women believed that "When you get your period in Germany, you don't have to work, you get those days off."[66] A Turkish woman remarked that "you'll find only cultured Turks there."[67] But the train bound for Germany carried almost all Turkish women, and they did not appear cultured. In a tone of self-parody, Özdamar writes: "It was a train of whores . . . . the train divided up into whores who combed their hair with men's semen and whores who spread men's semen on their bread and ate it."[68]

We can say, then, that the author fuels German perceptions of the Turkish "subordinated/subaltern pasts without ordaining these pasts with authenticity." Her focus is "neither the legend of the country of origin nor the lore of the country of residence but unevenly jointed bits of both."[69] This is not to say that she celebrates hybridity. In her works, hybridity, apart from allowing wordplay in different languages, is viewed as problematic and encumbering rather than purposeful and liberating.

Özdamar has written lyrically about her childhood on the border of Europe. Her parents had moved several times between the Asian and European sides of Istanbul. Whenever traveling to European Istanbul on business, her father would choose elegant trousers and a shirt the night before. "During the night the white of the shirt would shimmer before my eyes, and it seemed as if the trousers and the shirt were so excited about their forthcoming trip to Europe that they were unable to sleep."[70]

The author also recounts a time sunbathing topless on one of the islands near Istanbul. A motorboat suddenly passed by and one of the men remarked: "Today is a fine day for looking at European goods."[71] He assumed the sunbathing Turkish girl could not be anything but European.

Turkish Nobel Prize laureate Orhan Pamuk has captured the unique relationship Turks have with Europe. Twenty-four years after traveling to Europe the first time, Pamuk applied for a new passport in order to meet with his Turkish readers in Germany: "It was during that trip that I came to associate my passport with the sort of 'identity crisis' that has afflicted so many others in the years since then—that is, the question of how much we belong to the country of our first passport and how much we belong to the 'other countries' that it allows us to enter."[72]

SELF-LOATHING AND ANTIPATHIES
IN MASŁOWSKA'S POLAND

The fictional world of Dorota Masłowska is set in the Poland of capitalism without a human face. It is not a world marked by upward mobility, prosperity, overnight fortunes, country villas, or conspicuous consumerism. It consists instead of disempowered youth, junkies and alcoholics, wannabe rock musicians, racist skinheads, their vulgar language and uncouth habits, the bonds they forge with each other, and the dead ends they face in life.

Born in 1983 of Kashubian origin (Günter Grass's *The Tin Drum* is set among Kashubians), Masłowska was nineteen when she broke onto the Polish literary scene. Her voice was fresh and authentic. In her 2005 book *The Queen's Spew* (the title can just as correctly be translated as *The Queen's Peacock*, but it does not capture her literary intentions), she spoofs an acquisitions editor advising her: "What matters most to us is authenticity, truth . . . in the background 'Poland C', its harsh reality, the capitalism, the consumerism in its various manifestations, the general melee within society."[73]

Box 8.2. Poland's Dilemma as Seen at a Fruit Counter
"Basket A, that's expensive fruit imported from the distant West, coated in a thick layer of poisonous pesticides—germs spread by the blacks who touched them. And now let's look into Basket B, that's Russki fruit, a little cheaper than ours, but they're doctored fakes, certainly empty in the middle. Whereas in Basket C, there's genuine inexpensive Polish fruit, even the bruised Polish apples taste better than the apples of the putrid West, it goes without saying."

Source: Dorota Masłowska, *Snow White and Russian Red* (New York: Black Cat, 2005), 194.

Masłowska was awarded the NIKE, Poland's most prestigious literary award, in 2006 for "The Queen's Spew"—what she has called a song and others have labeled a rap poem or even lyrical hip-hop.[74] She inserts herself into the story as a character allowing her to criticize herself: "It's important to stop this book from being translated into other languages because the outlooks of its protagonists betray a low level of morality which puts Poland and the general values cultivated here into a bad light in the West."[75]

An example of Polish self-loathing is this bleak story. While riding her bike, Doris (the author) "wanted to forget in what a terrible country she lived, bearing the strange name Poland, in which a war of some kind, without a number, was still being fought, where you couldn't ride through because here or there someone is lying down, there's some broken glass, an unconscious person, the smell and stink of urine, filth—and try to keep your balance so that you don't do an endo because of that junkie."[76]

The most flamboyant character in the story is Stanisław Retro, a vocalist in a rock band, screaming homosexual, substance abuser—or so it is said. He dreams what young Poles since World War II have constantly dreamed about—"a simple and modest life in Sweden, about becoming a Swedish Jehovah's Witness pastor, about a good life helping sick people."[77] He returns later to this idea. "Ah fuck, to drop everything and leave for at least Germany, to be a fat German there with a fat wife named Gudrun or Gretchen, walk along sidewalks without cracks in them, best yet to be a Swede, having Pete as a second name, raise fish in a river and watch how they swim day after day, to be far from here."[78]

To be far, too, from the Polish ruling class—"collaborators" in Poland's ruin—is a sentiment expressed in an earlier novel. The main character, a punk called Nails, lashes out at "an annihilation prepared for the country by the fucking aristocrats, dressed in overcoats, in aprons, who, if only the conditions were right, would sell us, the citizens, to whorehouses in the West, to the German army, for organs, for slave labor."[79]

Masłowska's first novel (and her only book available in English) is called *Snow White and Russian Red*; the more descriptive Polish title is "The Polish-Russian War under the Red-and-White Flag." It presents a hyperrealistic portrait of small-town Polish society of the 1990s. Nails, a socially marginalized kid dumped by his girlfriend Magda, turns to drugs, gutter punks, and xenophobia as surrogates. The novel spotlights both the anarchic and Russophobic attitudes of young people in Poland—paradoxically, the generation that had suffered least at the hands of Russian-imposed rule.

Russkis—a pejorative word for Russians when used by Poles—are blamed for controlling the black market in knock-off cigarettes, pirated CDs, even Polish sand. These are some of their economic wrongdoings: they have raised the salinity of the Niemen river and are responsible for the arrival of gale-force winds—their part in environmental degradation. They also go off with grubby-faced dirty girls, demonstrating their lack of taste and culture.

Nails is haunted by the fear that Russians had broken into his apartment, "knocked the Mother of God of Lichen made of sky-blue plastic off the fridge, the head's gone, the holy water's scattered all over the place." They "brought in horses, ate up the Bird Milkies [a Polish chocolate treat], smoked the cigarettes, fucked up the upholstery, and good-bye, see you in a future life in Belarus."[80] Another post-Soviet nation, the Kazakhs, are called pigs.[81]

There are few insults that can be hurled in Poland worse than to say your "mother takes off her panties for the *Russkis*."[82] By contrast, the best testimonial a Pole can receive is: "radically anti-*Russki* with right-wing tendencies," which denotes "individual achievements in the advancement of Polishness."[83]

The thinking pervading much of Polish society is, then, "Either you're Polish or you're *Russki*. To put it more bluntly, either you're a person or you're a prick."[84] Masłowska accurately anticipates the heights that Russophobia was to reach under the Kaczyńskis five years later.

Let us not overlook the image of an enviable hateful West that the author imputes to her characters. Nails fantasizes about poisoning Magda because then "she couldn't go to the West to have a career as a secretary or actress"[85] The banality and yet power of the West is symbolized by the movie shown on a German porno channel: "Set in a castle, a guy in armor, and a German shit-eating glam-rock girl gave it to him in quite uninventive ways."[86]

There is even an anti-American undercurrent in Nails's world. He becomes a chain-smoker—"my way of expressing my opposition, my way of expressing my defiance to the West, against American dieticians, American plastic surgeries, American crooks, who are suave but betray our country on the sly."[87]

In 2006, Masłowska's first play, *A Couple of Poor Polish-Speaking Romanians*, was staged in Warsaw. The main characters are a middle-aged Romanian couple hitchhiking through Poland who encounter anti-Balkan antipathies. One Polish driver comments how he heard that "in that Romania they eat thorns, weeds, and rocks."[88] A Polish woman who gives them a lift wants to show how much she knows about the Balkans: "Fuck. Hungary, Romania, Turkia, I know, a beautiful country. Everyone says Romania, filth, shit, exrement, Islam, kids eating shit from the sidewalks, that tyrant Cincinnatus ruling."[89]

Eastern European self-loathing again makes its appearance in the play. Parcha, the Romanian husband, lashes out at his wife Dżina: "You have no shame! Woman, you're pregnant, you sniff glue, you curse, you stink up the car." He tells the first driver that picks the couple up: "You have to excuse her, she's a dumb Romanian, a lout, she worked her whole life in a factory of monkeys and dogs and doesn't know how to behave in public."[90] Later he explains to a drunken middle-class Polish woman driving to Warsaw:

"We're Romanians who speak Polish, we're lesbians, queers, Jews, we work in an advertising agency, like I said you know, we're going to Israel to plant trees."[91] In fact, the Romanian couple may well be Polish, as a 2008 London theater production intimated.

Self-loathing, self-parody, and self-typecasting are constant tropes, then, in Masłowska's works. The many antipathies that Poles hold are also identified. But a refrain in "The Queen's Spew"—probably a reference to funding the author may have received from the EU for her artistic work—raises the subject we have been concerned with. "This tune came into being with money from the European Union—though has anyone ever seen this supposed Europe? I doubt it."[92]

Another contemporary Polish novelist, Magdalena Tulli, employs a very different narrative style to address similar issues to Masłowska. In *Flaw*, she depicts a confrontation all too familiar in contemporary Europe—pitting the long-time residents of a town square against a group of refugees. The refugees arrive suddenly by streetcar and invasively take over the square. A respectable housewife peeking through lace curtains at the newcomers expresses her indignation. They "ought to realize that they are not at home here."[93] For Tulli, the refugees' costume more than their character brand them as undesirable outsiders: "The newcomers' attire does not blend subtly into the background; on the contrary, it is strikingly dark, and stands out in sharp contours displeasing to the eye. It can immediately be seen that they do not belong to this story."[94]

These refugees threaten to bring with them a harsh climate of bitter frosts and blustery snowstorms that are foreign to this place. They also bring additional work for officials, who "would have had to ask the official questions: who are these people, where are they from, and what ought to be done with them. Should they be dispatched without delay back where they came from, or, on the contrary, should a room be set up in the offices where they could turn in their applications and be issued residence permits bearing treasury stamps and a seal with the national emblem?"[95]

The unexpected appearance of destitute refugees in drab winter clothing lugging shabby suitcases in the carefully cultivated gardens of the unremarkable town square is not a Polish story. It is the story of Everyman, of Everymigrant. Conceivably this event could take place in the Place des Vosges in Paris or the Stortorget in Stockholm as seamlessly as in Warsaw's Plac Zamkowy. Local residents' reactions would probably be similar. The eastern Europeanness of Tulli's square lies in the costumes that are worn in it. The pervasive drabness of all its inhabitants marks the story as one of a society in transition in which all characters are struggling to put on a better costume, in which new Europe is striving to look as chic as old.

THE EQUAL-OPPORTUNITY ANTIPATHIES OF HOUELLEBECQ

Any novel from Michel Houellebecq invariably raises public controversy, and that is how the French author likes it. The "frank" depiction of Islam in *Platform*, published in 2002, even led to legal charges being filed against him for inciting racial hatred. When he was subsequently acquitted in a French court, his notoriety eventually equaled that of Salman Rushdie—not bad literary company to keep.[96] Both had been accused of blasphemous writing and both held themselves up as innocent victims of contemporary Islamo-fascism.

Houellebecq was born on La Réunion—an exotic French-governed island in the Indian Ocean with a largely Creole population. His coming of age in a tropical exotica and demographic gumbo did not seem to help him come to terms with the diversity in the world around him.

A Darwinist by orientation, it seems, the author holds Western liberalism and rationalism to blame for the spread of veniality, narcissism, and moral relativism. The Western world has become so flabby that it cannot defend itself any more against reactionary ideologies like Islamo-fascism. "Because of its need for rational certainty, the West finally sacrificed everything: its religion, its happiness, its hopes, and definitively its life."[97] The concepts of individual liberty, human dignity, and progress were also sacrificed over time.[98]

Neoliberalism is modern-day Darwinism, then: "Economic liberalism is the extension of the arena of struggle, its extension at all stages of life and for all classes of society. Similarly, sexual liberalism is the extension of the arena of struggle."[99] In order to illustrate the latter "struggle," Houellebecq grants himself license to engage in graphic descriptions of sexual activity.

It may seem paradoxical, then, that one of the few personages identified in his novels that comes in for praise is the Pope. "John Paul II was the only, absolutely the only one to understand what was taking place in the West."[100] His antimaterialism and rejection of moral relativism would have an obvious appeal to Houellebecq.

In his works, the author likes to examine not only the outrageous behavior of today's "postfeminist sluts" but also the sordidness of today's ethnic hatreds. There are few ethnic and racial groups that have not been skewered in one of his books. French society was deconstructed in earlier novels like *Elementary Particles*. The contrasting lifestyles of half-brothers Bruno, obsessed with sex, and Michel, a genetic engineer—both of whom have unfulfilled lives—is an indictment of the rudderless French society whose origins lie in the decadent 1960s.

Other nations of old Europe usually undergo gentler satire. Houellebecq takes the traditional condescending French view of its neighbor to the south: "standardization was doing its work . . . and Spain was approaching European, and especially English, norms. It was giving grudging acceptance to such extraordinary ideas as homosexuality, kindness to animals, vegetarian food, and New Age baubles."[101] Spain, where much of *Possibility of an Island* is set (and Houellebecq currently lives), is still not quite old Europe, however: "Spaniards don't like cultural programs at all, nor culture in general, it's an area that is fundamentally hostile to them."[102]

The German presence in the novel is represented by a cream which "by applying it to the glands before sexual intercourse and massaging it in carefully, sensitivity was diminished, and the rise of pleasure and ejaculation happened much more slowly."[103] Leave it to the Germans, says Houellebecq, to put sex into the service of science. Indeed, in *Platform*, Germans, with their ample money and little culture, seem crazed by sex tourism; for Houellebecq, Cubans and Thais are especially good at delivering the services. The one avenger of sexual anarchy and predation in *Possibility of an Island* is Gianpaolo, a handsome, heroic young Italian.

It would be inconceivable for a French author to leave the United States out of his skewering. But Houellebecq puts blame on the crassness of the Europeans themselves: "There was no case of a fashion coming from the United States that hadn't succeeded in swamping western Europe a few years later."[104]

The problems of EU standardization of national laws and of definitions—what is chocolate? champagne vodka? beer?—are a segue for Houellebecq to discuss sex workers. "As Europe becomes conceived of as a federation of states more and more, one nevertheless observes no uniformization in terms of legislation about mores."[105] His shining example is that of prostitution: it is legally recognized in Holland and Germany, but the French, following the Swedes, want to do away with it by penalizing the client.

On the subject of sex workers, Houellebecq takes direct aim at eastern Europe. In the brothels visited by Daniel1, the main protagonist of *Possibility of an Island*, "most of the girls were Romanian, Belorussian, and Ukrainian, in other words from one of those absurd countries that emerged from the implosion of the Eastern bloc."[106] The pornography industry "remained in the hands of shady Hungarian, or even Latvian, jobbers."[107] Aging tourists at a holiday club are entertained to a Miss Bikini Contest where the main contestants are a leggy teenage girl from Budapest and "a platinum-blond Russian, very curvaceous in spite of her fourteen years, who looked a right tart" and subsequently "began stuffing her hand down her bikini bottom."[108] After inevitably losing his slutty girlfriend to younger men, Daniel1 thinks to himself how "I could spend the night with a transsexual Slovenian whore."[109]

Houellebecq depicts the new little countries making up the new Europe in stereotypical terms. His narrator travels to the region: "The summer course was being held in Herzegovina, or in some such region, known primarily for the conflicts that had once drenched it in blood." The chalets had "red-and-white-checked curtains, and heads of boars and stags decorating the walls, all of it done with a Central European kitsch."[110]

Even in *Platform*, which describes Thailand's sex tourism industry, eastern Europeans make an appearance. The French sex tourist firm was going after clients from the former eastern countries: "Czechoslovakia, Hungary, Poland . . . very down-market."[111]

Box 8.3. Arab Modernity Projected Forward in Time
"When the Arab countries, after years of being insidiously undermined, essentially through underground Internet connections, could at last have access to a way of life based on mass consumption, sexual freedom, and leisure, the enthusiasm of their populations was intense and eager as it had been, half a century earlier, in the Communist countries."

Source: Michel Houellebecq, *Possibility of an Island* (New York: Alfred A. Knopf, 2006), 248.

The most controversial—and offensive—satires of foreigners in his novels are of Muslims. One character in *Platform* snarls: "Islam was born in the middle of the desert in the middle of scorpions, camels, and ferocious animals of all types. You know what I call Muslims? The scum of the Sahara. . . . Islam could not be born except in a stupid desert among filthy Bedouins who had nothing else to do but—pardon me—bugger camels."[112] There could be no doubt but that "the Muslim system was condemned: capitalism would be stronger. Already young Arabs dream of nothing else but sexual consumption."[113]

Overshadowed by *Platform's* Islamophobia is the fact that it describes an Islamic terrorist attack on a Western nightclub in southeast Asia; the book's publication date preceded the 2002 Bali bombings by just a couple of months!

Anti-Arab statements are made by characters in other Houellebecq novels. In *Elementary Particles*, Anne speaks of a holiday in Morocco where "the Arabs were disagreeable and aggressive, the sun was much too hot."[114] In *Possibility of an Island*, Daniel1's artistic output includes a rap record, *Fuck the Bedouins*, songs such as "Let's Fuck da Niggahs' Anus," and a creation called We Prefer the Palestinian Orgy Sluts.[115]

Houellebecq has been accused of misoxenia, blasphemy, and sexism—and also racism. Invoking the most classic of stereotypes, Bruno in *Elementary Particles* remembers as an adolescent measuring his penis, which was only 13–14 centimeters long, at most. "It was from that moment on that I started hating Blacks."[116] Elsewhere the French author speaks about a past colonial view of Blacks as "an inferior brother," which constituted "a kind of benevolent, almost humanist, racism." But "From the moment that whites began to consider Blacks as equals, it became clear that sooner or later they would consider them as superior. The notion of equality has no foundation with man."[117] Again blaming the West for encouraging jumbled ethnic hierarchies, "racial discrimination in reverse" also applied to Arabs, seen as inherently superior to Europeans.[118]

Raising the sensitive issues of racial and ethnic relations in western Europe and debunking the prevailing discourses on multiculturalism—as Makine has done—will inevitably make a novelist a "controversial" one. Whether Houellebecq himself thinks in ethnic and racial categories is less important than his conviction that that is how many western Europeans—as depicted in his many protagonists—think. The author's exposé of old Europe's xenophobic proclivities is valuable testimony, then, to a comparative study of xenophobia.

THE ANTI-RELIGIOUS VIEWS OF OLD EUROPE'S ESSAYISTS

Every country has a stable of journalists, essayists, and public intellectuals who produce commentary on the various malaises afflicting modern society. While it is true that risqué observations about relations between ethnic and religious groups may have more resonance in one country than other, the role of the pundit—an old profession pursued in all societies—is to be iconoclastic, to challenge conventional wisdom, and to draw provocative conclusions.

By the end of her life, the Italian journalist and television interviewer Oriana Fallaci had become one of the most outspoken and zealous critics of Islam in all of Europe. Her rage at Islam seemed atavistic. She scorned Muslims for their reproductive habits, their toilet habits, their practices of female circumcision.

In *The Rage and the Pride*, published in 2002 and a best-seller in many countries of old Europe, she added micturition to the list of faults she found in Muslims. Somalis in Florence's Cathedral Square, she claimed, were leaving "yellow streaks of urine that profaned the millenary marbles of the Baptistery." She marveled at their skill: "Good Heavens! They really take long shots, these sons of Allah! How could they succeed in hitting so well that target protected by a balcony and more than two yards distant from their urinary apparatus?"[119]

Fallaci, an atheist, believed in the fundamental incompatibility between Western and Islamic civilizations. Like Houellebecq, she was struck by the temerity of the post-Christian West in defending itself from Muslim extremism and in being so undemanding of and appeasing towards its immigrant Muslim population. The smugness and conformity exhibited by European elites in their discursive practices about diversity had been enabling to those Muslims whose attitudes did not reciprocate the West's hospitality. Moreover, Europeans themselves were incapable of presenting a united front because they were "inevitably poisoned by the differences of our many languages, by the discomforts and the suspicions that ensue from it, by the old rivalries and rancours rooted inside our tormented past of fratricidal wars."[120] In an Italy she idealized, she found comfort: "An Italy not tyrannized by the sons of Allah and by the parasites, the cicadas." She warned: "Woe betide those who invade it . . . Whether they come with troops and cannons or with children and boats, *idem.*"[121]

Fallaci was surprised at the speed with which Islam was steamrolling European identity. In great measure it was brought on, she contended, by the West's absurd self-abasement and its "penitential narcissism"—the term coined by French philosopher Alain Finkielkraut.[122] In *The Force of Reason*, published in English in 2006, she imagined a radically transformed Europe now called Eurabia, a colony of Islam with Italy as its base.[123]

According to Fallaci, Europeans, particularly on the left, subject people who criticize Islam to a double standard. "If you speak your mind on the Vatican, on the Catholic Church, on the Pope, on the Virgin Mary or Jesus or the saints, nobody touches your 'right of thought and expression.' But if you do the same with Islam, the Koran, the Prophet Muhammad, some son of Allah, you are called a xenophobic blasphemer who has committed an act of racial discrimination."[124]

Fallaci was not always logical in her views. One of the many famous political leaders that she interviewed was Iran's Ayatollah Khomeini. She was barefoot and wearing a chador—quite a compromise for an outspoken feminist—when she met him in Qom. She then described the Ayatollah as the most handsome old man she had ever met. She did reach a breaking point in the interview, however, and tore "this stupid medieval rag" off her face. Khomeini proved understanding and agreed to resume the interview the next day.

Fallaci's Islamophobic statements led to legal charges filed against her. The Federal Office of Justice in Berne asked the Italian government to extradite her so she could be charged under Article 261b of the Swiss Criminal Code. She faced litigation in France. Back home, an Italian magistrate indicted her. Cited in a European Arrest Warrant that charged her with xenophobia—sufficient grounds for extradition from one EU state to another—Fallaci had to take her chances in Italy. But she died of a terminal illness before any legal action against her proved successful.

In Britain, literary Islamophobia has been given a name—Blitcon. British literary neoconservatives consist of three of the most successful contemporary authors living in the U.K.: Martin Amis, Ian McEwan, and Salman Rushdie. All three supposedly believe that Islamism poses a fundamental threat to Western civilization.[125] Amis and his onetime fellow editor at the British journal *New Statesman*, Christopher Hitchens, who (like Rushdie) now lives in the United States, have especially become entangled in Islamophobic controversies in recent years.

It is said that when they were at Oxford together, Amis and Hitchens made an agreement to divide up the literary world. Amis would look after fiction, Hitchens nonfiction. Decades later, Amis has been accused of not holding to his end of the bargain.[126] Instead of concentrating on fiction, Amis began to dabble in essays. One paragraph in an otherwise well-reasoned essay published in 2006 established his "reputation" as Islamophobe.

> Islam, in the end, proved responsive to European influence: the influence of Hitler and Stalin. And one hardly needs to belabor the similarities between Islamism and the totalitarian cults of the last century. Anti-semitic, anti-liberal, anti-individualist, anti-democratic, and, most crucially, anti-rational, they too were cults of death, death-driven and death-fuelled. The main distinction is that the paradise which the Nazis (pagan) and the Bolsheviks (atheist) sought to bring about was an earthly one, raised from the mulch of millions of corpses. For them, death was creative, right enough, but death was still death. For the Islamists, death is a consummation and a sacrament; death is a beginning.[127]

Moreover, Amis's novella published that same year, *House of Meetings*, dealt unflatteringly with the psyche of a 9/11 hijacker.[128] The author's very obsession with Islamic terrorism seemed to his critics sufficient evidence that he belonged to the neocon anti-Muslim fringe.

In his turn, Hitchens was branded an anglo-Islamophobe after the 2007 publication of his book *God Is Not Great: How Religion Poisons Everything*.[129] To be sure, it is a self-styled "ecumenical" attack on all religions—not just Islam—because "Religion has retarded the development of civilization." In particular, "monotheistic religion is a plagiarism of a plagiarism of a hearsay of a hearsay, of an illusion of an illusion, extending all the way back to a fabrication of a few nonevents."[130]

Hitchens lists examples of the "retarded" nature of all religions. Saint Augustine was "a self-centered fantasist and an earth-centered ignoramus." Moses was "Commandingly authoritarian and bloody-minded," inclined towards "genocidal incitements." Gandhi was "A fakir and guru" whose belief in a simple agrarian way of life could have meant "millions of people would have starved to death if his advice had been followed." The Dalai Lama is satirized as "a hereditary king appointed by heaven itself. How convenient!"[131]

From Fallaci we know that insulting other religions does not give a pundit license to attack Islam. But Hitchens ignores this stricture. Islam is "a mask for a very deep and probably justifiable insecurity . . . not much more than a rather obvious and ill-arranged set of plagiarisms, there is nothing—absolutely nothing—in its teachings that can even begin to justify such arrogance." Regarding the Qur'an, "I simply laugh when I read the Koran, with its endless prohibitions on sex and its corrupt promise of infinite debauchery in the life to come."[132]

We can cite other examples of iconoclastic public intellectuals in Europe attacking the norms governing their societies. EU discourse on transnationalism and integration has become an easy target as, in the view of its critics, Europe reels under the weight of a population that often appears to be unintegrated, embraces parochial identities, and speaks in as many languages as on the Tower of Babel. The expression of xenophobic sentiments is, in this context, an overstated way of putting the lie to EU elites' discursive practices. Thus, in addition to far-away locals and foreigners, a target of xenophobic rage are the Eurocrats who manufacture what seems to be the false consciousness of our age.

NOTES

1. Melegh, *On the East-West Slope*, 92, 49.

2. Guido Schwellnus, "The Adoption of Nondiscrimination and Minority Protection Rules in Romania, Hungary, and Poland," in *The Europeanization of Central and Eastern Europe*, eds. Frank Schimmelfennig and Ulrich Sedelmeier (Ithaca, NY: Cornell University Press, 2005), 51–70.

3. Melegh, *On the East-West Slope*, 95.

4. Maria Todorova, *Imagining the Balkans* (Oxford: Oxford University Press, 1997), 188.

5. Todorova, *Imagining the Balkans*, 18.

6. This discussion is taken from Michael Osborn, "Culture in Romania and Bulgaria," BBC News, December 31, 2006, http://news.bbc.co.uk/2/hi/entertainment/6207758.stm.

7. "Britain to Review Romania, Bulgaria Migration Rules," *Eubusiness*, June 21, 2007, www.eubusiness.com/Employment/1182448816.11/.

8. James Slack and Matthew Hickley, "120 Immigrants from Romania and Bulgaria Arrive in Britain Every Day to Be Circus Stars," *Daily Mail*, May 23, 2007.

9. "Albanian Novelist Wins Inaugural Mann Booker International Prize 2005," www.themanbookerprize.com/news/release/1053.

10. Ismail Kadare, *The File on H.* (New York: Arcade, 1998).

11. Kadare, *The File on H.*, 91–92.

12. Kadare, *The File on H.*, 89.

13. Kadare, *The File on H.*, 198–99.

14. Kadare, *The File on H.*, 134.

15. Ismail Kadare, *Doruntine* (London: Saqi Books, 1988), 76–77.

16. Kadare, *Doruntine*, 22.

17. Kadare, *Doruntine*, 40.

18. Kadare, *Doruntine*, 65.

19. Kadare, *Doruntine*, 77.

20. Kadare, *Doruntine*, 151–53.

21. Kadare, *Doruntine*, 162.

22. Ismail Kadare, *The Three-Arched Bridge* (New York: Arcade, 1997), 70.

23. Kadare, *The Three-Arched Bridge*, 166.

24. Kadare, *The Three-Arched Bridge*, 162.

25. Kadare, *The Three-Arched Bridge*, 25.

26. Kadare, *The Three-Arched Bridge*, 172–73.

27. Kadare, *The Three-Arched Bridge*, 181.

28. Kadare, *The Three-Arched Bridge*, 183.

29. Kadare, *The Three-Arched Bridge*, 68.

30. Patrick McGrath, "Troubled Waters," *New York Times*, March 2, 1997, www.nytimes.com/books/97/03/02/reviews/970302.02mcgratt.html.

31. Ivo Andric, *The Bridge on the Drina* (Chicago: University of Chicago Press, 1977).

32. Ismail Kadare, *Broken April* (New York: New Amsterdam Books, 2007).

33. Ismail Kadare, *The General of the Dead Army* (New York: New Amsterdam Books, 2005), 27.

34. Kadare, *The General of the Dead Army*, 207.

35. Ismail Kadare, *The Concert* (New York: Arcade Publishing, 1998).

36. Ismail Kadare, *The Palace of Dreams* (New York: William Morrow, 1993), 24–25.

37. Kadare, *The Palace of Dreams*, 39.

38. Kadare, *The Palace of Dreams*, 104.

39. Kadare, *The Palace of Dreams*, 178.

40. Ismail Kadare, *Spring Flowers, Spring Frost* (New York: Arcade, 2002), 15.

41. Ismail Kadare, *Le crépuscule des dieux de la steppe* (Paris: Gallimard, 1996), 117.

42. Ismail Kadare, *Elegy for Kosovo* (New York: Arcade, 2000).

43. Kadare, *Elegy for Kosovo*, 3.

44. Kadare, *Elegy for Kosovo*, 36.

45. Kadare, *Elegy for Kosovo*, 119, 121.

46. Kadare, *Elegy for Kosovo*, 68.

47. Kadare, *Elegy for Kosovo*, 107.

48. Kadare, *Elegy for Kosovo*, 108.

49. Jonathan Finer, "Albania Takes Aim at a Deadly Tradition," *Washington Post*, August 23, 2007. Paperback copies of the full text were on sale in many kiosks in the country. Chapter 126 is titled "Blood Is Paid for with Blood."

50. In the first years of the new century, regular reports were published of revenge killings in the Albanian mountains. The institution of "sworn virgins"—women dressed as men with rifles on their shoulder wandering the Albanian mountainsides—also has persisted. See Joshua Zumbrun, "The Sacrifices of Albania's 'Sworn Virgins,'" *Washington Post*, August 11, 2007.

51. Kadare, *Spring Flowers, Spring Frost,* 72.

52. Kadare, *Spring Flowers, Spring Frost,* 170.

53. Kadare, *Spring Flowers, Spring Frost,* 96–97.

54. Quoted in Levent Soysal, review of David Horrocks and Eva Kolinsky, eds., *Turkish Culture in German Society Today,* H-SAE, H-Net Reviews, May 1998, www .h-net.org/reviews/showrev.cgi?path=23277895266619.

55. Emine Sevgi Özdamar, *Mother Tongue* (Toronto: Coach House Press, 1994), 113

56. David Horrocks and Eva Kolinsky, eds., *Turkish Culture in German Society Today* (New York: Berghahn Books, 1996), 47.

57. Özdamar, *Mother Tongue,* 57.

58. Özdamar, *Mother Tongue,* 157.

59. Özdamar, *Mother Tongue,* 96.

60. Özdamar, *Mother Tongue,* 72.

61. Özdamar, *Mother Tongue,* 78.

62. Özdamar, *Mother Tongue,* 81.

63. Özdamar, *Mother Tongue,* 100.

64. Emine Sevgi Özdamar, *Life is a Caravanserai—Has Two Doors—I Came In One—I Went Out the Other* (London: Middlesex University Press, 2000), 288, 290.

65. Özdamar, *Life is a Caravanserai,* 295.

66. Özdamar, *Life is a Caravanserai,* 289.

67. Özdamar, *Life is a Caravanserai,* 288.

68. Özdamar, *Life is a Caravanserai,* 295.

69. B. Venkat Mani, *Cosmopolitan Claims: Turkish-German Literatures from Nadolny to Pamuk* (Iowa City: University of Iowa Press, 2007), 117.

70. Emine Sevgi Özdamar, "Guest Faces," in *Writing Europe: What is European about the Literatures of Europe?* ed. Ursula Keller and Ilma Rakusa (Budapest: Central European University Press, 2004), 225.

71. Özdamar, "Guest Faces," 227.

72. Orhan Pamuk, "My First Passport," *The New Yorker,* April 16, 2007, 57.

73. Dorota Masłowska, *Paw królowej* [The Queen's Spew] (Warsaw: Biblioteka Twoich Myśli, 2005), 147.

74. The self-reference is found in Masłowska, *Paw królowej,* 147.

75. Masłowska, *Paw królowej,* 119.

76. Masłowska, *Paw królowej,* 31.

77. Masłowska, *Paw królowej,* 21.

78. Masłowska, *Paw królowej,* 22.

79. Dorota Masłowska, *Snow White and Russian Red* (New York: Black Cat, 2005), 20.

80. Masłowska, *Snow White and Russian Red,* 105.

81. Masłowska, *Snow White and Russian Red,* 250.

82. Masłowska, *Snow White and Russian Red,* 219.

83. Masłowska, *Snow White and Russian Red,* 255.

84. Masłowska, *Snow White and Russian Red,* 120.

85. Masłowska, *Snow White and Russian Red,* 158.

86. Masłowska, *Snow White and Russian Red,* 92.

87. Masłowska, *Snow White and Russian Red,* 29.

88. Dorota Masłowska, *Dwoje biednych Rumunów mówiących po polsku* [Two poor Romanians speaking Polish] (Warsaw: Lampa i Iskra Boża, 2006), 13.

89. Masłowska, *Dwoje biednych Rumunów*, 63.

90. Masłowska, *Dwoje biednych Rumunów*, 30.

91. Masłowska, *Dwoje biednych Rumunów*, 62.

92. Masłowska, *Paw królowej*, 119.

93. Magdalena Tulli, *Flaw* (Brooklyn, NY: Archipelago Books, 2007), 67.

94. Tulli, *Flaw*, 66.

95. Tulli, *Flaw*, 72.

96. Salman Rushdie, *The Satanic Verses* (New York: Picador, 2000).

97. Michel Houellebecq, *Les particules élémentaires* (Paris: Éditions J'ai lu, 2003), 270. The English edition is *Elementary Particles* (New York: Knopf, 2001).

98. Houellebecq, *Les particules élémentaires*, 309.

99. Michel Houellebecq, *Extension du domaine de la lutte* (Paris: Éditions J'ai lu, 1997), 100.

100. Houellebecq, *Les particules élémentaires*, 180.

101. Michel Houellebecq, *Possibility of an Island* (New York: Knopf, 2006), 51.

102. Houellebecq, *Possibility of an Island*, 216.

103. Houellebecq, *Possibility of an Island*, 143.

104. Houellebecq, *Les particules élémentaires*, 72.

105. Michel Houellebecq, *Platforme* (Paris: Éditions J'ai lu, 2002), 285. The English edition is *Platform* (New York: Knopf, 2003).

106. Houellebecq, *Possibility of an Island*, 72.

107. Houellebecq, *Possibility of an Island*, 110.

108. Houellebecq, *Possibility of an Island*, 181–82.

109. Houellebecq, *Possibility of an Island*, 223.

110. Houellebecq, *Possibility of an Island*, 80.

111. Houellebecq, *Platforme*, 198.

112. Houellebecq, *Platforme*, 243–44.

113. Houellebecq, *Platforme*, 339.

114. Houellebecq, *Les particules élémentaires*, 186.

115. Houellebecq, *Possibility of an Island*, 100.

116. Houellebecq, *Les particules élémentaires*, 191.

117. Houellebecq, *Platforme*, 112.

118. Houellebecq, *Platforme*, 195.

119. Oriana Fallaci, *The Rage and the Pride* (New York: Rizzoli, 2002). Cited in Mark Steyn, "She Said What She Thought," *The Atlantic*, December 2006, www.theatlantic.com/doc/200612/steyn-fallaci.

120. Fallaci, *The Rage and the Pride*,185–86.

121. Fallaci, *The Rage and the Pride*, 186.

122. Quoted in Margaret Talbot, "The Agitator," *The New Yorker*, June 5, 2006.

123. Oriana Fallaci, *The Force of Reason* (New York: Rizzoli, 2006). For other polemical works on the political and intellectual sellout of Europe to Islam, see also Bat Yeor, *Eurabia* (Madison, NJ: Fairleigh Dickinson University Press, 2005). Also Bruce Bawer, *While Europe Slept: How Radical Islam is Destroying the West from Within* (New York: Doubleday, 2006).

124. Quoted in Margaret Talbot, "The Agitator," *The New Yorker*, June 5, 2006.

125. These arguments are made by Ziauddin Sardar, "Welcome to Planet Blit-con," *New Statesman*, December 11, 2006.

126. This story was told to the author by Salman Rushdie, New Orleans, April 7, 2008.

127. Martin Amis, "The Age of Horrorism," *The Observer*, September 10, 2006.

128. Martin Amis, *House of Meetings* (New York: Random House, 2007).

129. Christopher Hitchens, *God Is Not Great: How Religion Poisons Everything* (New York: Twelve Books, 2007).

130. Hitchens, *God is Not Great*, 280.

131. The excerpted quotes are compiled in "One Hell of a Religious Read," *New York Post*, April 4, 2007, www.nypost.com/seven/04042007/gossip/pagesix/page-six.htm.

132. "One Hell of a Religious Read."

9

The Enduring Appeal of the Culturally Bounded Home

Observing the process of European integration through different lenses, as our analytic framework has enabled us to do, permits us to see things more clearly. And what we see is that things are muddled. The cold eye of the social scientist, or the critical eye of the cultural theorist, may have led to greater parsimony in explaining differences in Europe—but at the cost of appreciating complexity. Reductionism is the great danger when trying to make sense of the conflicting pulls of belonging, transnationalism, xenophobia, and nationalism within the EU. Institutions, discourses, attitudes, and narratives are all important in making Europe what it is becoming. To sacrifice any of these factors in the quest for an objective account of the state of contemporary Europeanness is to make the texture of the analysis the poorer.

In this final chapter, we return to a discussion of home and belonging. After all the phobias have been accounted for, can we nevertheless discover an inexorable and irreversible process taking place of building a European home that transcends east and west?

DIVERSITY AND INTEGRATION IN THE NATIONAL HOME

Home is a familiar, nonthreatening place. It is where people enjoy a sense of security and comfort level. It is a place of belonging for all who reside there.

The culturally bounded home is like that. It contains a familiar language, a habitual way of doing things, and people similar to you. The culturally bounded home brings together a community of people having a common ethnicity, religion, language, and history. Usually, therefore, it is a mix of primordial characteristics, like language, and socially constructed ones, like identity.

What a culturally bounded home is not is an all-inclusive site open to all newcomers without prejudice. Depending on how strictly gatekeeping norms are enforced, such a home will take in outsiders in the belief that they add to the life of the community. The carrying weight of a home, that is, how many people can be accommodated comfortably without adversely affecting the quality of life, is an important consideration in opening up the home to others.

From the perspective of these others—migrants who become the newcomers in what was for a long time other peoples' home—there is a risky presumption in their calculus. Salman Rushdie captures this in his deconstruction of the American film *Wizard of Oz*. "So Oz finally *became* home; the imagined world became the actual world, as it does for us all, because . . . the real secret of the ruby slippers is not that 'there's no place like home,' but rather that there is no longer any such place *as* home: except, of course, for the home we make, or the homes that are made for us, in Oz: which is anywhere, and everywhere, except the place from which we began."[1]

The modern state is a bit like Oz—a home that is made for people. It only roughly approximates a culturally bounded home. It is too large and specialized with too many functions to perform to be able to maintain cultural boundaries. Nevertheless, it recognizes the need to represent itself as homeland through a constant use of many "national" symbols, values, and invocations.

There is a point when the modern state loses credibility as a homeland, when it opens its doors to anyone making the effort to knock. The demographic balance between longtime residents of the state and newcomers shifts suddenly. The state will quickly claim that in an era of globalization it cannot do otherwise.

In some cities or their suburbs, the foreign-born population begins to outnumber the locally born. To add insult to injury, state leaders claim that this is a sign of modernity and progress even though they may do little to help the life chances of the foreign born. "Londonistans" arise in which second-generation Londoners of non-British ethnicities take to the peripheries while newcomers settle into traditional immigrant staging areas.[2] Soon there is little familiar, secure, and comfortable to such a place. Its hominess is breached and all its residents seem to have become mere denizens in this "Londonland."

Integration of newcomers into a host society can be a way of reinventing home. But integration has become ever more loosely defined. Lord Parekh, a social scientist in London who specializes in multiculturalism, asked: "Can minorities be said to refuse to integrate if they bring spouses from

Box 9.1. Searching . . .
"for a place
that can keep my soul
from wandering
a place where I can stay
without wanting to leave."

Source: Sujata Bhatt, "The One Who Goes Away," in *At the Round Earth's Imagined Corners: A Multicultural Anthology of Contemporary Poetry*, ed. Ken Watson (Melbourne: Phoenix Education, 2005).

their homelands, demand faith schools, choose to live together, or confine their cultural lives to themselves?"[3] Is wearing a veil, or a sari for that matter, a refusal to integrate? For Parekh, since "integration has become a vehicle of narrow cultural nationalism," the answer to these questions must be no.

Some welcome the dismantling of cultural boundaries, the setting of low thresholds for integration (discarding assimilationist measures, like learning the local language, altogether), and the establishment of communities whose one defining characteristic is diversity. For them, racial and ethnic diversity is "cool"—it is a value in itself that outweighs the attraction of a culturally bounded home. The ideologues of diversity add that it increases civic strength, that differences make a society stronger. They reject the argument that proximity of different groups to each other may produce tension and conflict and instead contend that close contact with those of other backgrounds leads to greater understanding and harmony between groups.

This xenophile position uses an array of familiar economic arguments to support itself. One is that labor costs are kept low when immigrants can freely enter the workforce. Another is that they do the jobs no one else wants. In addition, through their tax dollars they help pay for government programs like social security and health care. Their demand for goods and services stimulates economic growth. Diversity even helps drive up productivity and innovation, especially in high-skill workplace settings, since diverse teams produce more creative thinking and insights. Generally, therefore, where ethnic diversity is greatest, as in urban centers, more energy and enterprise emerge.[4]

Economistic arguments have a habit of not catching the public's imagination. Xenophilia is embraced by the public when it makes references to outsiders' success in the realms of popular culture or sports. Even in societies with significant xenophobic attitudes, exceptions are made for the "foreigner" or far-away local who has brought glory to the "nation" through athletic accomplishments. In Europe, soccer stars are at the top of the list.[5]

In France, Zinédine Zidane, born in Marseilles of Algerian parents, achieved iconic status as the player who helped France to unprecedented international soccer success. Swedes held Zlatan Ibrahimović, a member of their national team, in high esteem, especially after he was not allowed to play for Bosnia because he had been born in Sweden. In Poland, Emmanuel Olisadebe's image could at one time be found on everything from mobile phone advertisements to pizza shop sweepstakes. Born and raised in Nigeria, he came to Poland and his talent for scoring goals put him on a fast track for citizenship. In the 2002 World Cup qualifiers and tournament he scored more goals than any other Pole. Expressing the view of probably most "adopted" athletes about their "compatriots," Olisadebe was sanguine: "Poles are good and bad. Some throw bananas on the pitch and chant 'blackie' when I play, and some congratulate me and want my autograph when they meet me on the street."[6]

We can find examples of other foreign-born athletic stars who receive acclaim in their adopted, often otherwise xenophobic societies. Wilson Kipketer, onetime eight-hundred-meter world champion, was born in Kenya but recorded his greatest successes after becoming a Danish citizen. Monty Panesar, born in England to Punjabi parents, was a crowd favorite at international cricket matches. The first Sikh to play for a country other than India in Test cricket, he wore a black *patka* (a smaller version of the Sikh turban) that succeeded in getting many English fans to also wear *patkas*—and fake beards—while watching Panesar play. For their part, the Bulgarians welcomed Austrian Kilian Albrecht to their downhill ski team. Unable to make the powerhouse Austrian contingent, Albrecht was given Bulgarian citizenship just in time for the 2006–2007 Alpine season. Before him, Bulgaria had recruited two Ukrainians to their Nordic team. Today there are few sports left where outstanding foreigners are not recruited to strengthen a "national" team.

Xenophilic attitudes found in sports or pop culture are not an accurate indicator of a society's commitment to diversity. It certainly cannot be used as evidence—as public relations exercises sometimes do—that all foreigners and far-away locals are welcomed by their host societies. It simply tells us that even those who want to live in a culturally bounded home do not mind being entertained by outsiders.

There has been other discouraging news for diversity proponents. A broad survey of American public opinion found that the greater the diversity in a community, the less social capital, reciprocal trust, social solidarity, and civic engagement there is. Diverse communities seem to have a negative effect on everything from political engagement to social connectedness.

According to Harvard political scientist Robert Putnam, when social capital, that is, social networks based on friendships, religious organizations, and neighborhood associations, is high, so is civic well-being. Communities have a higher quality of life, neighborhoods are safer, people are healthier, and more citizens are involved in politics.

But his study of forty-one U.S. communities, whose residents were classified into four racial categories (Black, White, Hispanic, and Asian), found lower levels of social capital when diversity existed. Respondents were asked how much they trusted their neighbors and those of each racial category. They were surveyed about their friendships, civic attitudes, and involvement in community projects. Putnam reported that those in more diverse communities tended to

> distrust their neighbors, regardless of the color of their skin, to withdraw even from close friends, to expect the worst from their community and its leaders, to volunteer less, give less to charity and work on community projects less often, to register to vote less, to agitate for social reform more but have less faith that they can actually make a difference, and to huddle unhappily in front of the television.[7]

Particularly surprising were that levels of trust in more diverse communities were not only lower between racial groups but even among members of the same group. In more diverse settings, it seemed that there were neither close bonds formed across group lines nor increased ethnic tensions. Instead, a general civic malaise prevailed. More diverse populations extended themselves less in pursuit of collective needs and goals.[8]

Putnam's conclusion was that diversity produces discomfort. "People living in ethnically diverse settings appear to 'hunker down'—that is, to pull in like a turtle." More generally, "Diversity, at least in the short run, seems to bring out the turtle in all of us." At the same time, he believed that ethnic diversity as a line of social demarcation could fade with time. Social divisions could eventually be replaced with "more encompassing identities" engendering a "new, more capacious sense of 'we.'"[9]

Putnam's findings may not apply to Europe. Given different immigrant populations and different interethnic relations, diversity might still bring out competitive instincts and civic obligations in western Europe. It may also, however, bring out more antagonistic feelings than it does in the United States.

A TRANSNATIONAL HOME FOR OLD AND NEW EUROPE?

Cultural boundaries in Europe have not been removed or even, in some cases, blurred. Most nations continue to highlight what marks them off from neighbors as well as from non-European populations. To be sure, transnational attitudes emphasizing European identity have become more widespread. Eurobarometer polls show a steady increase in most countries in attachment to European identity.

Transnational events appealing to publics across all Europe are usually those having nothing to do with the EU. These include the Champions League (football), the Eurovision Song Contest, and perhaps even the Ryder Cup (golf). Discount airlines (like Dublin-based Ryanair) allow Europeans to travel cheaply to even small towns in each other's countries. The motorway system, train networks, and bus service have become steadily integrated into a European grid. Europeans of all nations holiday with each other more often at the major resorts. With so much travel, there is now even an egalitarianism to the carbon footprints that Europeans are leaving.

But as we have found in this book, national stereotypes, antipathies, phobias, rivalries, and biases still affect mutual attitudes and behavior in old and new Europe. As reprehensible as they may be, individual nations have constructed unofficial ethnic hierarchies. Xenophobic orientations are stronger in some countries than others. There is a fundamental difference between accusing foreigners of running an unhygienic pizza parlor and bombing their hostel. There is a major difference between banning a techno rave and sterilizing minority women.

In recent years, western European publics have become more concerned about their immigrant populations. Eastern European citizens have tended to remember ethnic and religious squabbles of the past. If Muslims are now most often othered in old Europe, it is by contrast Russians, Romanians, Roma, and Turks who are what much of central Europe regards as its alterity.

Therefore, a different set of ethnically driven recriminations, perceptions, and misperceptions prevails in old Europe compared to new. But these differences by themselves do not constitute a cultural or normative divide between the two parts. Instead, the impression in the east that old Europe is socializing, controlling, even colonizing new Europe has become reified into a continental divide.

Many postcommunist societies have lost much of their admiration for western Europe—and the United States—as they have experienced the hardships that the economic and political systems they borrowed from them have caused. It is significant that radical right parties in new Europe target not just their country's traditional ethnic rivals but also particular western European nations, in many cases the Germans. By contrast, russophobia is palpable across nearly all eastern Europe while the west finds it difficult to get worked up about it.

Attitudes towards foreigners are not, of course, the only orientation that may set off old from new Europeans. The ways that people in each part imagine their social networks may differ. Surveys have shown how citizens in select eastern European countries pride themselves on being compas-

---

Box 9.2. The Tin Drum

"[A]fter much effort I was issued a visa for Poland in March of '58 and traveled from Paris via Warsaw to Gdańsk, a city still emerging from rubble, to seek out the former Danzig. . . . I went to see the surviving relatives in the countryside. I was greeted at the door of their cottage by the executed postman's mother, with the irrefutable: 'Ginterchen! My, how you've grown!'

"We had become so foreign, so alien to each other, that at first I had to assuage her doubts by producing my passport, but then she took me to see her potato field, which today lies underneath the cemetery of Gdańsk airport."

Source: Günter Grass, *Peeling the Onion* (New York: Harcourt, 2007), 11.

---

sionate, religious, and patriotic. They feel they fit well in closely knit communities. Western Europeans supposedly take greatest satisfaction in working hard and in being well-educated, honest, confident, and cultured. These are qualities that say more about the individual than about social networks. Such auto-types may be eroding as common political and economic structures have shifted into place across Europe, demanding similar behavior and attitudes.

For citizens east and west, viewing the other half of Europe as alien is self-defeating. Emphasizing markers, distinctions, and borders in the enlarged EU is unlikely to produce personal gains. This is not to say that they do not remain salient and influential, only that using them is not a good game plan. Saying you are Welsh or Latvian or Slovene is unlikely to impress anyone in a Europe become more knowledgeable about itself. There are no affirmative action considerations to speak of and it is the marketplace that determines one's place in the enlarged community. As one esoteric example, Latvia has become a favorite destination for people from England because they can throw cheap stag and hen parties there—not because they are Latviaphiles.

Despite, or perhaps precisely because of, such travel, it is sometimes said that old Europe still knows little about its new counterpart while eastern Europeans for many reasons have had to learn about the advanced western states. A knowledge gap may exist, affecting perceptions of each other.

Constructing a transnational home where both eastern and western Europeans feel they belong faces many obstacles. Institutional engineering is a start, but crafting cognitive, cultural, and normative structures is important for the longer-term success of such a project. Societies with ethnic

pecking orders at home will find it difficult to embrace transnational egalitarianism among states. In turn, supranational democratic institutions do
not in themselves ensure the elimination of a hierarchy among EU states—
a hierarchy that is unspeakable yet sensed in both parts of Europe.

THE MYTH OF UNITY OUT OF DIVERSITY

Eurodiscourse praises diversity within a member state but criticizes polyvocality within the arena of the EU. Put differently, for EU elites multiculturalism should govern in the national home (making it non-national) while
metaculturalism should structure the transnational one (making it into an
organic whole).

Should it not be the other way around? Taking as a given that most countries in the world are multinational—about 80 percent of them are—a more
expedient discursive EU approach would be to stress that most countries are
made up of a titular nation—the people after whom the country is named.
This works most of the time: for Austrians, Danes, French, Germans, Hungarians, Poles, Romanians, Slovenes. It does not work for Belgium—symbolically, the EU capital. An apocryphal story relates how at a military con-
scription center a recruitment officer asks all Belgians to raise their hands.
Only the far-away locals—those of African, Arab, and Asian descent—put
up their hands. No Flemish or Walloon would do so.

Integration, acculturation, and especially assimilation have become pejorative terms. They are contested ideas that over the last decades nontitular
groups have largely succeeded in discrediting. An important source of xenophobic attitudes in Europe is a backlash to the loss of the power of this sociological language. In this context, discursive practices praising diversity
are counterproductive.

In turn, affording greater recognition to the existence of many Europes
seems a politically prudent way to cement cooperation among all EU states.
As Ralf Dahrendorf noted, the "habit of cooperation" can be a force for integration because it transcends institutional structures and looks to soft
power influences—culture, knowledge, education—for momentum.[10] Europeanization should be based on this habit of cooperation.

In addition to cooperation, given deep-seated and intensely felt public attitudes on identity and belonging, the construction of an appealing transnational home needs more closely to mirror citizens' identities rather than to
reflect self-interested elite preferences. Failure to do this can leave the "nationalist card" in the hands of cynical, dangerous, and misoxenic right-wing
movements. The anxieties that ordinary EU citizens have about unmanaged
and unplanned immigration have stood in stark contrast with the policy
preferences of EU elites and business interests. These anxieties need, there-

fore, to be taken into account in the policymaking process—not just in electoral campaigns—if an anti-immigrant backlash is not at some point in the future to turn more virulent and even violent.

Unity out of diversity has for long been a populist slogan. But as a project it also entails risk: that unity will not result, or that diversity will be steamrollered. At times it has appeared that Europe's political elites have invoked the mantra without calculating what its consequences might be.

NOTES

1. Salman Rushdie, *The Wizard of Oz* (London: BFI Publishing, 1992), 57.

2. Melanie Phillips, *Londonistan* (London: Encounter Books, 2007).

3. Bhiku Parekh, "Where is Britain Going?" (London: Commission for Racial Equality, 2006), http://www.cre.gov.uk/anthology_05.html.

4. Scott Page, *The Difference: How the Power of Diversity Creates Better Groups, Firms, Schools, and Societies* (Princeton, NJ: Princeton University Press, 2007).

5. Of course, the rest of the world, including Europeans, call "the beautiful game" football—not soccer.

6. "Olisadebe," 2002 FIFA World Cup, ESPN Soccernet, http://soccernet.espn .go.com/wc/player?id=14781&lang=en.

7. Robert D. Putnam, "*E Pluribus Unum*: Diversity and Community in the Twenty-first Century; The 2006 Johan Skytte Prize Lecture," *Scandinavian Political Studies* 30 (2), 137–74. A similar finding on the negative impact of diversity on social capital was reported by Dora L. Costa and Matthew E. Kahn, "Civic Engagement and Community Heterogeneity: An Economist's Perspective," *Perspectives on Politics* 1 (2003), 103–11.

8. Putnam, "*E Pluribus Unum*."

9. Putnam's preliminary research findings were summarized in Michael Jonas, "The Downside of Diversity," *Boston Globe*, August 5, 2007.

10. Ralf Dahrendorf, "The Future of Europe," in *Whose Europe?* eds. Dahrendorf et. al (London: Institute of Economic Affairs, 1989), 9.

Sources and Suggestions
for Further Reading

Chinua Achebe. *Home and Exile*. New York: Anchor Books, 2001.

Richard Alba, Peter Schmidt, and Martina Wasmer, eds. *Germans or Foreigners? Attitudes Toward Ethnic Minorities in Post-Reunification Germany*. London: Palgrave, 2003.

Arjun Appadurai. *Modernity at Large: Cultural Dimensions of Globalization*. Minneapolis: University of Minnesota Press, 1998.

Wil Arts, Jacques Hagenaars, and Loek Halman, eds. *The Cultural Diversity of European Unity: Findings, Explanations and Reflections from the European Values Study*. Leiden, Netherlands: Brill, 2003.

Étienne Balibar. *We, the People of Europe? Reflections on Transnational Citizenship*. Princeton, NJ: Princeton University Press, 2004.

Rainer Bauböck, Eva Ersbøll, Kees Groenendijk, and Harald Waldrauch, eds. *Acquisition and Loss of Nationality: Policies and Trends in 15 European States*. 2 vols. Amsterdam: Amsterdam University Press 2006.

Zygmunt Bauman. *Europe: An Unfinished Adventure*. London: Polity, 2004.

Seyla Benhabib. *The Claims of Culture: Equality and Diversity in the Global Era*. Princeton, NJ: Princeton University Press, 2002.

Mabel Berezin and Martin Schain, eds. *Europe Without Borders: Remapping Territory, Citizenship, and Identity in a Transnational Age*. Baltimore, MD: Johns Hopkins University Press, 1999.

Robert Bideleux and Richard Taylor. *European Integration and Disintegration East and West*. London: Routledge, 1996.

József Böröcz and Meliinda Kovács, eds. *Empire's New Clothes: Unveiling EU Enlargement*. Budapest: Central Europe Review, 2001. e-book.

Rogers Brubaker. *Citizenship and Nationhood in France and Germany*. Cambridge, MA: Harvard University Press, 1992.

Sheila L. Croucher. *Globalization and Belonging: The Politics of Identity in a Changing World*. Lanham, MD: Rowman & Littlefield, 2003.

Riva Castoryano. *Negotiating Identities: States and Immigrants in France and Germany.* Princeton, NJ: Princeton University Press, 2001.

Herrick Chapman and Laura L. Frader, eds. *Race in France: Interdisciplinary Perspectives on the Politics of Difference.* New York: Berghahn Books, 2004.

Maria Green Cowles, James Caporaso, and Thomas Risse, eds. *Transforming Europe: Europeanization and Domestic Changes.* Ithaca, NY: Cornell University Press, 2001.

Ralf Dahrendorf et al., eds. *Whose Europe?* London: Institute of Economic Affairs, 1989.

Joan DeBardeleben, ed. *Soft or Hard Borders? Managing the Divide in an Enlarged Europe.* London: Ashgate, 2005.

Gerard Delanty and Chris Rumford, *Rethinking Europe: Social Theory and the Implications of Europeanization.* London: Routledge, 2005.

Andrew Geddes. *Immigration and European Integration: Towards Fortress Europe?* Manchester: Manchester University Press, 2000.

John Gillingham. *European Integration, 1950–2003: Superstate or New Market Economy?* Cambridge: Cambridge University Press, 2003.

Mérove Gijsberts, Louk Hagendoorn, and Peer Scheepers eds. *Nationalism and Exclusion of Migrants: Cross-National Comparisons.* Aldershot: Ashgate, 2004.

Agata Górny and Paolo Ruspini, eds. *Migration in the New Europe: East-West Revisited.* London: Palgrave, 2004.

Akhil Gupta and James Ferguson, eds. *Culture, Power, Place: Explorations in Critical Anthropology.* Durham, NC: Duke University Press, 1997.

Ernst B. Haas. *The Uniting of Europe: Political, Social and Economic Forces 1950–57.* Stanford, CA: Stanford University Press, 1958.

Loek Halman, Ruud Luijkx, and Marga van Zundert. *Atlas of European Values.* European Values Studies 8. Leiden, Netherlands: Brill, 2005.

Michael Hanagan and Charles Tilly, eds. *Extending Citizenship, Reconfiguring States.* Lanham, MD: Rowman & Littlefield, 1999.

Lawrence Harrison and Samuel Huntington. *Culture Matters: How Values Shape Human Progress.* New York: Basic Books, 2000.

Ulf Hedetoft and Mette Hjort, eds. *The Postnational Self: Belonging and Identity.* Minneapolis: University of Minnesota Press, 2002.

Jost Hermand and James Steakley, eds. *Heimat, Nation, Fatherland: The German Sense of Belonging.* New York: Peter Lang, 1996.

Richard Herrmann, Thomas Risse, and Marilynn Brewer, eds. *Transnational Identities: Becoming European in the EU.* Lanham, MD: Rowman & Littlefield, 2004.

David Horrocks and Eva Kolinsky, eds. *Turkish Culture in German Society Today.* New York: Berghahn Books, 1996.

Tony Judt. *Postwar: A History of Europe Since 1945.* New York: Penguin, 2005.

David H. Kaplan and Jouni Häkli, eds. *Boundaries and Place: European Borderlands in Geographical Context.* Lanham, MD: Rowman & Littlefield, 2002.

Michael Keating, John Loughlin, and Kris Deschouwer. *Culture, Institutions, and Economic Development: A Study of Eight European Regions.* London: Edward Elgar, 2003.

Pamela Kilpadi, ed. *Islam and Tolerance in Wider Europe.* New York: Open Society Institute, 2007.

Will Kymlicka. *Politics in the Vernacular: Nationalism, Multiculturalism and Citizenship.* New York: Oxford University Press, 2002.

Gallya Lahav. *Immigration and Politics in the New Europe: Reinventing Borders.* Cambridge: Cambridge University Press, 2004.

Walter Laqueur. *The Last Days of Europe: Epitaph for an Old Continent.* New York: Thomas Dunne Books, 2007.

Jonathan Laurence and Justin Vaisse. *Integrating Islam: Political and Religious Challenges in Contemporary France.* Washington, DC: Brookings Institution, 2006.

Daniel Levy, Max Pensky, and John Torpey, eds. *Old Europe, New Europe, Core Europe: Transatlantic Relations After the Iraq War.* London: Verso, 2005.

Nadia Lovell, ed. *Locality and Belonging.* London: Routledge, 1999.

Neil MacMaster. *Racism in Europe: 1870–2000.* London: Palgrave 2001.

Mikael af Malmborg and Bo Stråth, eds. *The Meaning of Europe.* Oxford: Berg, 2002.

Anthony W. Marx. *Faith in Nation: Exclusionary Origins of Nationalism.* New York: Oxford University Press, 2003.

Donald McNeill. *New Europe: Imagined Spaces.* London: Arnold, 2004.

Attila Melegh. *On the East-West Slope: Globalization, Nationalism, Racism and Discourses on Central and Eastern Europe.* Budapest: Central European University Press, 2006.

Robert Miles and Dietrich Thränhardt, eds. *Migration and European Integration: The Dynamics of Inclusion and Exclusion.* London: Pinter, 1995.

Cas Mudde, ed. *Racist Extremism in Central and Eastern Europe.* London: Routledge, 2005.

———. *Populist Radical Right Paries in Europe.* Cambridge: Cambridge University Press, 2007.

Francis Mulhern. *Culture/Metaculture (The New Critical Idiom).* London: Routledge, 2000.

Andreas Musolff, Colin Good, Petra Points, and Ruth Wittlinger, eds. *Attitudes Towards Europe: Language in the Unification Process.* Aldershot, UK: Ashgate, 2001.

Umut Ozkirimli, ed. *Nationalism and its Futures.* London: Palgrave, 2004.

Bhiku Parekh. *Rethinking Multiculturalism: Cultural Diversity and Political Theory.* Cambridge, MA: Harvard University Press, 2000.

Scott Page. *The Difference: How the Power of Diversity Creates Better Groups, Firms, Schools, and Societies.* Princeton, NJ: Princeton University Press, 2007.

Susan Parman, ed. *Europe in the Anthropological Imagination.* New York: Prentice Hall, 1997.

Craig Parsons. *Immigration and the Transformation of Europe.* Cambridge: Cambridge University Press, 2006.

Bo Petersson. *Stories about Strangers: Swedish Media and the Constructions of Sociocultural Risk.* Lanham, MD: University Press of America, 2006.

Bo Petersson and Eric Clark, eds. *Identity Dynamics and the Construction of Boundaries.* Lund, Sweden: Nordic Academic Press, 2003.

Sandra Ponzanesi and Daniela Merolla, eds. *Migrant Cartographies: New Cultural and Literary Spaces in Post-Colonial Europe.* Lanham, MD: Lexington Books, 2005.

Allan Pred. *Even in Sweden: Racisms, Radicalized Spaces, and the Popular Geographical Imagination.* Berkeley: University of California Press, 2000.

Romano Prodi. *Europe as I See It.* London: Polity Press, 2000.

John E. Roemer, Woojin Lee, and Karine Van der Straeten. *Racism, Xenophobia, and Distribution: Multi-Issue Politics in Advanced Democracies.* Cambridge, MA: Harvard University Press, 2007.

Rosemarie Sackmann, Bernhard Peters, and Thomas Faist, eds. *Identity and Integration: Migrants in Western Europe.* London: Ashgate, 2003.

William Safran, ed. *The Secular and the Sacred: Nation, Religion and Politics.* London: Frank Cass, 2003.

Edward W. Said. *Out of Place.* New York: Vintage Books, 2000.

Saskia Sassen, *Guests and Aliens.* New York: New Press, 1999.

Frank Schimmelfennig and Ulrich Sedelmeier, eds. *The Europeanization of Central and Eastern Europe.* Ithaca, NY: Cornell University Press, 2005.

Dieter Senghaas. *The Clash Within Civilizations: Coming to Terms with Cultural Conflicts.* New York: Routledge, 1998.

Yasemin Nuhoglu Soysal. *Limits of Citizenship: Migrants and Postnational Membership in Europe.* Chicago: University of Chicago Press, 1995.

Jeff Spinner-Halev. *The Boundaries of Citizenship: Race, Ethnicity, and Nationality in the Liberal State.* Baltimore, MD: Johns Hopkins University Press, 1994.

Pierre-André Taguieff. *Force of Prejudice: On Racism and its Doubles.* Minneapolis: University of Minnesota Press, 2001.

Ray Taras. *Liberal and Illiberal Nationalisms.* London: Palgrave, 2002.

Ray Taras and Rajat Ganguly. *Understanding Ethnic Conflict: The International Dimension.* 3rd ed. New York: Longman, 2008.

Göran Therborn. *European Modernity and Beyond: The Trajectory of European Societies 1945–2000.* London: Sage, 1995.

Ronald Tiersky, ed. *Euroskepticism: A Reader.* Lanham, MD: Rowman & Littlefield, 2001.

Maria Todorova. *Imagining the Balkans.* Oxford: Oxford University Press, 1997.

Anna Triandafyllidou. *Immigrants and National Identity in Europe.* London: Routledge, 2001.

Milada Vachudova. *Europe Undivided: Democracy, Leverage, and Integration after Communism.* New York: Oxford University Press, 2005.

Andrew Baruch Wachtel. *Making a Nation, Breaking a Nation: Literature and Cultural Politics in Yugoslavia.* Stanford, CA: Stanford University Press, 1998.

Andrew Baruch Wachtel, *Remaining Relevant after Communism: The Role of the Writer in Eastern Europe.* Chicago: University of Chicago Press, 2006.

Meredith Watts. *Xenophobia in United Germany: Generations, Modernization, and Ideology.* New York: St. Martin's Press, 1997.

Sally Westwood and Annie Phizacklea. *Trans-nationalism and the Politics of Belonging.* New York: Routledge, 2000.

Maureen Whitebrook. *Identity, Narrative and Politics.* London: Routledge, 2001.

Jan Zielonka. *Europe As Empire: The Nature of the Enlarged European Union.* New York: Oxford University Press, 2006.

Index

About the Author

Ray Taras has served on the faculty of a number of universities in Europe and North America. A specialist on nationalism and international politics, he is the author of *Liberal and Illiberal Nationalisms* (Basingstoke, U.K.: Palgrave, 2002), *Understanding Ethnic Conflict: The International Dimension*, 3rd ed (New York: Longman, 2008; with Rajat Ganguly), and the forthcoming *Europe's Rising Islamophobia: The Impact on Foreign Policy* (Salt Lake City: University of Utah Press, 2009). He lives in New Orleans and Salt Lake City.

Made in the USA
Monee, IL
10 January 2021